INNER ROME:

POLITICAL, RELIGIOUS, AND SOCIAL.

BY THE

REV. C. M. BUTLER, D.D.,

PROFESSOR OF ECCLESIASTICAL HISTORY IN THE DIVINITY SCHOOL, PHILADELPHIA;
AUTHOR OF "THE BOOK OF COMMON PRAYER INTERPRETED BY
ITS HISTORY;" "LECTURES ON THE APOCALYPSE;"
"ST. PAUL IN ROME," ETC. ETC.

PHILADELPHIA:
J. B. LIPPINCOTT & CO.
1866.

PREFATORY NOTE.

THE author of this work has no explanations to make additional to those contained in the introductory chapter, except to state that the last three chapters were contributed by a lady, a member of his family, whose opportunities for observation of the subjects of which she treats were greater than his own.

WEST PHILADELPHIA,
Dec. 1st, 1865.

CONTENTS.

CHAPTER I.

Introductory.

CHAPTER II.

Internal Administration of the Papal Government.

CHAPTER III.

The External Policy of the Papal Government.

CHAPTER IV.

Persecution for Political Opinion.

CHAPTER V.

The Imprisonment of the Advocate and Deputy, Signore Vincenzo Tergolina.

CHAPTER VIII.

The Government of Priests, and its Anomalies.

CHAPTER IX.

The Papal Government after the Restoration.

CHAPTER X.

Rome and Brigandage.

CHAPTER XI.

Rome and Brigandage.

CHAPTER XII.

Napoleon III. and Rome.

CHAPTER XIII.

The Issue, the Situation, and the Solution.

CHAPTER XIV.

Intolerance toward Jews and Protestants at Rome.

CHAPTER XV.

Indulgences.

CHAPTER XVI.

Lay Confraternities.

CHAPTER XVII.

A Chapel of Dead Men's Bones.

CHAPTER XX.

A Visit to Loretto.

CHAPTER XXI.

Morals of the Priesthood.

CHAPTER XXII.

Sickness and Death.

CHAPTER XXIII.

Sickness and Death.

CHAPTER XXIV.

A Chapter of Fragments.

INNER ROME.

CHAPTER I.

INTRODUCTORY.

I CALL my book "Inner Rome," because it professes to disclose more of the real inner character of Rome—its government and administration, its religious and social state—than can be obtained from a temporary sojourn in the city, or from information to be found in the ordinary guide books, and works of travel and description. Of making books on Rome there is no end. Descriptions of its art, its religious ceremonies, its ruins, its customs, and its costumes, abound and superabound. I do not touch these topics, except in an incidental way, and as illustrative of other subjects which I may have in hand. My aim is to answer some of the queries which arise in many minds as to what lies beneath the surface of what is seen, after the eye and the mind have been satiated with the wonders of art and the splendors of ceremonial. I wish to convey to my countrymen a true picture of the actual workings of the Papacy and of the state of religion and society which it produces, such as is not to be found in the books of tourists, and cannot be obtained by those who have access to only English sources of information. I wish to demonstrate that the usual impression which prevails that Rome is, of all civilized States, the most wretchedly, cruelly, and stupidly misgoverned, and undergoes an unparalleled amount of mental terror and torture, is well founded, and rather falls short of than transcends the truth. I desire to create or to increase an interest in that noble Roman people, who are exhibiting heroic traits of character under circumstances well calculated to debase and crush them, and in the triumph of that grand cause of United Italy, with Rome for its capital, which would lead to the downfall of the temporal power of the Papacy, and to the renovation of the entire Italian peninsula.

The conquest of the Æmelia and Romagna, by Victor Emmanuel, and their annexation to the Kingdom of Italy, put the Italian Government in possession of many archives of the Papacy, which furnish the most damaging demonstrations of its atrocious character. It would be difficult for an enemy to invent anything worse than what Rome officially proclaims of herself. It is true that these documents were not intended for Protestant eyes, and it was not supposed that irreverent heretics would ever see them. They would all have been destroyed had not the rapidity of the revolution, in many cases, prevented the attempt. In Faenza, the populace rose in a rage and destroyed the archives. From Ravenna, the documents connected with "the great causes" were sent to Rome. In Ferrara, a secretary-general, Tellarini, spent three days in burning papers. But a greater loss to history occurred in the disappearance of all the minutes and decisions of the tremendous Council of Censure, of which some account is given in Chapter IX., and of the "most reserved" correspondence contained in registers marked P. P., and kept by the legates themselves.

Yet, notwithstanding the disappearance of these documents, enough remain to show unmistakably the dreadful character of the Papal despotism. Two ponderous volumes, containing sixteen hundred pages, have already seen the light. Others will follow. They were published by the direction of Farini, Dictator of Æmelia, accompanied with notes and explanations by the editor, Cavaliere Gennarelli. My statements of the character and administration of the Papacy are drawn, for the most part, from these documents, or from the works of Cav. Gennerelli, which are based upon and confirmed by them. They are therefore official and authentic. Nothing can be more fair and satisfactory as evidences of the character of the Papal Government. They have not been translated into English, and the only book in which I know that they have been made use of, to a certain extent, is "Italy in Transition, by the Rev. Wm. Arthur," published in London in 1861.

More than two years' residence in Rome, it may well be believed, has afforded the author some peculiar facilities for penetrating to the knowledge of the inner religious and social state of Rome. The truth of his statements on such subjects derived from Roman friends, and from the friends and the banished citizens of Rome in other parts of Italy, must rest upon his own character. A citizen of the United States is more readily admitted into the confidence of a Roman patriot than one of any other country. It is believed that he will be thoroughly in sympathy with the Italian aspirations for Independence, and that he will be less liable, than a citizen of any European State, to make disclosures which might tend to compromise individuals, or the cause to which they are devoted.

Such have been the author's facilities for studying the "Roman question" and the state of the Roman Government and Church and people. While he trusts that his work may not be without interest for the statesman and the theologian, it is essentially popular in its character and form. It enters into no elaborate political or religious disquisitions. It describes rather than discusses. It is narrative and descriptive rather than polemic or didactic. Without observing any very strict system of arrangement, the author finds that his miscellaneous chapters fall naturally into the threefold division of political, religious, and social, and that what may probably be regarded by readers generally as the most entertaining, though not perhaps the most instructive portion of the work, will be the later chapters. With these preliminaries as to my purpose, I proceed in the next chapter to speak of the internal administration of the Papal Government.

CHAPTER II.

INTERNAL ADMINISTRATION OF THE PAPAL GOVERNMENT.

THE Papal theory of the origin of its temporal power makes the Pope's grant to the Roman people of a constitution in 1848 a sacrilege. The Roman State, in all its parts and as a whole, is a religious property, *an ecclesiastical benefice.* As such, the separate parts of which it is composed have been given to Popes in trust, for the benefit of the church. It is a vast *estate*, given at various times, consisting of many farms and houses, and property of every kind, and of 3,000,000 of tenants, who are not indeed slaves or serfs in the ordinary meaning of those terms, but who can hold and transmit property and enjoy civil rights, only on the conditions affixed by the infallible head of the church for *her* welfare, and not their own. Whatever benefits the inhabitants of this domain may enjoy, are not *rights*, but only gracious privileges and immunities granted by their sacred sovereign, and to be withdrawn when demanded by the interests of the church. The sovereign has no right to grant any privileges inconsistent with the purposes of the original donation. The people have no right to demand or expect them. Infallibility, therefore, slumbered for a moment, when, in forgetfulness of this solemn deposit, it granted a constitution to the Roman people. But the sin has been expiated by the after-suffering. The Pope has resolved to sin no more. Infallibility is wide awake, and will never more sleep nor slumber. The Pope cannot and will not permit the sacrilege of alienating any part of the sacred deposit. No portion of the Roman States is in fact alienated. It is true that the Æmelia and the Romagna are now in the possession of an excommunicated and sacrilegious robber, by the name of Victor Emmanuel; but this is only a temporary and forced withdrawal. The Papacy has survived darker crises than the present. The gates of hell shall not prevail against it. At every appeal to alienate any part of his sacred estate, or to grant any privileges to his subjects, on the ground of their inherent rights, the Pope talks of Constantine and Pepin and Charlemagne and the blessed Countess Matilda, and shaking his infallible head, doggedly thunders "*Non possumus.*"

This solemn formula is not always treated by the Roman people with the reverence which the government and the priesthood think it should receive. On one occasion, while I was in Rome, a priest endeavored to induce a hackman to take him at a lower than his usual fare. The man majestically waved his whip, and said, "*non pos-*

sumus," and drove off. He paid, however, for his irreverent wit the penalty of several weeks of imprisonment. It is thus that the priests of Rome make the people love them.

In the statement of the above theory of the Papal power, it is forgotten that some portions of the Sacred States were acquired by the rapine and treachery of the remorseless Borgias, and the ambitious Julius II. But, no doubt, being mixed with the holy Papal lump, they too have become equally sacred and inalienable.

The government of these States is certainly peculiar. When bachelors and old maids and childless persons assume the government of children, we sometimes admire their theories, but we always pity the children. When priests assume civil powers—woe to the people!

If the Roman States constitute a benefice, then it is subject to the conditions of a benefice. Its fundamental law is not a written constitution; not a series of precedents; not even the collected decrees and bulls of the supreme authority, but it is the laws which regulate church property and endowments. This is logical. The Papacy does not shirk this conclusion. It broadly announces it. It actually refers its fundamental law to the *Council of Trent—the eleventh chapter of the twenty-second session.* Let no man say that the Roman States are destitute of a fundamental law!

As a specimen of the style of government

adopted by those who place the throne upon the altar, I refer to two documents, not of the dark ages, but, as it were, of yesterday. One is from Fra Filippo Bertolotti, "Inquisitor-General of the Holy See," in the Dioceses of Pesaro, Rimini, Fano, and the adjoining territory, and "special delegate against heretical pravity," and is addressed to those under his jurisdiction. The document bears the date of September 15, 1851, at Pesaro.

In an interminable sentence, in what may be called the Papal style, the Inquisitor strictly commands, under all the penalties prescribed in "the canons, decrees, constitutions, and bulls" of the Popes, those whom he addresses to make known to him such persons and crimes as he proceeds to specify. Among them are the following:

"All heretics, or persons *suspected or reported* to be heretics, or who have favored, or defended, or *described and explained heresies.*"

"Those who have done, or do, acts from which can be inferred *a compact, express or tacit, with the Devil.*"

"Those who have hindered, or *hinder in any manner whatever, the proceedings of the office of the Holy Inquisition.*"

"Those who have composed satires, or divulged writings against the High Priest, the Sacred College, Superiors, Ecclesiastics, or against the Regular orders."

"Those who without license retain writings and prints, which contain heresies, or the books of heretics."

"Those who without necessity or license have eaten, or given to others to eat, meat, eggs, *latticini* (the products of milk), on forbidden days, in contempt of the precepts of the Church."

Whoever fails to denounce the above criminals to the Holy Inquisitor and special delegate against "heretical pravity," shall be subject to excommunication.

This frightful document was to be hung up in all taverns, coffee-houses, shops, book-stands, and frequented places of every kind. What a horrible instrument placed in the hands of evil and revengeful men! What an agency for disseminating distrust and terror and deception and degradation through a community! What tortures of mind and heart, what struggles between compassion and a sense of justice on the one side, and a misinstructed conscience or an inevitable terror on the other!

The other document to which I refer is an edict issued by the Cardinal Archbishop, Cardinal Bishop, and other Archbishops and Bishops of the Marches and of the province of Umbria, as recently as 1850. It refers to the sins of "blasphemy, inobservance of the sacred days, profanation of the churches, and violation of fasts, and immorality," and reminds the faithful that the penalty of these crimes, according to the degree of delinquency, and according to the circumstances and the times, are "excommunication, or imprisonment, or fines, or castigation, or exile, or even death." But, without following all these provisions, in which there is an absurd confusion of civil and ecclesiastical crimes and penalties, I notice one feature of the edict, which runs through the whole Roman administration, and is the source of untold woes and gross injustice to the citizens of the Roman States.

"*Art.* 54. In all the cases above mentioned, where a penalty *merely correctional* is to be applied, a speedy and summary process shall take place, when the character of the delinquency shall be established, and *the names of the informer and the witnesses shall be kept secret.*"

"*Art.* 55. Half of the fines imposed shall be applied to the benefit of holy places, and the other half shall be divided between the informer and the officers who shall have executed the law."

Nothing could exemplify better than these provisions the evils of the priestly government. In the first place, under the head of immoralities, are mentioned crimes which come properly under the cognizance of the civil power. But as the Cardinals and Archbishops, representing the Pope, are the civil power as well as the spiritual, they mix together in most admired confusion, violations of the moral, canonical, and civil law, and distribute penalties *pell-mell*, penances and prayers, imprisonments and fines.

Indeed, it is the constant policy of the Papal Government to obliterate the distinction between violations of the laws of the Church and the moral laws of God, and the civil laws of man. Authority is one—crime is one—penalty is one. The Pope concentrates authority; disobedience to him as Pope or king, or Pope-king, is crime which bears the character of blasphemy. Punishment is equally a holy penalty, whether it be in its form a prayer-repeating penance, or long fasts, or imprisonments, or fines, or death. Such is the Papal theory.

Again, provision is made that when a penalty *merely correctional* is to be applied, the punishment is to be speedy. This provision enables Archbishops and Bishops, when they will, to dispense with all the forms of law. They are to judge whether a *merely correctional* penalty will suffice. They may make such a penalty more severe, if they please, than a penalty strictly penative might be. Moreover, the names of informers and witnesses are to be secret! False informers run no risk of contradiction, exposure, confutation, or the revenge of their injured and slandered victims. If they have enemies, here is a means of cheap and safe revenge. If they are needy, or greedy of baiocchi, here is a means of obtaining them—for a quarter of all fines go to the informer! Nothing can be conceived worse than the position of a citizen of the Papal States under such a system. If he fails to observe any of the rules of the Church, he is in a worse position than the violator of the civil laws of other States. His position is worse, because he is subject to both civil and spiritual penalties. It is worse, because he may find himself convicted, without having been tried, on secret testimony, which he cannot meet and confute; and he may be punished as severely on the plea of a merely correctional penalty, without trial and condemnation. And, above all, his position is immeasurably worse, because a direct premium is offered to needy and malignant spies and informers, and to brutal carbinieri,—many of whom are convicts pardoned in order to be made the instruments of Papal justice,—to conspire together to ruin the innocent, and especially to persecute those who are suspected of a want of bigoted devotion to the Church. It is a horrible system.

A case of the administration of justice at Rome, which was due directly to the Pope, which occurred the year before my arrival in the city, produced a profound impression throughout Italy. The history of the case is briefly as follows:

On the evening of the 29th of June, 1861, there was a great crowd in the Corso and in Monte Citorio, who raised the cries of "*Viva Italia! Viva Vittorio Emanuele!*" The gendarmes rushed into the midst of the crowd, and struck and fired right and left. A man by the name of

Locatelli, well known to the police as a partisan of Victor Emmanuel, was in the crowd. A gendarme was stabbed in the melée. Locatelli was struck down and arrested by the gendarmes as the author of the crime. But he constantly and loudly denied it. He declared that he was arrested only because the police could not find the author of the deed, and were determined to have a victim. He testified that he had just left the Corso, and was going toward Monte Citorio, when he was set upon by several of the pontifical gendarmes. But he was put on trial for the crime. The witnesses were "*ten pontifical gendarmes*," three French and one pontifical soldier—a Swiss. In the official account of this trial, the *names of the witnesses are not given.* They are designated by initials. They testified that the murder took place in a general and crowded melée. They agreed that it was about ten o'clock at night, cloudy, and the moon in her fourth quarter. They differed in their account of the height and size of the murderer. They found in his pocket, when arrested, his knife closed, and with no marks of blood; while one of the witnesses testified that the knife of the murderer fell to the ground, and was taken up from the ground by the gendarme Z. This gendarme Z. testified that he found a knife, but did not see it fall from Locatelli's hand, who was four or five steps from him when he took it up.

It was on this vague and contradictory testimony that Locatelli was executed. He died crying *Viva Italia!*

A correspondent of *La Presse*, in Paris, after an account of this trial, wrote: "There is no man of sense, who, upon reading the principal depositions of the witnesses, does not declare that this condemnation is monstrous. But in Rome, everything is done *en famille;* they have a horror of publicity. They judge everything with closed doors; witnesses are examined privately, interrogated separately, and never confronted with each other, or with the accused."

To show how exceedingly unsatisfactory this proof must have been, nothing more is needed than the fact that the President of the Sacra Consulta himself addressed these words to Pius IX., when he presented to him the sentence of death:

"Your Holiness, here is the sentence of death against Locatelli. I believe that I discharge a duty of conscience when I observe that the crime was committed at night, in the midst of a crowd, so that witnesses might easily have been deceived, or have seen imperfectly, and that consequently *this is a case in which to exercise clemency, which may relieve us from the danger of committing a great injustice.*"

The warning was in vain. The Pope, who cannot sign a sentence of death, laid over this document the fatal black ribbon.

It had been well if Pius IX. had listened to the

representations of M. Sagretti, the President of the Sacra Consulta, for a few days after the execution, the following statement appeared in the *Siecle* of Paris, from its correspondent at Florence:

"The *Nazione* of Florence announces that Jacques de Castrucci, a Roman emigrant, presented himself before the commissioner of the king, and avowed himself the author of the homicide committed upon the Papal gendarme in the conflict on the 29th of June. The object of this declaration was to prevent the execution of Locatelli. The news arrived at Rome too late. *Locatelli had been already executed.*"

Such are some specimens of Papal administration and Papal justice.

CHAPTER III.

THE EXTERNAL POLICY OF THE PAPAL GOVERNMENT.

WE have seen that the *form* of the Papal Government permits the exercise of excessive tyranny. But some governments are worse, and some better, in their administration than in their theory. A great poet has not hesitated to write:

> For forms of government let fools contest;
> *That which is best administered is best!*

It is certain, at least, that a bad theory and a good practice is better than the opposite. But when the theory is bad, and the practice worse, the case is grievous for a nation.

Let us see in what spirit, and according to what maxims and modes the Papal Government is administered.

When Pius IX. fled to Gaeta, he carried with him the conviction, never since shaken, that the exercise of absolute despotism is the first duty of popes and kings, and submission to it the chief right of nations. The Tuscan Ambassador, in a dispatch to his court from Gaeta, wrote: "All here is hesitancy and perplexity. In one thing only there is firmness, and that is in the absolute determination not to hear a word in reference to a constitution or guarantees." And again, in a conversation with him, the Holy Father declared that "the pretended rights which constitute the foundation of Constitutional Governments, are utterly irreconcilable with his convictions, which are decidedly averse to a constitution."*

Hence, on his return to Rome, the Pope not only annulled the "*Statuto*" in the Roman States, but exerted his influence to banish all such pestilent documents from Italy. In a diplomatic note addressed by Prince Schwarzemberg, from Vienna, to Baron Hagel, at Florence, in which he exhorts the Tuscan Government to abolish the Statuto Constitutionale, we find that one of his most urgent arguments is, *that the Pope desires it.* He writes thus: "The Pontifical Government avows that its repugnances (to constitutional governments in Italy) have, moreover, foundation in reasons which refer particularly to its own well-being. The Pope does not seek to disguise the fact that constrained as he feels by duty to recognize and declare *every form* of parliamentary government as directly threatening to the free exercise of the spiritual power,

* Le dottrine civili e religiose della corte di Roma, in ordine al dominio temporale. Considerazioni e documenti, etc. del Cav. Achille Gennarelle, Avo. nella curia Romana. Firenze, 1862.

he cannot without alarm observe the constitutional principles, which are the ordinary fruits of revolutions, propagated and embodied *all around his States*, nor even the most mitigated forms of representative government, the contagion of which seems not less inevitable and disastrous."

That is sufficiently explicit! *All* representative governments are, by their very nature, hostile to the free exercise of the Pope's spiritual power. To enjoy the free exercise of that power is the first right and the highest duty of the Pope and all his faithful subjects. Hence he, and all his subjects who are logical and consistent, should exert themselves to prevent and destroy constitutional and representative governments. Such faithful and logical and loyal children of the Pope as the Emperor of Austria, Francis of Naples, Leopold of Tuscany, and divers little princelings of Modena and Parma, are consistent, and have done their utmost not only to keep all constitutional institutions out of their own kingdoms, but from all conterminous States, in order that the "contagion" of this pest may not infect the atmosphere of holy despotism, which was wont to rest so peacefully over those favored lands.

How much perplexed these faithful subject-monarchs of the Pope sometimes are in reconciling their supreme duty to him with the subordinate duty which they owe to themselves and their subjects, appears conspicuously in the case of the poor Duke Leopold of Tuscany. Among the secret archives of the Grand Duke, which were thrown open to the cognizance of the Italian Government when Tuscany became part of the Kingdom of Italy, there was found a remarkable correspondence, of which I will give a brief account.

By the revolution of 1848, Tuscany obtained a constitution. By that constitution, all Tuscans, without distinction of religions, were equally admitted to civil and military appointments. The Holy Father communicated to the Duke his disapproval of this provision. "The Holy Father," said the note of Mons. Massoni in his name, "is decidedly of opinion that an organic law should be proclaimed declaring the intrinsic incapacity of the Jews to discharge any offices whatever which have any relation to the Catholic religion. If, however, there should be a difficulty on the part of the Duke to issue such a law, his Sanctity is comforted by the thought that inasmuch as to *him* (the Duke) is referred the confirmation of all appointments, he will not sanction those to which he (the Pope) has referred." Inasmuch also as such persons might, according to the *Statuto*, belong to the Senate or House, or even the Council of the Duke, the Holy Father advises the Duke of the absolute necessity that they should be prohibited by an organic law from having any voice in matters pertaining to religion and the Holy Catholic Church.

To this note a timid and submissive reply is sent, in which the Grand Duke declares that up to the period of the dispatch he has admitted to employments which have any relation to the Catholic religion, none but good Catholics.

Again, a month later, another representation is made to the effect that by the Statuto, "Ecclesiastical persons in causes, *civil and criminal*, may be called before judges, who are not Catholics, nor even Christians," and the Duke is earnestly desired,—nay, is rather commanded,—to prevent this dreadful scandal.

Observe in the tone of the reply the obedient spirit of a true son of the Church. "The undersigned (Monsignor Boninsegni) begs to assure your most religious Eminence, that his Imperial and Royal Highness, the Grand Duke, protests that in the use of his prerogative he has constantly remembered not to admit those exercising a worship different from the Catholic, to any employments which have, or can have, any relation to the religion of the State, or to the discipline of the Church. And this, it seems, ought to tranquilize the Holy See in reference to the apprehension which it has conceived, that civil causes regarding the Church and ecclesiastical persons may be called before judges who are not Catholics nor even Christians."

But, notwithstanding this assurance, it seems

that the Pope's anxieties continued, and were increased after his return from Gaeta. In February, 1852, he wrote personally to his son Leopold. It seems that Leopold hated the constitution as cordially as the Pope. Stimulated, no doubt, by the Pope's creatures, he wrote to the Holy Father asking his advice. The poor Duke was in much perplexity. The letter of Pius IX. opens with a precious specimen of the style of address to sovereigns which prevailed in the days of Hildebrand and Innocent the Third.

"The grateful memory which your Highness is pleased to preserve of my counsels given on another grave contingency is full proof of your right-mindedness; and the fidelity with which you now resort to the Head of the Church for enlightenment in a moral doubt, is perfectly consistent with those decided sentiments of religion and piety with which we know you to be pervaded."

The Duke thought that other than Catholics might be admitted to all functions, except the judicial. The Pope is alarmed by this laxity. He advises the Duke that the true spirit of the Church is always "to keep as far as possible aloof from contact with unbelievers." Faithful rulers "should regard as full of danger those associations which take place between clients and lawyers, the sick and their physicians, which create and foster a respectful esteem and confidence in the former toward the latter." Nothing, it seems, is more dangerous to the faithful than to entertain esteem and respect for heretics. Hence the Pope, inexorably logical, counsels the Duke to abolish, by a sovereign act, "pure and simple," that article of the constitution, in order that affairs may be restored to their old condition.

The bewildered Duke professes, and is yet afraid to obey the Pope. He writes: "It was my design to except from the new laws of the Constitution, promulgated 15th of July, 1848, the first article, which makes equal before the laws the heterodox and Catholics. Your Sanctity will observe that I could not be tranquil in conscience if I should sanction this article, and you explain the embarrassments to which the sanction of this article would expose me, by making it necessary for me to sanction other equal privileges with the faithful which the heterodox would claim. I will, therefore, cheerfully annul this article, and by this means the former state of things will be restored."

Yet the perplexed Duke begs indulgence especially for the physicians, who have been admitted under the Constitution since 1848. He would have these permitted still to exercise their functions. "No more shall be appointed, but please allow *them* still to exercise their profession." Such is the representation to the Father. He assures the Pope that they are extensively employed, that they have, according to the regulations, always advised the friends of the dying in time to have the offices of the Church performed. That, because of their skill and high reputation, many persons, "profoundly pious," have preferred them; that they have never taken an undue advantage of their position. The Duke hints to his Holiness that as these persons adopted this profession in reliance upon the fundamental law of the State, it would scarcely be just to dispossess them. And then he adds the following words, the abjectness of which could not have been surpassed in the darkest mediæval days:

"To abolish the Statuto of the 15th of July, 1848, a special decree of the Government is necessary, and this shall be done *in accordance with the desire and command of your Holiness.* But, before I promulgate such a decree, I beg your Holiness to reflect that having made it the subject of consultation, I anticipate serious divisions, great diversities of opinion, and momentous consequences. It is my duty to make this observation, while *I leave the decision of the matter to the enlightened prudence of your Holiness.*"

But the minister of King Leopold saw that it would be madness to adopt this course; that another revolution would be the inevitable result. He drew up another letter, in which the inconveniences of obeying the Pope's injunctions were meekly represented. But Leopold refused to adopt and send it.

In answer to the submissive and deprecating suggestions of Leopold, the Pope consented that those admitted to the profession of law and medicine under the Constitution of 1848, should be permitted to retain and exercise them on condition that the Jews in these professions should *be employed only by Jews!* He adds: "It grieves me greatly to observe that the opposition made to your Highness in the Cabinet, has become bruited abroad, and that it seeks support through the whole of your kingdom, and even beyond it, exciting anew passions which are scarcely calmed, and exaggerating, falsifying, and villifying for the purpose of producing a breach between you and the ministry."

Comment on this correspondence is not needed. It shows what is the relation of the Pope to princes, when affairs are in what his Holiness considers a normal condition. It is on the one side a relation of authority and dictation; and on the other of awed and reverent submission.

There was once a prophet riding upon a faithful ass, who seeing an angel with a drawn sword in his hand, recoiled, and bruised his master against a wall, and who, when abused for thus starting back, addressed to his master a gentle and affectionate remonstrance. They all—prophet and ass and angel—have their counterparts in Pius and Leopold and the avenging angel of Revolution. We hear repeated the reproach and the acknowledgment that it was undeserved, which is recorded in the sacred story.

"And the ass said unto Balaam, Am I not thine ass upon which thou hast ridden ever since I was thine ass until this day? Was I ever wont to do so to thee? And he said, Nay."

CHAPTER IV.

PERSECUTION FOR POLITICAL OPINIONS.

IN the effort to detect political plots, and to discover some clew to the hated and dreaded National Committee at Rome, the Papal Government proceeds with an infatuation and a disregard of humanity and right and common sense which are truly astounding. It ignores all law and all the ordinary forms of justice under which decent despotisms usually veil their outrages, and blind to all that stands out distinctly in the sunlight of modern civilization, is sharp-sighted only in those dark labyrinths where intrigue and espionage track and entrap their victims.

The Papal Government is the only one in the world where men are banished and imprisoned, simply because their sentiments and feelings are known or surmised to be adverse to the Government. In other governments such persons are watched, and not put in offices of trust; but by none other are they banished or disfranchised simply because their general influence is dreaded as unfavorable to the policy of the State. But this is done constantly by the Papal Government.

In many cases which have come to my personal knowledge, gentlemen have been banished from Rome with no charge made against them, and with the explicit or implied admission that there were no charges to be made, on the single ground that they were unfriendly to the Government, and exercised an influence against it. Now when it is remembered that in Rome there is no press in which political hostility can express a syllable of dissatisfaction, no rostrum from which a whisper of discontent is ever heard, no permitted clubs or gatherings where public affairs are canvassed, it will be evident that gentlemen are banished from Rome, not for saying or doing anything disloyal, but from simply *being* liberal in politics and dissatisfied with the Government, and *being unable to seem contented.* The influence of silent disapprobation is counted as a crime. And, as a matter of course, the higher is the moral and social position of this negative offender, the greater is his offense.

The Government seems to have a special spite against physicians. It knows that the influence of a beloved physician in the family is second only to that of a venerated pastor. It knows, moreover, that in common with all the educated and intelligent population of Rome, the physicians almost unanimously detest the Government. Hence the persecutions and banishments of this class have been numerous, incessant, and irritating, no less to the people than to themselves. The banishment of no individual could create such wide-spread dissatisfaction as that of a popular physician. The celebrated Dr. Panteleone was banished for no other cause than that of acting in behalf of a city, of which I believe he was a native, in presenting to the Government a petition for the redress of some grievances to which they were subjected. Another, Dr. Maggiorani, Professor of high standing for many years in the medical school at Rome, after suffering tortures from the successive banishment and imprisonment of several of his sons, was at length banished, and now holds a distinguished position under the Italian Government, as professor in the same department at Palermo. I remember to have read a bitter review in the "*Osservatore Romano*" of his inaugural address, which called out replies from Palermo, in which the Roman organ of the Government was challenged to produce any reason for the banishment of the Professor, which would justify it in the eyes of any other despotism in the world. I remember no less the squirmings, and the malignant insinuations, and the poor evasions of the organ, which could make out no other case against the Professor than that he was suspected to be an enemy, and known not to be an earnest friend of the Government. The case of the excellent Dr. Franco, now practicing at Paris, is quite the same. The Government alleges nothing against him, and admits virtually that there is nothing to be alleged. He was a man of well-known prudence in reference to the expression of his political sentiments, even with most foreigners, as no doubt some of his American patients will remember. He has in vain petitioned to pass one day at Rome to assist at the nuptials of a beloved relative. He was a man of high character and of wide influence, and hence his silent disapprobation of the Priestly Government could not be tolerated. Never was the rule, "He that is not with us is against us," more rigidly applied. And these banished Romans, how they pine for their home!

In some cases a course of procedure is adopted more cruel than that of banishment. A case occurred early last winter which will illustrate the remark. A young physician was subjected to a domiciliary visit of the police, who expected to find papers which would show him to be connected with that dreaded secret organization, the thought of which is a terror when they wake and a nightmare when they sleep to the priests and the officials of the Government. It is impossible for the Papal police to act otherwise than brutally, for they are brutal. No Roman will enter into this hated service. No Roman would probably be trusted in it. It is made up of foreigners of various nations. Many of them are criminals and disbanded soldiers of Francis II. So detested are they by the Roman people that it is not considered safe for them to make arrests during the day. They are made at night or in the early dawn. Indeed, they are in such peril from the indignation of the Roman people that regulations were made a few years since, after the assassination of several of them, that they should never go on their rounds alone. Every recent visitor at Rome will remember always to have seen them in groups of from two to five. At night it is exceedingly ludicrous to see a Pontifical gendarme, with his cocked hat and large military cloak, looking as stately as a field-marshal, slowly stalking through the streets, *protecting the city*, while three or four little, lithe French soldiers walk some distance behind this majestic personage in order to protect *him*. He protects the citizens from thieves and robbers, and the French soldiers protect him from the *citizens*.

The visit of the police to this young physician was made in their usual mode of mixed cruelty and cunning. His wife was within a week of her first confinement. In the early morning, as the maid unlocked the door of the apartment to go out for milk, she found four men standing ready to enter. They were policemen in citizen's dress. They pushed by her and entered into the bed-room of the physician and his wife, and ordered them to rise and aid them in the search they were about to institute. They would not leave the chamber to allow the physician and his wife to dress lest they should take that opportunity to destroy or secrete some papers. Two of the men hurried the physician off to prison before the search was begun, and the other two remained for the examination. They emptied all drawers and closets, and tore up cushions and mattresses, and found only one prohibited article in the apartment, and that was a *printed life of Cavour*. The terror of the young wife can only be conceived by those who know how often persons thus hurried off to prison, with no crime, and no real political offense, but only on suspicion or false information of spies or enemies, have languished in some unknown cell or dungeon for years without being permitted to receive or send a message. The effect of this shock upon the poor lady was fatal. Much interest was made to have her husband restored to her until after her confinement. He was released after thirty-six hours, but it was too late! She never rallied, and died a few days after in childbed! With such memories in Roman homes, who can wonder at the intensity of hatred and indignation with which the Government is regarded! Nothing more was done. The Government had killed an innocent wife, embittered, as we may suppose, almost to madness, one of its citizens, had offended all of his friends, and, as a compensation, had secured a copy of the life of Count Cavour. It cost too much.

But worse things than these sometimes occur. Besides petty persecutions of lads and youths—such as seizing cravats and breast-pins and tearing them off in the street, when the device or color is supposed to have a political meaning, they too are sometimes subjected to the rigor with which grown men are treated. Innumerable instances I have heard in which a youth, belonging to a family of *whites* or liberals, has been made to suffer disabilities in school or college. In one case, a youth, who wore a Victor Emmanuel breast-pin, was not only dismissed from college, but had every avenue to an education in any institution in Rome closed to him. One of the young sons of Professor Maggiorani, only seventeen years of age, was imprisoned for a considerable period, and for what was not known. But another case, the story of which I give in the words of my wife, on whose mind it made a painfully indelible impression, is still more harrowing.

"Spending the evening with an English acquaintance in Rome, my attention was arrested by the countenance of one of the casual visitors, as being very intellectual but profoundly sad. Finding strangers with our host he sought a quiet corner near one of the ladies whom he knew, which brought him accidentally near to me also, and I soon heard her ask him what had happened to depress him to such a degree. At first he seemed unwilling to speak in my hearing, but introducing him to me she assured him that he might safely say in my hearing whatever he could say in hers. Then he poured out his grief. A youth, I think of seventeen years of age, a mere boy, the son of a dear friend, had been suspected of connection with the unknown and much-dreaded National Committee. Hoping, as some supposed, to get at some information through the confession which he might make, he was arrested, deprived of the usual blessings of life and light and home, and thrown into a solitary cell, noisome and damp, seven feet by nine. Here, denying all knowledge of anything treasonable, he was kept until four wretched months had passed, when, worn out by confinement, bad air, and bad food, and intolerable distress of mind, he had become ill. Begging the jailer to send the prison physician to him, that worthy had made him a short visit, and said that he would send him something. In due time medicine came marked with the number of another cell, not his own. He waited for the jailer, pointed out the mistake, showed him that the patient in the other cell must have his medicine, and that an exchange had been made. It was all uselessly spent breath. The surly, cruel wretch would do nothing. Very ill, the poor lonely boy concluded to take the medicine, right or wrong. Its effect upon him was terrible, and when, at length, the attention of the authorities was directed to him, he was pronounced to be dying. Then, inasmuch as nothing had been found against him, and as he prayed so earnestly to be taken home to die in his family, and as their grief, overcoming their fear, was making itself clamorously heard, his prayer was granted, and he was conveyed to his home. The gentleman who mentioned these facts had just come from his bedside. 'Will he live?' 'I think not.' Innocent, amiable, intelligent, most affectionate, guilty only of desiring with all the youth of Italy a free government, he dies, murdered! And the gentleman who narrates the story, although to a group of friends, seems either afraid or too much accustomed to such scenes to be *indignant*, and appears to be impressed by the tragedy, as by a fate, only with a profound sadness."

Another history, which also came to the knowledge of my wife, and is told in her words, is as profoundly affecting as the former. It shows that where the interests of the King of Naples and his cherished brigands are involved, the rights and the lives of Romans are held in small regard.

"In the summer of 1862 I formed one of a party, mounted on donkeys, going from Albano to the fair at Grotta Ferrata. The hot sun and the fatigue had made me unequal to the return journey on the donkey, and my friends had introduced me to an Italian gentleman, who kindly invited me to take a seat in his carriage. He was about thirty years of age, of noble connections, and pleasing manners. Shortly after leaving Grotta Ferrata, this gentleman, who had been thoughtful heretofore, and had said only what kindness had rendered necessary, suddenly turned to me and said, 'And so, madam, you are the wife of a priest—a Protestant priest?' 'Yes,' said I, 'that strange thing in Rome. I suppose I am a great curiosity to you.' 'Madam,' said he, most energetically, 'would to God that every priest in Rome had his own wife and family!' I was surprised, and said, 'St. Peter certainly had his, but your church has made many laws and introduced many customs since the time of St. Peter. Whether such innovations are right or wrong, we must decide for ourselves.' 'Decide! Yes; and I assure you that all Italy is *Protest*-ant at this moment—that is, all thinking Italy—and especially upon this matter of the celibacy of the clergy. There is scarcely a man in the country but would be glad if every priest were married.' After a good deal of conversation, all tending to the same point, he added: 'The less the priests have to do with our domestic and political affairs, the better for us.' Frightened by such bold utterances, I remarked that he and I were quite strangers to each other, and that in view of the present condition of public affairs I wondered that he should talk thus to me, and I wondered that he had no fear of imprudent disclosures on my part. 'Fear,' he said, 'I have passed long ago; I have left it far behind me,' waving his hand with expressive gesticulation. As this, however, was by no means my own case, as I had a horror of Papal spies, and as I could not be sure that the coachman or the footman, or both, had not understood every word which had been or might be uttered, though we spoke in French, I resolutely changed the subject of conversation.

"I afterward asked of my friends his history. With lowered voices they told me a terrible story of brigand horrors. The young men of the family were all known as liberal, or anti-temporal power men, or in the common language of Rome, as *whites*, as distinguished from the priestly party known from the prevailing color of their dress as blacks. They had, however, taken no offensive steps and indulged in no offensive words. No cause for their arrest could be ascertained, though it was diligently searched for. A party of pleasure was at this time formed for a visit, I think to Naples. If I remember rightly it was a bridal party. Among the number was this gentleman with whom I had been riding, his favorite brother (and only those who know the Italians intimately can know how strong are their family affections), and a young sister and brother-in-law. On the road they were stopped by a party of brigands, robbed, and subjected to frightful outrages. The young sister succeeded in escaping into the woods, and, after great hardships, reached a town, from whence she could return to Rome. The two brothers were soon overpowered, pinioned, and threatened with death. In an agony of distress the elder brother offered to save the life of the younger by a ransom, and to bring the money in person, and then give himself up to the threatened death. The offer was accepted, the elder brother left, obtained the money, and returned. But something had occurred to change the plans of the band. Perhaps they had heard of soldiers in pursuit of them in the neighborhood. At all events they had disappeared, but the mutilated remains of their poor victims were strewn upon the ground, here a hand, there an ear, further on a mutilated trunk. Worn out by fatigue and anxiety, the sight was too much for him. He was carried back to Rome in a state of insensibility, and a long and terrible attack of brain fever ensued. After many months of gradual recovery his every other feeling seemed to be merged in a desire to avenge the murder of his innocent, beloved brother. To this end he laid the whole affair before the Papal Government, but was met at every turn by political accusations against himself and family, concerning which he challenged the fullest examination, and was obliged at length to desist from all further effort as worse than useless, convinced that the Papal officials were in league with the system of brigandage, and that he saw in them the real murderers of his brother and his friends. Despairing of anything good in Rome, so long as it was swayed by priests and haunted by ghastly memories, life had become worthless to him, and hence his remark to me that he was past all fear. His friends were, however, striving to distract his mind and to engage his attention to the ordinary occupations of life, and to some extent they had succeeded."

I conclude this series of individual histories with another, of which I was also personally cognizant. Well acquainted myself with the gentleman whose painful history is here described, but knowing that an American friend had been longer and more intimately acquainted with him, and was probably better informed of the details of the events which I wish to describe than myself, I requested him to furnish me with his recollections. In answer to my request he has kindly sent me the following information:

"DEAR SIR,—I take great pleasure in sending you, as you requested, the facts connected with the arrest and imprisonment of Signor ——, as far as I can remember them.

"In the latter part of the winter of 1852 and '53, we received a visit, in our rooms on the Corso, from Signor ——, who had, that very morning, been liberated from one of the subterranean prisons of Rome, devoted exclusively to political offenders. The sudden change from the dark prison to the bright light of day, the joy of seeing once more his family and friends, and the effects of several months of imprisonment had so unstrung his nervous system that his hands were in constant agitation, and his voice trembled in telling us the history of his arrest and imprisonment.

"He was driving in his carriage from the city to his country-place, and had almost reached one of the gates of the city, when suddenly several gendarmes presented themselves, stopped the horses, and ordered him to dismount immediately. Thinking that they had mistaken him for some one else, he mentioned his name, and expostulated with them for having stopped him so arbitrarily. Instead of an answer to his expostulation he was ordered to follow them. He was conducted immediately to prison and placed in a small, dark cell, entirely alone, without having any accusation preferred against him, and without any reason being assigned for his imprisonment. For several weeks he saw no one but the jailer who made his regular rounds in distributing bread and water to the prisoners. The minutes seemed like hours and the hours like weeks. To break the dreadful solitude, he begged the jailer to send for his favorite flute, but he met with a surly denial. He then petitioned the inspector, the chief of the prison, that he might be permitted to have some musical instrument, as he was very fond of music. He was again refused. He was soon transferred, however, from his solitary cell to a part of the prison where a large number of political prisoners were confined. The air was so unhealthy, and so little attention paid to cleanliness, that many were ill. Notwithstanding the liberty they enjoyed of seeing each other and of talking together, and of playing different kinds of games allowed by the regulations of the prison, the time hung so heavily upon their hands that they were reduced to all kinds of shifts to fill up the hours of the day. One of the number, perhaps of a more delicate organization than the others, yielding to the influences of the place, became exceedingly melancholy. His companions, fearing the fatal consequences of the continued depression of mind, attempted in vain to arouse him. Their efforts commenced too late. His reason, already unsettled, soon abandoned him completely. To the dangers of illness and fear of death was now added something worse than either, the fear of the loss of reason. They immediately bound themselves by a solemn agreement to do everything in their power to prevent a recurrence of this dreadful calamity. As soon as one of their number became pensive, the rest combined immediately to distract his thoughts and cheer his spirits in every possible way that they could devise. After several months' imprisonment, Signor —— was visited by a lawyer employed by the Government for his defense. He was not allowed to choose his own advocate. After considerable delay he was brought before a tribunal composed of priests, and as no charge was brought against him, and as he was only suspected of liberal sentiments, he was liberated from prison with the condition that he would remain but one day in Rome, and then go to his house in the country to remain there until he received other orders from the Government. It was on this day that we first saw him. A few hours after our interview, and after taking leave of his family, he set out for his country-place, escorted by some of the Papal police.

"Ten years afterward we were again in Rome, and again saw Signor ——, who, freed from his condition of remaining upon his farm in the country, was allowed the privilege of coming to Rome, with the condition, however, annexed, that he was never to go outside of the walls of the city. To see that this condition was not broken, the police visited his house constantly, and very often woke him up at midnight in order to be certain that he was still in Rome. Constantly watched by the Papal spies, a prisoner within the circuit of the walls of Rome, with most of his property either confiscated by the Government or paid in fees to his advocate, he was, the last time we saw him, still cheerful, with the hopes that the time is not far distant when Rome freed will become the capital of a united Italy.

"Yours very truly, R. N. T."

The facts as above narrated correspond to my own less perfect recollection of them. In one point, however, I am persuaded my friend has fallen short of the full statement of the case. He says that it was "after considerable delay" that his case was brought before the tribunal. That which is most distinctly impressed upon my mind in connection with this case was the fact that this gentleman's hair was turned prematurely gray, and that his eyes wore that blanched aspect which plants acquire which are deprived of light, and which was due to his *long imprisonment* in a dim prison.

CHAPTER V.

THE IMPRISONMENT OF THE ADVOCATE AND DEPUTY, SIGNORE VINCENZO DI TERGOLINI.

THE apologists of the Roman Government deny that political prisoners are treated with severity. Last winter, the Hon. Mr. Corcoran, a member of Parliament, inserted a letter in the *London Times*, in which he declared that he had visited the political prisoners, and that their number was less than fifty, and that nothing could be more comfortable than their situation. He had conversed with them, and they had declared that they had nothing to complain of, and admitted that the delay in their trial was generally due to their own remissness. It was quite a fascinating picture which he drew of the life of a political prisoner in Rome. Some of my English and Scotch friends went with him and confirmed his statements. They were surprised at what they saw, and feared that the good Pope and his kind government were the victims of political and Protestant slanders.

It was a *show prison* which they saw. It is possible that Mr. Corcoran believed that it included all the political prisoners of Rome. If so, it proves that his charity was greater than his sagacity and knowledge. It may be that his unconsciousness of the hundreds of political prisoners in San Michele, in the horrid fortress of Paliano in the Sabine Hills, and of various lonely prisons on the sea-shore, did not arise from his being "willingly ignorant."

Let us turn from this rose-colored account of a Catholic partisan, who only saw one prison for a few moments, to a story of a political prisoner, a man of high character, education, and position, who had a bitter experience of several of them for the space of four years.

Signore Vincenzo di Tergolini has published an account of his imprisonment by the Roman Government. It bears all the marks of truthfulness. It is dedicated to the Rev. Mr. Gurney, of Paris, a friend of the author, and well known as a gentleman of high character and standing.

His father was for many years a highly honored judge in Padua, Vicenza, and Venice. He became an advocate, a doctor of law, a judge, and finally a deputy to the Venetian Parliament.

In 1848, Venice became independent of Austria. Signore Tergolini became prominent by his patriotic writings and speeches, and self-sacrificing pecuniary contributions for the Republic.

Sent as a commissioner to Florence, to establish with her a firm and friendly alliance, he was just on the eve of a successful termination of his mission, when the reaction in favor of the Grand

Duke broke forth in that city. It was part of that general movement which restored Venice to Austria, Rome to the Pope, and Florence to Leopold. He was compelled to escape. Unable to return to Venice, he concluded, for precisely what reason does not appear, to take refuge in Rome. It was for him a fatal determination.

It was impossible that his history should remain unknown. He was suspected and watched by the police. At length he was denounced to the authorities. To escape from the city without a passport was impossible. To remain undetected within the city seemed to be impracticable. And yet he baffled the police for months, sheltered by his friends, and sleeping in coffee-houses, theaters, stables, in the dark angles of remote quarters, and among the ruins. In October, 1851, he was at length arrested.

He was a political prisoner. He was a gentleman of high education and position. Certainly he did not fare like those favored prisoners whom Mr. Corcoran saw, surrounded with comforts and books and the society of equals. The brutality which he experienced was such as no Christian Government should exhibit to thieves and murderers, and the utter disregard of all legal forms of which he was the victim could have a parallel only in the despotism of the worst of the Cæsars.

He was thrust into a little, dark, and filthy watch-house, in which common criminals and thieves and murderers were temporarily placed previous to their imprisonment. It was exceedingly damp as well as dark. A voice accosted him,—"Who are you?" "An unfortunate creature like yourself," was the reply. His companion kindled a match. By the fleeting light he saw a man of middle age lying on a bare table, supported by iron feet. He observed, also, the disgusting filthiness of the floor. As night drew on, he expected food and a bed, or a transfer to another prison. In vain! His companion, a servant of a marquis, committed for an alleged theft, kindly relinquished his table to the new-comer. At four o'clock in the morning five other persons were thrust into the same vile hole. One of them brutally demanded and obtained his resting-place. His little money had been taken from him. For three days he was left without food. During this period other prisoners came and went and were provided for. At length, on the fourth day, he was allowed eight baiocchi a day for food. In this dreadful place he remained thirty-two days. A constant succession of thieves and assassins came and were again removed in the course of a few hours. He alone was compelled to remain. And the captain of this band of carabinieri, as one of those who showed him some kindness assured him, had himself been a robber, and bore upon his shoulder the brand with which it is the custom of the Roman Government to mark such criminals. Such is Roman justice. Thieves and robbers promoted and put in charge of political prisoners. And why? Because no upright citizen will discharge this hateful function.

The Roman law, for there is law in Rome, requires that an accused person should undergo a preliminary examination within twenty-four hours after his arrest. But it was not until ten days had elapsed, that Signore Tergolini was examined. Even then it was not properly an examination. No evidence, written or oral, was produced against him. He was simply questioned. Hope was held out to him that if he would give certain information to the Government, he should be released. But he declares that he was absolutely ignorant of the matters concerning which he was questioned. The Government knew his history. They inferred that he must be connected with those secret societies which have for their object the overthrow of the Papal Government. They hoped by cruelty and imprisonment, and the despair produced by them, to extort information. A system this, worthy of Tiberius or the Borgias. It is not at all improbable that some other prisoner, weaker or less honorable than himself, had thus been induced, by suffering and the desire to escape horrible imprisonment, to give on mere suspicion or pure invention the name of Signore Tergolini, as one of those conspirators which the Roman Government so earnestly seeks and never finds. Who can tell how many persons in

Rome, liberal indeed in sentiment and longing for a change in the Government, but utterly free from conspiring against it, are the victims of secret informers! Who can tell the agony and self-reproach of those informers, who, in hours of weakness and temptation and despair, have saved themselves by the sacrifice of others equally innocent with themselves of the crimes imputed to them!

Signore Tergolina, still hoping for release and exile, was struck with horror upon finding that he was to be sent to the prison of San Michele. Conducted thither in the garb that he had not changed for thirty-two days, he was placed in a little cell, narrow and dirty, and swarming with vermin. It was six feet high and five feet broad, with a window three feet wide, into which the sun shone but a few minutes in the morning. "God must have restrained me," he writes, "from dashing my head against the wall, and thus putting an end to my uneasiness and suffering of body, and the tortures of my almost broken heart." In the cell next to his own there was a young man, of about twenty years of age, condemned to death. He heard his groans by night and day. Communicating with him as they were marched from the cells to the yard each day, he was assured by him that he had committed the murder of a liberal, at the solicitation of his parish priest, with the promise of impunity and absolution. In such a cell, and with such accompaniments, he continued to share all the pains and penalties inflicted upon robbers and murderers and assassins. It is characteristic of the policy of the Roman Government, the fact which he mentions, that on one occasion he heard the voice of some English person praising the commodiousness and airiness of the large hall around which the cells were ranged. "But," he adds, "none of the doors of the cells were opened, where he would have found a scene revolting to humanity."

In this connection I cannot omit Signore Tergolina's account of the Papal law in the case of those who are condemned to death. Persons accused of crimes whose penalty is death, are closely confined until that penalty is pronounced. Then they enjoy greater privileges. They are placed in a larger prison, and with other prisoners. Their straw sack is changed for a mattress of wool, and this is called the *bed of death.* Better food and wine are furnished for them, and this is called the *food of death.* Four baiocchi a day are paid to them, and this is called the *wages of death.* Thus they pass days, weeks, months, and sometimes years, not knowing but each day may be their last. On the day of execution the lock of their cell is oiled, and at night six men enter noiselessly, spring upon the prisoner, put him in chains, drag him to a priest to confess, and then, the execution! The author declares that he knew several prisoners whose death had been delayed in this manner, from two to seven years. What a cruel and wanton aggravation of the already sufficient agonies of the condemned!

It was not until seven months after his first imprisonment that he was again examined. The judge announced to him that *nothing* was elicited by the examination. He knew not for what reason he was arrested. He could not answer and disprove charges, for none were made. He simply answered questions.

Political crimes, after this first examination, come before the tribunal of the Sacra Consulta, from which there is no appeal. It is composed of six monsignori, and the procurator, who corresponds to our attorney-general, or district attorney. They sit on an elevated platform, before a large table, on which is placed a crucifix. The accused stands before them, guarded by a soldier, and with his advocate by his side. The advocate has no power to control the proceedings, to elicit the charges, and to confine the inquiry to the indictment. The accused is asked all sorts of questions which the suspicions of his judges or the tales of informers may suggest. The advocate dare not demand a strict indictment, or a close adherence to the question, before this awe-inspiring tribunal. He can but timidly suggest explanations of the conduct of his client, from which his innocence may be inferred. The accused, after such a process, waits for his written sentence, which is delayed sometimes ten months, and which renders no reason for his condemnation, and which is without appeal. Signore Tergolina declares that as he writes he has under his eye a sentence of the 31st of Dec. 1851, of ninety persons of Senigallia (the Pope's native province), of every condition in life, upon which are printed the words "Sacra Consulta," "Invocato il nome santissimo di Dio." Of these ninety persons, ten were condemned to ten, fifteen, twenty, and forty years in the galleys, and twenty-four to death. And yet the Pope—the minister of God's mercy to the world—cannot sign a sentence of death. But when it is submitted to him for ratification or pardon, he places upon the sentence, if he approves of it, a black ribbon, and if he reverses it, a red ribbon.

It was before this tribunal that Signore Tergolina was at length brought, after nine months of delay, for trial. The advocate assigned him came to him and made many inquiries, and expressed his conviction that he could not be condemned. He was brought before his judges with his hands bound in irons, between two soldiers. His indignation at thus being led as a common criminal with thieves and murderers through the streets overcame his prudence. He broke out against his judges with earnest remonstrances. "Certainly," he said, "God enabled me to hurl just invectives against these malignant hypocrites in that tremendous hour. Notwithstanding the feebleness produced by poor and meager food, and broken sleep upon a bed of straw for so long a period, besides my agony of mind, I did not allow myself to forget what was due to the dignity of man." One would like to have witnessed that scene, and heard that invective!

Matteucci, cruel and stealthy and soft as a tiger, asked him many questions in a gentle and insinuating way. Signore Tergolina freely admitted his agency as a Venitian patriot. But his conduct in that respect was not a matter for the jurisdiction of Rome. Only one point was made against him. He was in Rome without a passport. He proved that he had deposited it in the police office, according to law, and had been refused the ordinary card of sojourn. He was dismissed with the assurance that his trial would be resumed. But, no! He was removed to the "*Carceri Nouve.*" On the 3d of August he received his sentence, following that trial in which only one slight offense was charged, and that disproved. He was condemned to the galleys for twenty years. They professed in the sentence, although the charge was not made in the trial, to have found in his possession a prohibited paper, relative to a secret society. Signore Tergolina solemnly declares that he never had such a paper, and never belonged to such a society.

Such was the treatment and trial of a political prisoner, not a citizen of Rome; a man of high position and distinction; a patriotic, learned, and religious man.

I cannot dwell upon the cruel and revolting circumstances of his imprisonment at the Carceri Nouve, and subsequently of his transfer to the dreadful fortress of Paliano, among the Sabine hills. When, on a pleasant summer evening, a year ago, I sat at Oleavano, opposite to this grim old medieval fortress, I heard from an artist who had visited this region for many summers, some harrowing tales of the treatment of political prisoners within its walls. I was assured by him that they were mixed with other criminals, and fared worse rather than better, and that they were there by the hundred. And now this book, "*Quattro Anni delle prigione del S. Padre*," of the Avvocato Tergolina, confirms the statement that I then heard.

It would be a matter of painful interest, if my space permitted me, to give some of the details of his continued imprisonment for more than three years after his condemnation. He was never consigned to the galleys. He made himself exceedingly useful to his fellow-prisoners by giving them regular instructions, and by preparing memorials for them to the Government. He occupied much of his time in legal and moral writings. His mind received in prison those first impressions of religious truth which were subsequently matured in England into the full conviction of the great truths of the Gospel as they are set forth in the Church of England. His book is written in a spirit of almost childlike Christian simplicity. It was by his exemplary conduct, and his unwearied representations of his innocence, that he at length obtained his freedom.

I conclude this account with the statement of some other punishments for political offenses, of which Signore Tergolina was cognizant, and with a description of his food and his condition at Paliano.

On the 30th of April, 1850, five young men sent up from the roof of a house the tricolor of Italy in Bengal lights, in commemoration of the victory gained over the French troops on that day of the previous year. For this offense they were arrested, imprisoned, and condemned to the galleys for twenty years. At the date of his writing (1860) Signore Tergolina knew that one of them was still undergoing that sentence.

The young man, Henry Ruspoli, cousin of the prince of that name, fell under the suspicion of having taken part in that demonstration. Walking with his young wife in the streets, he was suddenly struck by carabinieri, and separated from her. As she raised a loud cry, one of these brutes struck her with his hand and silenced her, while another prostrated her husband with his baton. He was conducted first to the guard-house, and thence to San Michele, where he was detained several months, and whence he was at length released for want of any evidence against him, and from the influence of his illustrious relative.

In the same year, 1850, the celebrated sculptor

Rinaldi was suspected of having received a Lombard exile in his house. The carabinieri having searched his house and not found the person for whom they were in search, conducted to the prison all the inmates of the house at that time. Rinaldi, his wife and sons and daughters and domestics, a lady visitor, a physician, then making a professional call, fourteen persons in all, were detained eight days in prison. Truly does Signore Tergolina remark that the Papal Government at that time was like a famished tiger whose appetite it seemed impossible to satisfy.

After mentioning other similar cases, Signore Tergolina remarks that he cannot refrain from describing two ridiculous instances of Papal persecution which show the extent to which priestly fear proceeded.

A poll-parrot, who had been taught to utter disrespectful words concerning the Pope, was banished; and another which sang a patriotic song was killed by the police.

The manner of living to which Signore Tergolina, equally with the vilest criminals, was subjected, is thus described:

"In fact many died there, and none can say in consequence of what disorder. Our daily food was such as to leave us half famished, and often, when half famished, it was impossible for us to eat. Black bread, which was half full of dark, heavy matter; soup, which was filthy and only half cooked; rice of the most inferior quality, with gravel and nameless impurities mixed with it; beans, with ashes carelessly mixed in, and so old and decayed as to be full of great black bugs, and the other vegetables in like manner filled with vermin; and water, bad and full of extraneous matter, and sometimes swarming with little living fish,—such was our sustenance at Paliano." "For four years I suffered the horrors of famine, and after my liberation for a whole year, it seemed as if my hunger never was satisfied. For all that period I had not seen nor tasted a piece of pure bread nor a drop of pure water."

After this testimony of a man of pure and honorable character, singularly void of a spirit of bitterness and revenge, as his whole book shows him to have been, we can judge what value is to be attached to the testimony of those visitors, who are led by sleek monsignori and zealous perverts through a clean and cheerful and well-furnished show prison, and are told that it is thus that the Roman Government treats political offenders.

The story proves several points which place Rome far in advance of all other civilized despotisms in cruelty, and put her by the side of the worst of Oriental and ancient tyrannies.

It proves that men are arrested in Rome on the mere suspicion that they may belong to secret societies against the Government, or on the information of spies, or of prisoners, who invent crimes for others, to escape penalties, just or unjust, inflicted upon themselves.

It proves that not only Roman citizens, but the citizens of other States, who have been known as the friends of freedom, are regarded as criminals at Rome, and as destitute of the rights, which belong even to the guiltiest wretches, of an accusation and trial, and opportunity for defense.

It proves that political prisoners are treated not with less but with greater inhumanity than any other class.

It proves that arrests are made of many persons not so much for the purpose of punishing them as of extorting from them information.

It proves that in the case of political offenders all the ordinary maxims and forms and proceedings of law are utterly and arbitrarily set aside.

It proves that for the purpose of guarding the temporal power of the Pope, every dictate of common humanity and of decent respect to our common nature, is set aside, and that the poor victim, often entirely innocent, is given up to a malignant, remorseless, unchecked, omnipotent will.

All this in the name of the religion of the blessed Saviour!

Oh Lord—how long? how long?

CHAPTER VI.

THE SECRET NATIONAL SOCIETY AND COMMITTEE.

The Pope and the Priests may be afraid of the Devil, but they are not so much afraid of him as they are of the Secret Society and its committee, which lie under the whole of the Roman population as the catacombs lie under Rome—dark, sinister, penetrating everywhere, and everywhere charged like a mine, with explosive materials. It is indeed a marvel, a master-piece of Italian subtlety—the Secret Society. It is everywhere felt, and nowhere seen. The wonder is that so impulsive a people can keep such a mighty and wide-spread secret so close that all the appliances of Papal power and priestly craft are utterly unable to get any clew to it. Of course, a mere visitor who at once described it as absolutely inscrutable, and professed to know much about it, would stultify himself. And yet, from some facts well known, and from others fairly deduced, and from special information derived from friends who, I was morally certain, belonged to it, I felt that I had acquired a pretty correct general notion of its character, objects, and operations.

Its object is well known from its own published annals. The National Committee has its press, and publishes, from time to time, its manifestoes. It indicates its policy and the duty of its members, and publishes its appeals, its warnings, and its words of encouragement to its friends in Italy and throughout Europe. These are facts well known. But who the committee are, and where the printing-press is, are facts not known, and, so far, not discoverable. The efforts to get a clew to that press are incessant and unavailing. The police, the confessional, the whole army of Jesuits, the *Serventi* and *Servente*, all are employed in vain in the hopeless task. During the last winter that I was in Rome, the police fancied that it could be found in some subterranean chambers within the gardens of the French Academy of Arts. They claimed the right to examine. The French authorities were indignant. But the Papal Government insisted that the examination should be made. It was made, and nothing was found, and the French were more angry than before. It is just as likely to be in some old Roman chamber under the palace of a Cardinal who is searching for it as anywhere else. It may be under the special charge of the minister of police who professes to make frantic efforts for its discovery. Or it may be in some catacomb, or some wine vault of a ruined Roman villa, on the Campagna. But wherever it is, the entire power and craft of the Papacy are insufficient to find it.

The present National Committee has for its watchword, "United Italy under Victor Emmanuel, with Rome for its Capital." After the restoration of the Pope in 1849, the Secret Society which was formed was republican, and contemplated the unity of Italy as a Republic. When the masterly policy of Count Cavour made Napoleon's triumphs inure to the unification of Italy under a constitutional monarchy, a new society in the interests of Victor Emmanuel was formed. It gradually absorbed the best portion of the Roman patriots. At length, within the past year, knowing well, what the Papal Government in vain endeavored to discover, the *locale* of the rival Republican committee, it threw it open to the light, destroyed its printing-press, and put an end to its existence. There is now but one patriotic organization in Rome which has any real power. The old friends of Mazzini have, for the most part, joined the new organization, and adopted the new watchword. Its object is utterly to destroy the temporal power of the Pope, and to make Rome the capital of United Italy. It is in constant communication of course with the Italian Government.

There is probably nothing more remarkable in history than the absolute inscrutableness of this wide-spread association, under a government which has unrivaled instrumentalities for *espionage.* Men lie imprisoned for years under the suspicion that they belong to it—mere boys are seized and cast into narrow dungeons—property is confiscated, rewards are offered, the police stimulated to its utmost, the confessional plies its subtlest and most terrifying agencies, spies are paid to join it and disclose it—and yet not one person has hitherto betrayed it. This is certainly most remarkable. When I have expressed my wonder at this state of things, and my doubt of its possibility, and therefore of the existence of any extensive association of this kind, I have been referred to considerations such as the following:

I have been reminded that ever since the period of the French Revolution the Italians have had constant experience in secret societies, and have learned, after many failures and disclosures and betrayals, the secret of guarding them on every side from discovery by treachery or indiscretion. The Italians have a genius for subtle secrecies and intrigues; and it has been sharpened by the societies of the Carbonari and of Young Italy which have existed all over Italy for more than fifty years. Their organizations and operations have been miracles of skill. Their long training in secret societies, and this perfect knowledge of the sources of danger and betrayal, it is contended, are sufficient to account for the marvelous immunity with which this wide-spread association carries on its work.

I have been told too, that the leaders of this organization have studied in the Society of Jesus such models and methods of secret operations as have enabled them to put to defiance all efforts for its discovery. Three hundred years of keen study, by the sharpest wits in Europe, of all possible methods of disguise—study which penetrates into the deepest mysteries of human thought and motive and passion—have, no doubt, brought this evil skill to its utmost perfection.

Yet, notwithstanding these explanations, it still seems a wonder that this million-eyed Roman Government, with the training of centuries in *espionage*, has never been able to detect and bring to light this remarkable organization. The utmost that it has ever accomplished has been to obtain moral, or even in some cases absolute certainty, that certain individuals belonged to it; but from none of them have they been able to learn what it is, where it is, and who are its leaders and members. They have found the key-hole to this adamantine *safe*, but they cannot find the key; and they cannot penetrate into and possess its archives by breaking it or burning it. The fact seems incredible, when we remember what is involved in this obstinate secrecy.

In the first place, it is evident that all the thousands of Romans who belong to this association must be guilty of constant and repeated perjury. Simple falsehood, it must be confessed, comes easy to an Italian. But this is in cases which his religion will either sanction in advance or subsequently absolve. But perjury to the priest—perjury which cannot be confessed and absolved—it would seem as if no Romanist could possess a patriotism robust and daring enough to confront this awful sin. And yet nothing is more clear than that the priesthood make searching inquisition for this society in the confessional. The sacraments of the church are refused to those who do not disavow all connection with the new order of things in Italy, and express their readiness to co-work for its destruction. Secret instructions were issued by the Grand Penitentiary, in the early period of the revolution, to this effect. A copy of this document found its way into the Italian press and was the subject of much and indignant comment.

This curious paper bore the date of the 10th of December, 1860. Its directions were stringent and peremptory. The confessor was commanded to regard every act of political adhesion, however remote, to the new Government, as a sin which needed special expiation before the guilty party could be admitted to enjoy any religious privileges or consolation. The expiation demanded was a solemn engagement to turn, at the first favorable opportunity, against the Italian Government. The penitent was permitted to defer active opposition to the Government until he could do it with personal safety. Thus persons in the employment of the Italian Government might be permitted to remain as secret foes and prospective traitors. The soldier might continue to serve until an opportunity should offer to surrender his post or his command. The clerk might remain in office, if he would betray the secrets of the Government.

When such instructions were given to the priesthood in the Italian Kingdom, we may be sure that others, still more monstrous, would be issued at Rome. I have heard repeatedly, and from sources entitled to my entire confidence, that constant inquisition was made at the confessional into political opinions, and that the expression of doubt as to the lawfulness of the Pope's temporal power was treated as the sin of sins. But I confirm my own testimony by that of an able writer in the North British Review for June (1865), who is evidently thoroughly conversant with the "state and prospects of Italy." He writes thus:

"Confessors were not content with imposing a special penance on those who stood convicted of connection with political authorities deemed unholy. They were directed to constitute themselves inquisitors, not into the acts but into the speculative opinions, on political matters, of their penitents. During Lent, 1862, in Rome, the question came to be addressed to penitents, What they thought of the Pope's temporal dominion? and absolution was refused to such as either declined replying to what they considered a question affecting a point foreign to religion, or answered in a spirit not in accordance with the view that it was a divine institution. It is to be expected that our statement will be set down as an Exeter Hall fancy by those who make it their business to cry up the court of Rome. The facts we allude to are of too private a nature to be given in detail, but we stake our credit on the perfect authenticity of the statement; and we know that one of the most eminent members of the Roman Catholic hierarchy who then happened to be in Rome inveighed in unmeasured terms of reprobation against this monstrous proceeding. Since then the system has not been abandoned. It has only been modified."

It should be remembered, in this connection, that it is not possible for any Roman to avoid this perjury, by abstaining from confession. He must confess at stated festivals, or a certain number of times during the year. The city is divided into a certain number of *Rioni*, or wards. Every householder is compelled to return to the police, and to the parish priests, the name of every inmate of his house. The first ceremony, which even every foreigner undergoes, upon hiring an apartment or a room, is the rendition to the police department of an accurate account of his name, profession, age, and country. There is every day at the police department in Rome a precise knowledge of how every chamber, large enough to contain a bed, is to be occupied on that night, in hotels as well as in private apartments, in the case of all persons except those who may have arrived in the city later than three o'clock. Now as every priest knows of every Roman citizen within the bounds of his parish, so he is under bonds to see that every one comes to confession. If he should neglect that duty, he would soon find himself in the priest's prison, near Civita Vecchia, or subjected to some other hard discipline. In like manner every citizen of Rome is compelled to present to the authorities a certificate of the priest to the effect that he has confessed, and is a good Christian, and has been absolved. If he should fail to do this, he will be fined, and if he persist he will be imprisoned or sent to the galleys; if he should die unshriven through obstinacy, he will be denied Christian burial, and his property will be forfeited to the State. It is true that these rigorous exactions are occasionally somewhat relaxed through the kindness or treachery or corruption of the priest.

There are also cases in which confession is evaded by collusion with the priests. A poor man is hired to personate one whose repugnance to the confessional or to sacrilegious falsehood is unconquerable, and the priest, for a consideration, or from sympathy with the patriotism of the party (for there are some such priests) sends him a certificate that he has made an excellent confession. I was told that this system of substitutes for confession is quite common, but I am inclined to think it is rare, although I know of instances in which it was adopted.

Now in view of this enforced confession, and this inquisition into political opinions, and this consequent necessity for perjury, which from its very nature cannot be confessed and absolved, and which therefore it would seem would create a superstitious terror in a Catholic conscience, it certainly seems passing strange that this great secret society should remain so long utterly unbetrayed. It indicates either a very enfeebled religious principle, or a conviction that, under the circumstances in which the Romans are placed, patriotism is itself a religion of higher sanctions and obligations. Both of these reasons may operate, but the latter is probably most effective. The Roman patriot no doubt satisfies his conscience by the plea that the priest has no right to penetrate into his political convictions and actions, and to brand that as sin which is for him lofty duty, and hence, that what the priest in his spiritual character has no right to demand to know, he himself has a perfect right to conceal. Such questions are not always easy to be resolved. In our own war, patriotic spies and religious soldiers escaping from bondage, have felt it a solemn duty, or at least an unquestioned privilege, to lie fearfully to the enemy. In a land of casuistry and of Jesuits, there is no lack of high authority for conscientious deception and dishonesty. Rome has taught her children how to deceive her, and yet retain a good conscience.

But however difficult it may be to account for this marvelous secrecy, there can be no doubt of the *fact* of the existence of the National Committee, of its numerous membership, of its effective working, and of the utter inability of the Government to discover its leaders, or break up its press, or impede its operations.

That which is most unaccountable in the whole matter is, not that multitudes have been found faithful, but that there has not been a single person to betray the association, and that no spies of the Government have been able so to connect themselves with it as to disclose its secrets. Doubtless enormous bribes and rewards have been offered. Rome would count a million of scudi cheaply spent if she could lay her hand on the head, or even on the members of this organization. Nor do we doubt that there are many connected with it, who, for high pay, or under the terror of imprisonment, or the stings of conscience, or from superstitious fears, would betray it—*if they could.*

If they could! Here we believe that we hit the true secret of this impenetrable society. The organization of the association is said to be new and peculiar. The Freemasons and the Carbonari and the Illuminati were societies of individuals known to each other through secret signs and watchwords. Their object was to make known to each other the members and the officers of the society, and to combine for associated action.

Each member was acquainted with the authority directly above him, and with a group of co-members with whom he was to act. The liability, however, to discovery and betrayal involved in this arrangement gradually led to a new method, by which only so much of mutual knowledge of the *personelle* of the association was allowed, as was essential to efficient action. The problem to be resolved was to bring to bear the momentum of the entire combined association, and yet to keep each member so isolated as that he should not know personally and positively any other member. An analogy to this may be found in material substances whose particles, however compact they may appear, are said never actually to touch each other. In order to a perfect security against betrayal, it was necessary that no member should have knowledge or proof, though he might have a moral certainty to his own mind, that any other particular individual was a member of the same association. This system the National Committee is said to have brought to marvelous perfection. The committee is small, and its *personelle* is unknown to the members. It has an absolute power of direction. Its double work is, on the one hand, to increase the number of partisans of the Italian Government, to advise them of such a policy in its interests as they can safely pursue, to obtain from them such information as will forward its objects, and to have all things ready for united action when the hour of deliverance shall strike, and, on the other hand, to confer with the Italian Government, conveying to it the secrets of the Papacy, advising it of the state of the Roman mind, and accepting from it counsels and suggestions as to the method and policies which it should pursue.

The advantages of such a system, if practicable, are obvious. He would be a bold man who should say that it is not practicable in the deft hands of these most subtle masters of finesse and craft. Moreover, it is evident that the thing to be accomplished needs nothing more. The immunity from betrayal induces the most timid patriots to join the organization. If the Government obtains moral or positive proof that an individual citizen belongs to it, even then it can do no more. Racks and screws cannot squeeze out of a man what is not in him, and even the utmost that can be found against *him* is that he received a printed communication from the National Committee, or that he wrote "*Viva Vittorio Emmanuele!*" on the walls of a cardinal's palace; or that he threw a harmless bomb between the legs of a particularly black and obnoxious priest, or that he tossed into a carriage in the Corso, during the Carnival, a bouquet with squibs against the Government, or that a picture of Garibaldi was found fixed in a frame *behind* that of the Pope or the Madonna, or something equally atrocious. It is sufficient for the National Committee to know who are its friends, on whom it can rely in the decisive hour, and to keep them encouraged and faithful to the cause by advising them of the situation and the prospects, and permitting them to make such occasional demonstrations as shall keep the Government in a state of alarm, and shall amuse them by the mixture of the comic with the serious which always attends these little patriotic *escapades*.

How pervasive and intangible and terrifying to the Government this national organization is appears from an incident that occurred just before I left Rome, in the winter of 1864. The city was startled one morning by the report that the long-trusted and confidential private secretary of Cardinal Antonelli had been arrested. He was charged with being in communication with the Italian Government and in complicity with the National Committee. An agent of Victor Emmanuel at the very source and center of the Papal power, in the midst of its innermost *penetralia*, and in the person of the private secretary and inner *confidante* of the Pope's Pope! Could anything be more mortifying or alarming? And it proved to be true! He was tried by the court of the *Sacra Consulta*, and convicted on evidence that was vague, and which led to nothing and to nobody beyond himself, and was sentenced to many years, I have forgotten how many, of close imprisonment. This august court, of about twenty judges and officials, held secret sessions, and each member was strictly forbidden to publish or reveal a word of its proceedings. And now mark the result! Lo! on the day after the trial closed, a record of all the proceedings, *printed by the National Committee*, was laid upon the table of every cardinal and high church dignitary in Rome! The impalpable National Committee and association were no more affected by this blow than Milton's loyal angels were by the swords of the hosts of Lucifer, which passed through their ethereal bodies and left them as they were.

Which of these officials was a member of the National Association, or from the cabinet of which of the cardinals or officials these records were nightly abstracted and copied through the agency of another secretary, or cook, or major-domo, or mistress; or where they were printed, or through whom the delicate attention of presenting them to the cardinals was paid, are points on which the Government is far more in doubt than it is as to the authenticity of the handkerchief of St. Veronica and the resting-place of the bones of St. Peter.

In another chapter on the same subject I will give some incidents which will illustrate the mode in which this Committee and its agents operate.

CHAPTER VII.

THE SECRET NATIONAL SOCIETY AND COMMITTEE.

THE work of the National Committee, and the society which it directs, is, as was seen from the last chapter, one of preparation and readiness to act in the future, rather than of present action. Yet the irrepressible patriotism of the Romans often breaks forth in most hazardous and useless, yet withal often comical manifestations. Although parties are frequently arrested and imprisoned on mere suspicion, the hatred of the patriots to the Government and the priests often finds imprudent and laughable expression.

When I arrived in Rome in June of 1862, just after the canonization of the Japanese saints, the air was full of whispers of the new designs of Garibaldi. The hopes of the patriots were at their height. The belief in Garibaldi's star was unbounded. The Romans were fully aware of the determination of the French Emperor to protect Rome and the Pope. But they knew as well that Napoleon had been opposed to the liberation of Naples and its union to the Kingdom of Italy —but it had been done by the irresistible Garibaldi. They knew of the diplomatic bonds which tied Victor Emmanuel—but they had been cut by the victorious hero. Hence they believed that the stern attitude of opposition and threatening which the Italian Government assumed toward Garibaldi was a comedy well understood by both parties. They were convinced that in some way, quite out of the usual tenor of European politics, but perfectly in harmony with Garibaldi's romantic career, the Emperor would be propitiated or baffled; and that the red shirt of the Liberator would soon be seen ascending the Quirinal, and heralding the victorious entrance of the stalwart King of Italy into the long-designated palace where many Pope-kings had been made, but which was henceforth to hold a King of Popes! What a day for Rome that would be! What a passion of patriotic joy would shake the seven hills! The thought almost set the Romans wild. Self-restraint was difficult in the extreme. Hope and exultation would escape in some form of expression. Patriotic demonstrations became rash and frequent. The patrols of French soldiers through the streets of Rome were increased. Murders of obnoxious gens-d'armes were multiplied. Terrifying messages were sent to many priests. They went softly and spoke gently, and recalled the horrors of the French Revolution, and looked pale and frightened. The patriots were at that time particularly exasperated with the Government and the priesthood, because they knew well that the canonization of the martyrs was only a pretense for assembling and reanimating the partisans of the temporal power, and rallying to its support with new zeal the Catholic powers of Europe. It was a period of intense suppressed excitement, of anxious expectation, of high hope on the one hand, and of a fearful looking for of wrath and vengeance on the other.

Such was the state of feeling during the summer months which I spent at Albano. Walking often under the grand old avenue of Ilexes which led to the Pope's summer residence, or strolling on the borders of the blue, deep-down dimpled lake, in company with an Irish-American priest, our talk was alternately of "the situation" at home, and at Rome. He was at the same time a high ultramontane as a Catholic, and a strong patriotic Unionist as an American; and the singular combination often produced perplexities of feeling and opinion which were peculiarly and deliciously absurd. He was spending the summer at a convent which overlooked the lake, and looked like an abode of tranquillity which no mundane anxieties could disturb. But the rumor of Garibaldi hovering on the Papal border created such a flutter among these nested Franciscans, as the appearance of a hawk on the horizon produces in a cote of doves. But the talk of the good fathers was not dove-like. Their common name for the King of Italy was "the Piedmontese Hog;" for Garibaldi, "The Brigand;" and for Napoleon III. any and every objurgatory and villifying epithet that came to hand. It is a curious fact that the priests hate their Imperial protector more even than those formidable foes from whom he is supposed to protect them. The good fathers were alarmed from observing on the Alban and Sabine hills signal-fires, which burned into their souls like an anticipated purgatory. These signal-fires could be traced all the way along the central mountain chain, the back-bone of Italy, from the neighborhood of Rome to the region where the daring Liberator had begun his adventurous and disastrous march. My location would not permit me to see these fires by night; but I saw their smoke by day. Intense as was my interest in the fortunes of my own land at that time, my heart bounded at the thought that I might possibly see Garibaldi enter Rome in triumph. Yet it was a hope rather than an expectation. From the first I have always believed that Napoleon would never relinquish his hold on Rome until he should be constrained by force, or by irresistible, and long-resisted, political necessities.

From time to time we heard of the anxious and troubled state of Rome—of the number of arrests, which on one day amounted to forty, and of the still continued, ill-judged, irritating and damaging demonstrations of the Roman patriots. On one occasion a dog was painted in the colors of the Pope, and with a tin pail tied to his tail, was sent down the Corso, and went out of the

Porto del Popolo—the same gate from which Pius IX. escaped in 1848, and from which, according to this symbolical representation, he would soon be compelled to escape again. At the opera, in the midst of the performance, a number of birds suddenly flew about the area with the Italian tricolor ribbons fluttering from their necks. This dreaded and hated tricolor was flaunted everywhere in the face of the priests and the police. Young men were stopped in the Corso, and their breast-pins and cravats torn from them. Ladies whose toilets combined the three colors, were peremptorily bidden to return home and change their dresses. Even the bouquets for sale at the corners of the streets often breathed treason; and the very vegetables lay under suspicion of conspiracy and rebellion. One of the regular occupations of the police in the morning was to efface from the walls patriotic watchwords, and the national emblem. The mischievous patriots delighted particularly in thus marking the walls of priests and princes, and conspicuous partisans of the black party. One of its most frequent demonstrations was in the evening to throw bombs made of stout pasteboard, and with an alarming charge of powder, between the legs of priests as they paused to talk with a friend or sip a glass of lemonade at the open stalls; and the delight of seeing the agile jumping of those consecrated legs must have been immense, for it was a dangerous pastime, and when discovered, severely punished. Men who leaned long against a wall were closely watched—for it was discovered that they often left a printed or a painted tricolor behind them. One method of baffling the effacing operations of the police was curious. Eggs were emptied, and then filled with tricolored paints, and thrown at night high upon the walls of buildings, and at points difficult of access. It made it necessary for the police often to procure ladders, and the sight of these majestic gens-d'armes, with their cocked hats, high up on ladders scraping off these moral plague-spots, must have been a matter of huge glee to these childlike and playful, even when earnest, Romans. Until the time of my departure, I noticed in my walks past the Coliseum, that there were some of these marks high upon the walls, which the police had never effaced, and which no doubt still proclaimed to the undying faith of the Roman patriots—"Garibaldi is coming!"

At this period and subsequently, there were other demonstrations which were peculiarly annoying to the Government. The Government insists that the great body of the Roman people are extremely contented and happy. It is accustomed to contrast their favored and peaceful state under the paternal government of the Pope, with that of the wretched and degraded population of Protestant nations. Hence it loves to show off the hilarity of the people on festivals and at the carnival. But the great body of the respectable Roman citizens take no part in, and do not even witness the festivities of the carnival. They are given up to foreigners, to French soldiers, and to the lowest of the populace. There is no heart, no abandon, no genuine fun, no characteristic national life in them. It is a dreary gibbering ghost of past hilarity. It annoys the patriotic Romans to see this farce enacted in the eyes of foreigners, and the modes which they employ to give their testimony against it have an air of decorous and solemn absurdity which is very diverting. Notice may be given in some way to which no clew can be obtained, or by little printed slips of paper with unintelligible figures and letters scattered in the street, to the effect that it is the purpose of many citizens *to take a walk*—that is all!—on the Pincian Hill, or at the Coliseum, or in the via Porta Pia. Accordingly, at the height of the carnival at one season, an immense number of citizens, gentlemen and ladies, *in black*, or in very sober suits, were seen solemnly walking—that was all!—on the Pincian! The police dispersed them, when suddenly the Piazza San Lorenzo was filled with the same somber and meditative crowd, to be dispersed again. At another time the same thing occurred at the Coliseum; and at still another at the Porta Pia. On the anniversaries of the Pope's accession, or of his birth-day, there is an immense turn-out of the people and of carriages;

and in spite of all the precaution of the baffled police, some demonstration is usually contrived which testifies unmistakably that the only anniversary which they would keep with their whole heart would be that of the Pope's passage into purgatory. On such occasions it is astonishing to see the imprudence with which demonstrations are made from which no good practical result can come, and which subject those who make them to espionage or arrest.

A remarkable instance of this imprudence on the one hand, and of the severity of the Government on the other, occurred on the opening of the railroad from Rome to Naples. It was a whole year after the Roman road was ready to be connected, before the Pope could be induced to consent that the road should be opened. Shortly after it was opened, a party of about forty Romans obtained permission to make a trip to Naples. When they crossed the Roman frontier and came in sight of the flag of the Italian kingdom—the view was too much for their prudence and self-restraint. They broke forth into enthusiastic and irrepressible cheers. Only one of the party was permitted to return! Many of them were married and business men; and for this imprudent act they were not only banished but beggared!

The patriots of Rome are not without their poets. Many satires and epigrams and patriotic odes in manuscript are circulated among them.

I have in my possession two of them, written in a round clear hand. One of them is on "The Excommunication of the King of Italy." I translate, as well as I am able, a few of the verses.

THE EXCOMMUNICATION OF THE KING OF ITALY.

To the lucent dawn of a Roman day,
  Our mitred and white-robed Sovereign turns,
And a dreadful awe in his heart makes way,
  And a thought of fire within him burns.

Be still—for the lips of our holy Jove
  Are moving with words divine and high;
Be still—lest the prayer of faith and love,
  Marr'd by your noise, shall not reach yon sky!

Perchance he pleads with earnest zeal,
  That our sins may be all forgiven;
That the angel *Grace* may come and seal
  To our troubled hearts the peace of heaven.

Perchance he commits to God's kind care
  The welfare of peoples new born and free,
And prays that *Italy*, one and fair,
  Like our Rome of olden time may be.

What! Italy *one?* that league of hell?
  It makes him fume, and threaten, and fret,
And hurl at Victor Emmanuel
  The bolts—that have never hit him yet!

They are shining nothings in the air;
  They can break no more a monarch's crown;
Our God does not hear a cursing prayer,
  But strikes the black *anathema* down.

And thus the poem continues through a dozen stanzas more with increasing vehemence, reproaching the Pope for employing mercenaries to persecute and murder his own subjects, and for subjecting to foreign nations that Italy which it was his first duty to emancipate.

Another poem, entitled the "Adieu of Rome to the Hero of Niagara," is much more spirited. It is impossible for me to transfer to a translation the ease and point and sarcastic ring of these mocking and biting verses. The hero of Niagara, Blondin, had drawn immense multitudes to witness his performance in the old Pretorian Camp-ground of Tiberius. It was one of the few allowable frivolities in which the Romans could be indulged; because it was one which could not be turned to any political account. But it will be seen that Blondin's performances did something more than amuse the people and add several thousand scudi, in the form of tax for licenses, to the Papal treasury.

The following is a close and faithful, if not a happy, rendering of this sharp doggerel:

Great Quirinal Father!
  In mercy pray bend,
And to this bad world
  A moment attend.

Surely our Frenchman
  A Canon should be
Of John Laterano,
  Oh, Holy Padre!

He's the genius of Rome
For twisting and turning,
And sets all the city
To gazing and learning.

The people, astounded,
Admire every squirm
Of this quick, bright-spotted
And flexible worm,

Which France the renowned
Of heroes the nurse,
Has sent for our joy—
And also our purse.

We are but poor creatures
Of song and of dance,
And hence all our heroes
Are sent us from France!

Applaud, ye great people!
Crowd all in one bunch,
And throw up your caps
To Blondin and Punch!

Since hero and robber
In French mean the same,
Our hero shall be
A creature more tame.

A brave lofty tumbler,—
Economical too,
Whose cost will not be
Beyond a few sous.

Hero of Gymnasts!
The old land of Brutus
Returns the gay greeting
With which you salute us.

We hail your grand advent,
  For well we remember
You're like the great hero
  "*Del due decembre!*"

Your feats are the same;
  You are not strangers!
Alike in your fame,
  Alike in your dangers.

We dub you a Canon;
  You have enough grace,
And your prince will do better
  Than you in your place.

Our rulers and tumblers,
  While they walk the tight rope,
Expect not to fall—
  At least so they hope!

CHAPTER VIII.

THE GOVERNMENT OF PRIESTS, AND ITS ANOMALIES.

When the Papal Government is spoken of as a government of priests, it is said by its partisans to be a gross and conscious misrepresentation. The number of lay persons in the employment of the Government, compared with that of priests, is adduced as a triumphant confutation of the charge. The statistics, for instance, of the year 1856, prove that the entire administration of the Roman States was conducted by 7157 persons, of whom only 303 were ecclesiastics, and the remaining 6854 laics. We may allow the figures to be true, and yet adhere to the statement that the Government of the Roman States is a government of priests.

A crowned priest is at the head of the State. He constantly proclaims it as the first and most sacred of his duties, as a civil ruler, to administer the affairs of the State with a view to the welfare of the Church. He is supreme, in the sense and to a degree that no other ruler in the world claims to be. He is directly empowered and is infallibly directed by the Spirit of God to govern the Church for its best interests; and hence, as the interests of the Church are inseparably bound up with those of the State, he is equally directed and empowered in the Government of the State. This fact makes the administration of the Roman States a priestly government.

But it is, moreover, a government by priests, as well as a priestly government. The *governing* is done by priests. Let us see.

All the high offices, in which the *governing* functions are discharged, are in the hands of the priests. The heads of departments govern; the subordinate officers serve. It would be a singular confusion of things that differ to call Earl Russell the Secretary for Foreign Affairs, and the tide-waiters and the porters at the custom-houses the *governing class* of Great Britain. We are accustomed to say that the aristocracy constitute the governing class in Great Britain. And yet, if we should count all the clerks and laborers in the employment of Government, who are, equally with Lords Palmerston and Russell, officers under the Queen, and decide the question by preponderance of numbers, we should conclude that the middle or the lowest class is the governing class of Great Britain.

If we turn to the official Annual Almanac published at Rome, we find the following positions occupied by ecclesiastics. They are at the head of all the *departments* (as we should term them), including, at this time, the ministry of war. They occupy the prefectures, or legations of the provinces; the embassies, and all diplomatic functions; the principal offices at court (such as Maggiordomo, Maestro di Camera, etc.); the higher judicial tribunals of the Sacra Consulta, the Rota, the Segnatura di Justicia, il Tribunale Lauretano, and in part the criminal Tribunals. They are at the head of the congregation or committee of public instruction; occupy the presidency and vice-presidency of the Council of State; of the *consulte* of the finances, of the police, of the public health, and of prisons; of the committee on the public land, the presidency of the commission of agriculture, etc. They are, in short, at the head, and in the controlling position, of all the departments and all the agencies of the State. Wherever there is honor, influence, control, profit, there they are! Wherever there is labor, subordination, service, no honor, small pay, there they are not! Where the carcass is, there the—*crows*—are gathered together.

Again: the total amount of money paid to the laity in office has been contrasted with that paid to ecclesiastics, and the inference drawn from the figures that the former receive far the greater benefit from the Government. But we find that the *average* of the salaries of ecclesiastics is about four times that of the laics. The truth is, that the offices held by the laity are such as the priests would not accept, or the duties of which they could not discharge with any decent regard to propriety, and to the respect which they expect from the people. They could not or would not become clerks in custom-houses, laborers upon the public roads, or servants and *custodi* in palaces and museums, at prices below what they receive for the easier and more honored function of saying mass.

And yet the partisans of the Church insist that it is a perversion of the truth to say that laymen are excluded from high offices at the Papal court. The author of the "Storia degli Stati della Chiesa," etc., issued at Rome in 1860, as an elaborate vindication of the Papacy, refers to the fact that, after the Pope's return from Gaeta, provision was made that laymen might be employed in some high functions. But we do not need the testimony of Mons. About to the effect that in point of fact very few are thus employed. My author, with charming naïveté, admits the fact, and accounts for it on the ground that very few laymen equal to their posts can be found; and, moreover, that it would have been very difficult to have passed by prelates "who had hitherto administered affairs with as much prudence as disinterestedness." Hear him!

"Gregory XVI., and his Secretaries of State, Bernetti and Lambruschini, acted upon the principle that no concession should be made to liberalism, which when it obtains one privilege becomes emboldened to demand others which cannot be granted. In this sentiment they were confirmed by Austria. If we can confide in the statements of Coppi, Gregory XVI. absolutely refused to establish a Council of State composed of laymen, in order that there should be no infringement of the prerogatives of the cardinals ; in like manner he rejected the device of allowing the people to elect their municipal and provincial counselors. Neither Gregory XVI. nor Pius IX. permitted a lay administration. Even the lay ministry instituted by Pius IX. before the revolution, was presided over by the Cardinal Secretary of State. In the lay ministry, if we except Mamiani, who was a demagogue ruled by his imagination, and Rossi, who was so ignominiously massacred, there remained not a single one who by capacity or education was fit for a high position. Ambitious men, indeed, who were continually seeking for office, were not wanting—Italian liberals, of superficial knowledge, and having no capacity but for declamation and intrigue, but wanting in firmness and intellectual sobriety, and in that self-abnegation which is essential to the right conduct of political affairs. Besides these there were some subaltern functionaries who are familiar with subordinate branches of administration, but are utterly unfit for comprehensive views. Besides this, it would have been very difficult to pass by prelates who had administered public affairs with equal prudence and disinterestedness."

Now it certainly seems a little singular that while laymen are found quite equal to the administration of the vast affairs of such large kingdoms as France and Austria and Russia and Great Britain, there are not found in the Roman States men capable of holding high offices, even under an infallible head, in a kingdom which numbers less than a million and a half of inhabitants. This is especially unaccountable when we are told that they have been trained by the best of systems, administered by the holiest of men. But Rome is full of these practical contradictions, which while they confound reason, give ample scope and development to faith.

Moreover, our author proceeds to show that the laymen are largely employed in those subordinate offices for which they are fit. The Gendarmerie, the Guarda Nobile, the clerks of the departments, employees in post-offices, railroads, and telegraph offices, the firemen, the postillions, the street scavengers, are they not all officers of the Government? Do they not all wear certain uniforms and gilded badges, some of them a foot square? Unreasonable men! what more can you desire? You should not aspire to an equality with the officials of the Heaven-designated Theocracy. Do you not know that even when you die your *feet* are placed toward the altar, whereas the priest's *head*, when he is dead, occupies that position? If the priest enters heaven *head foremost* and you can enter it only *feet fore-*

most, would it not be utterly incongruous that you should occupy any other than a subordinate position upon earth?

This double government, spiritual and temporal, has made it necessary to *invent* a class of men who have no counterpart in any other nation or government in the world. The *prelatura* are not laymen; they are not priests. They are a *tertium quid*—a combination of the two. They have the training and the dress and some of the restrictions of priests,—such as the inability to marry while in the service of the Pope,—and they have the functions and the freedom and the worldly life of laymen. The problem to be resolved was to secure men who would discharge, in a thoroughly priestly spirit, civil functions which it might not be suitable for the priesthood to perform, or which might need a special training for their discharge. Young men, if they have an income of 1000 or 1500 scudi a year, are employed in some subordinate position in a court of justice, or in the office of a cardinal connected with the Papal Court, or as secretary or clerk to a Papal Nuncio. Hence they are for the most part from the ranks of the aristocracy, or from the *new rich* men who appear even in Rome in the character of "the country merchants." A way is then opened to the *prelatura*. They are in the line of the highest dignities. Yet even while fulfilling those functions which are not priestly, they are not permitted to marry. It is difficult to describe this class, because they are a species so peculiar. They can occupy the office of *monsigniore*, which can be held also by priests and bishops and archbishops; and they can, if they please, advance from their inchoate or initial *orders* to the diaconate or priesthood, or the episcopate, if attractive preferments are presented to them. They cannot be advanced to the cardinalate, unless they are ordained deacons. But they can remain in that order as cardinals, and never perform mass or any of the functions of the priesthood. Cardinal Antonelli was a deacon until recently, having been ordained priest and performed mass for the first time last winter. Those who look for reasons in his conduct were malicious enough to suggest that they were to be found in the fact that the health of Pius IX. was failing, and that no one below the order of priest could be elected Pope. As *monsigniori* they hold many of the highest offices of the State. They are in the judicial, financial, and executive departments. Yet none the less do priests and bishops hold those offices, which are indiscriminately assigned to the *prelatura* and the priesthood. The association is calculated and intended to *priestify* the *prelatura*, and make them equally in spirit and feeling consecrated to the interests and policy of the Pope-King. It is possible for them, while they remain in an order below that of deacon, to marry; but, in that case, they cease to belong to the *prelatura*, and to exercise the functions they have hitherto discharged. They pass into the class of laics. The regular militia of the Pope must have no interests but those of the Papacy. They must be without wife and family. By this contrivance, some of the anomalies arising from the exercise of civil functions by priests are avoided; and yet those functions are discharged in the full priestly spirit. They belong to the priesthood in feeling and in interest. They have their bigotry, if not their piety. The laity feel that this class is more distant from them than the priesthood are, for with the latter they have some sacred associations and some affection and respect, arising from the offices which they have rendered, and the good character which many of them sustain; while with the latter they have no other associations than that they are the agents of that priestly government which they detest They see in them only that side of the priestly character which they abhor, and not that other side which they respect. Hence, so far as their agency in public affairs is concerned, it is pre-eminently priestly; though in their personal character they are almost universally destitute of that purity of character and life which attract reverence and regard for many members of the priesthood, and especially for those who confine themselves to their sacred functions.

Farini thus gives his judgment upon this class of mongrel priests: "The *prelatura*, and especially that part whose functions are connected with the court and with politics, and which is composed of men too laic to be ecclesiastics, and too ecclesiastic to be laymen, merit no consideration for their knowledge, and no respect for their manners. Their reputation is very indifferent. They are accused of making use of their power of patronage to corrupt the families of their dependents. They are the objects of the special detestation of the Roman people. It is obvious that their character and position must have a tendency to induce in them the faults of both the clergy and laity, without the virtues of either."

In estimating the relative emoluments of the clergy and the laity, it should be remembered that while the average of the salaries of the former is four times greater than that of the latter, they are, at the same time, in possession of rich benefices, dotations, abbacies, canonries, and of unnumbered offices of profit and honor without labor, connected with hospitals, museums, convents, and other institutions.

Whoever else may doubt whether the government of the Roman States is a government of priests, it is very clear that *they* at least have no doubts upon the subject. Their bearing and relation to Romans and to strangers indicate their consciousness that they are a governing class. Their insolence to strangers and visitors sometimes passes all endurable bounds. On one occasion I was standing in a group toward which a procession, carrying the host, was approaching. On such occasions it was my custom to take off my hat, but not to kneel. A little priest by my side, observing that I did not uncover at the precise moment that he did, rudely snatched my hat from my head, with violent expressions and gesticulations. After the procession passed, I turned to him and told him, as well as my scant Italian would permit, that he was an impertinent fellow; that he was not a policeman, and had no right to assume his functions; and that if he should do this thing to some of my countrymen, instead of a mere rebuke for his insolence, he would be likely to receive a castigation. He was livid with astonishment and rage, and replying not a word, went and spoke to two gendarmes that were standing near. They, however, seemed to think it was no case for their interference, and I passed on. A party of English and Scotch friends were in the crypt of St. Peter's, and, as the air was chill, and they did not suppose it was a consecrated place, the two gentlemen, who were clergymen, retained their hats. While there, the notoriously bigoted and violent Monsignore Talbot met them, and in a great rage accused them of purposely insulting the sacred place, and the feelings of the faithful; and insisted upon their immediately leaving the place. He would not listen to the assurances of these gentlemen—who gave him their cards—

that they were unconscious that it was expected of them to uncover; that the *custode* did not advise them of the fact; that they had seen other parties doing the same thing, and that they were incapable of consciously insulting the convictions and feelings of any one. The arrogant priest gave no heed to their assurances, but turned them out with rudeness and indignity, and ordered that they should not be again admitted.

The anomalies of this priestly government are almost ludicrous. Think of bishops and archbishops passing from sacred functions to regulate the war department, the lotteries, the theater, the police, and the prisons. Imagine a venerable ecclesiastic, with his spectacles on his nose, reading that lightest of all trash, a Roman comedy, and deciding how much of indecency and innuendo he could allow to remain, in consistency with the claims of morals on the one hand, and the interest of the prince-proprietor of the theater and of a government which must allow the people to be amused, on the other! Imagine another signing an order to a detachment of troops to proceed at once—for instance to Perugia—and shoot the unfaithful and disloyal children of the Holy Father back into loyalty and love! The *absurdity* of this government, as well as its tyranny, is profoundly felt by the Roman people. They are mortified and humiliated, as well as indignant, to be the only people in the world governed by priests. It is something like the feeling

6

which men have who are under a petticoat *régime*, from which they fain would but cannot break.

The priests are a privileged class, not only in securing to themselves the best emoluments of the State, but also in the right which they enjoy of being judged by an ecclesiastical tribunal, even in criminal cases. When the interests of a class are different from those of the rest of the community, and its crimes are to be tried and condemned only by itself, we may well expect a lenient judgment. The priesthood have exclusive jurisdiction in regard to all crimes committed by ecclesiastics of every grade.

But the anomaly of their functions in civil life is most perceptible when we observe the questions and associations into which they are introduced.

"The Cardinal Vicar of Rome, with the assistance of lieutenants and assessors, and *every bishop* in his diocese, with the assistance of his vicar, and one or more assessors, are judges in certain civil and criminal causes. Their jurisdiction extends to matters and persons,—that is to say, all contests which concern properties, whether ecclesiastical, or administered by ecclesiastics, or involving the interests of the tonsured class, come under their cognizance. Moreover, they exercise the police of morals, and judge all cases which have reference to them. Thus the priest is mixed with a crowd of courtezans and those abandoned persons who minister to vice and sell their own children for purposes of lust; thus he penetrates all the secrets of illegitimacy and of impure amours; thus he diminishes his own dignity and exposes himself to temptation which feeble human nature knows not always how to flee; thus he draws upon himself suspicions, murmurs, calumnies, and sometimes deserved outrages if it happens that the censor and judge of the irregularities of others yields to his perilous enticements, or if, by an unwisely directed zeal, he provokes scandal in families and cities, and introduces suspicion and discord where there existed previously, if not the reality at least the appearance of an honorable and respected union. The episcopal judge takes cognizance of all causes of rape and of illegitimate pregnancy, giving sentence according to the formula: *either endow or marry*, or—*to the galleys:*—a formula which often does nothing but subserve the purposes of abandoned women; a sentence which, in making the origin of the family to be compulsion, violates the moral principles of love and esteem and choice, which are its only true basis. Moreover, these inquests and condemnations for evil manners are very frequent; there are scarcely any bishops who have not cases of adultery of which to make trial and example."*

And this is the class of men to whom the in-

* Farini.

spired injunction is addressed—"Preach the Word; be instant in season, out of season"!

A striking instance of the *inconvenience*, to say the least of it, of the exercise of civil power by the Pope, was brought to light by the publication of the documents that were found in Bologna, after it came in possession of Victor Emmanuel, to which we have had, and shall have, frequent occasion to refer. Among these documents is a copy of the license given by the municipal authority, which was at the time directly under the control of the Cardinal Legate, the well-known Bedini, to women of bad life to ply their trade. Immediately on the entrance of the Austrian troops into Bologna (in 1854), the military commandant of the city, having regard, as he declared, "to the health of the troops," demanded that the Government should assume the direction of these women, and provide medical care for them. Although licenses had been issued by the municipal authority to this class of persons, and although the municipality was under the direct control of Cardinal Bedini, and although the sick among them were received into the "l'Ospital Civico" (a municipal institution), yet there did seem to be some awkwardness in completing this system at the demand of the Austrian authorities, by the payment of salaries to doctors for the special purpose of attending to such cases. Hence "*Excellenza Reverendissima*," the Secretary of State at Rome, was addressed upon the subject, and the inconvenience of this state of things was represented. Lo! behold the devices of holy infallibility. The "Illustrissimo and Reverendissimo Signore," at Bologna, was addressed in this wise: "The sanctity of our Lord has benignantly deigned, at an audience held this morning, to nominate the Doctor Pietro Zuola to be the first fiscal surgeon of Bologna, with the monthly allowance of 15 scudi per month, and in place of Zuola has nominated Dr. Giselio Bergazi, with the pay of 12 scudi per month, on condition that both shall render services gratuitously to the care of women of bad life, *the extraordinary gratuity which they have hitherto received for this service no longer being allowed.*" How beautiful and profound! What holy alchemy to turn leaden vice into golden goodness! It would not do for the "sanctity of our Lord" to permit physicians to be paid for attending those who had been licensed under his authority, to lead the life which brought on disease; but he could give them a nominal office with a salary and then direct them to discharge *gratuitously* the service for which they had hitherto been paid.

Such are the positions and the necessities imposed upon the Papacy, by becoming a kingdom of this world, and, as such, subjecting herself to the dictation of a power like that of Austria.

CHAPTER IX.

THE PAPAL GOVERNMENT AFTER THE RESTORATION.

THE form of the Papal Government admits of the most absolute despotism in case policy or passion prompt to its exercise. There are indeed laws, but they are only the rules of ordinary administration, which can be set aside at the pleasure of the Pope.

But in truth the principles of the Papacy make civil despotism a religious duty.

The first dogma of the Papacy is that God has revealed and bestows salvation only within one form of truth, in one church, under one head. It claims that temporal power has also been bestowed on this one infallible head of the church, in order that it may second and secure this great blessing of the salvation of those committed to its care. It becomes then the duty of the temporal power, in the service of the spiritual, not to permit any other dogma or church or ministry to exist within the range of this authority. This duty Rome most faithfully discharges. It becomes equally the duty of the temporal power to watch and regulate and coerce the whole life, outward and inward, of thought and speech and action of all its subjects, in order that they may be preserved from the danger to which their souls may be exposed. Its first duty is to the soul. As a spiritual power it must furnish it with truth, and put it in the Ark of Safety. As a temporal power it must keep it there by laws and pains and penalties. Hence, because of the *object* for which it exercises temporal power, it assumes the same sort of sanctity as the spiritual power. Its exercise is an obvious duty on the part of the Pope, and submission to it an equal duty on the part of his subjects. This is the theory of the Papacy. It claims to be absolute. It declares that in this fact lies its efficiency and blessing. But it contends that in practice it is a merciful and paternal power.

We do not pause to confute this theory; but we propose to show that in practice it is not holy and beneficent, but that on the contrary it is one of the most unrighteous, cruel, remorseless, and disgusting despotisms that the world ever saw. This is not the conviction alone of Protestants and Liberals, but no less that of a vast majority of those who admit the spiritual claims of the Papacy. Says one of the last and most able of the advocates of Rome as it is: "It is reserved for our age, the worthy child of Voltaire, to be the witness of another scandal; to see children arming against their mother; independent Catholics, that is to say, hypocrites employing against Rome their venomous fangs, recoiling before no violence, no calumny, no infamy. They have represented the Holy City as the sink of all the vices, as the rampart of despotism, as the Babylon, and the prostitute of nations."

We are quite aware that such charges should not be made on the authority of vague rumors. They should not rest even on individual testimony. They should have the support of authentic documents. We have related circumstances which have come to our own knowledge, on testimony that is to our mind perfectly satisfactory. But we have, moreover, conclusive documentary evidence that similar things, and worse things, by the hundreds, are constantly going on in Rome and the Roman States.

Pius IX. abolished the Statuto or Constitution of the Roman States, by his own arbitrary decree, soon after his return from Gaeta. The French occupation of Rome, and the Austrian occupation of the provinces, enabled him fully to carry out his system, notwithstanding that French honor often felt itself wounded, and even Austrian brutality was shocked by the remorseless cruelty of his Government. There was no revenge too small and brutal, there was no cruelty too wide-reaching, for the rage for punishing and repressing, with which the Papal Government seemed to be possessed.

The touching story of the heroic Garibaldi's wife has been often told. When he left her dead, in charge of a family of laborers, and rushed in agony into the woods to escape from his pursuers, with the charge that they should give her decent burial, even he, with all his knowledge of priestly vindictiveness, could not have imagined that these poor people would have been persecuted for an act of humanity which it would have been brutal to have declined. But they *were* persecuted. The delegate of Ravenna, the representative of the Pope, ordered them to be imprisoned, and the order was executed. But, so revolting even to an Austrian military governor was this proceeding, that General Marziani, then exercising that office, ordered their release, in the following rebuking words: "Considering that the brief reception of Garibaldi and his dying wife in the house of the brothers Ravaglia was granted through a sense of humanity, the delegate of Ravenna is ordered immediately to release the brothers Ravaglia from prison!"* When an Austrian general in Italy rebukes an official for inhumanity, the case must be bad indeed!

No city seems to have suffered more cruelly from Papal rule than Ferrara. We remember its gloomy, desolate, depressed aspect, as we saw it in 1853. Since we have read these documents we understand the reason. It had been, and was then, the scene of atrocities which filled its inhabitants with horror. Not long previous to that visit, the Austrians had arrested, on a rumor of

* *I lutti dello Stato Romano*, by Cav. A. Gennarelli. p. 14.

conspiracy, forty of the citizens. These persons, arrested on suspicion, were subjected to tortures in the stocks, by hunger, and by bastinading, to force them into confession of a conspiracy of which they knew nothing, and which was never proved to have had any other existence than in the fears and imaginations of the priests. It is now known by the documents to which I have referred, that the Papal Government, instead of repressing, lent its aid to this cruel outrage. The Austrian general demanded and received the aid of the Pontifical police, and of three "taciturn and firm priests!"*

One of those priests has left an account of his interview with some of these persons who had been thus tortured into confession of crimes of which they had not been guilty, and who solemnly, in their last hours before execution, declared to him that they were innocent. Succi declared the confession was wrung from him by bastinading, under which he believed that he would die. Malagatti declared that he confessed what was put into his mouth, because his tortures were so horrible that they caused a violent hemorrhage of blood. Parmeggiani gave a similar testimony. This priest, and one of the Confraternity of the Dead, related these facts to the Papal authorities. They were not conveyed to the Austrian governor! These poor men, inno-

* *Il Governo Pontificio, etc.*, vol. ii. p. 550.

cent, but not strong enough for martyrs, were executed.

No one in Ferrara believed them guilty. On the day of the execution in the fortress, the city looked deserted as if smitten by the plague. A student of the University, Annibale Bonaccioli, hearing, as he left his home, of the execution, persuaded some of his fellow-students to absent themselves with him from the University, and return to their homes. He and his father were tried, condemned, and imprisoned for this crime. Released and permitted to go to Turin, on condition of returning no more, they unwisely did return. Monsignor Matteucci, Governor of Rome, directed that the young man should be imprisoned for a year. The poor youth pined and failed in health, and a fellow-student wrote a most touching application to be permitted to visit and spend the nights with him. No notice was taken of this application. After a few months, this young man, only eighteen years of age, died in prison.

What the means of torture were which were employed to extort these confessions, appear from the statements of some of the forty, who, notwithstanding them, were able to stand firm. "The Brigadier Paganini took me to the grates where I could hear every night the beating of some of the other prisoners; and he called my attention to the barking of his great mastiff, whom he loosed against these poor captives, and who bit them. I was beaten by whips, which have left indelible marks upon me. Armed with a knife, he threatened to cut my throat; and did make some slight wounds in it. To make me confess crimes of which I knew nothing, he pulled me by the hair, and kicked and beat me most unmercifully."* All this only ten years ago! All this in behalf of and with the sanction of a Government which professes to wield the power of the Saviour of the world!

One of the persons arrested, Gaetano Ungarelli, underwent the most frightful tortures by the bastinado (a banished barbarity which Cardinal Antonelli has the credit of reintroducing)† with heroic fortitude. His account of his examination by this torture, and of his manly, indignant, and spirited replies to his tormentors, is extremely interesting.‡

The conclusion of that account we translate below. And let the reader remember that he had been convicted of no crime—except that of heroically refusing to confess one of which he was not guilty! Not one particle of proof—only suspicion—was ever adduced against him.

"Bound to the same chain with convicted malefactors, I was confined for eighteen months in the bagno of Ancona; then transported to Paliano, a castle of infamous memories, where I remained little less than four years. I was then

---

* *Documenti, I lutti dello Stato Romano,* p 87.

† *Idem,* p. 123. ‡ *Idem,* p. 113.

liberated, but my vexations did not cease, for I was forbidden to pursue my studies in my native place, or in the Roman States; and when I had resolved to go to Piedmont to continue them there, and demanded my passport, it was given to me on the condition of perpetual exile, and under the penalty of imprisonment if I should return.

"I will say a few words of some others more unfortunate than myself. Succi and Parmeggiani, fathers of families, were shot, together with Malagutti. The prosecutor, Grau-Shak, bore a particular hatred to Battara because he had been a Pontifical soldier, and he felt spiteful toward him because on account of a grave disease with which he was afflicted, he could not be bastinadoed. Battara was condemned to fifteen years of forced labor. He is still at Paliano, notwithstanding that the Pope, on occasion of his journey to Ferrara, pardoned him. It is pretended that he only substituted a penalty of three years for the fifteen.

"Signora Annetta Banardi, mother of a family, a lady of masculine understanding, has defied the rage of these tyrants, who could not overcome her constancy. She also has sustained four years of imprisonment.

"I might narrate also the trials at Bologna, in which many were condemned to death, which sentence was afterward commuted by Radetzky, into forced labor for a time. Frederico Comandini de Censena, seeing that he was likely to undergo the bastinado, endeavored with the fragment of a glass goblet to destroy his life. He is now wasting away in Paliano.

"Behold a single brief page of that ten years' chronicle of two governments, one of which arrogates to itself the title of *just*, and the other that of *holy!*"

At Bologna the cruelties exercised against the citizens were, if possible, still greater than at Ferrara. A blind frenzy of cruelty and revenge, a headlong and indiscriminating rage to find victims and make victims, in punishment of the well-known detestation by the Bolognese of the Papal Government, seemed to have taken possession of the ruling power at Rome. The tribunal of the first instance at Bologna, composed of persons devoted to the Papacy, protested against the action of the Papal police, for inflicting tortures upon the accused, for extorting confessions by tortures, beatings, and by acts degrading to humanity against prisoners who were only accused, but against whom no evidence had been adduced. They even accuse them of stimulating persons to the commission of crime, as a means of discovering the crimes of others.* Gennarelli declares that it would take a volume succinctly to tell the story of the atrocities of the Papal Government in Bologna, from the period

* *I lutti*, p. xxxvi. *Documenti*, p. 91.

of its restoration, until it was destroyed and superseded by that of Victor Emmanuel.

One of the most revolting of all these histories is that of the murder of three young men in Fermo.

A venerated old priest, Corsi, was stabbed in Fermo, in 1849, while the Republic was still in power. He was beloved and honored by all the citizens. Public fame accused two wretches of this crime, and they were put in prison. After the Papal restoration, although many persons were subjected to surveillance, imprisonment, and the galleys by Cardinal D'Angelis, the Government was not satisfied. It seemed to crave blood. Three young men, known to be earnest liberals, were especially obnoxious to the ruling power. They were arrested as accomplices in the murder of the old priest Corsi. One of the two criminals already in prison, Testori, was well known to be steeped in crime. It was soon seen that he had become a favorite of the police; and was allowed the luxury of a mattress, wine, and cigars. He had been induced to give evidence against these three young men, on the promise of pardon. One of them proved that on the evening when the crime was committed he was lying ill of a fever. The doctor and his nurse testified to the fact. The doctor was won by Papal promises of patronage, but the faithful girl, and old chemist who had supplied his medicine, stood firm to their first testimony. Yet all this availed nothing.

The three young men were shot. A cry of grief and indignation went up from the city. Testori felt sure of his release. But finding that he too was about to be executed, he confessed to some of the "Confraternity of Pity," whose function it is to attend the condemned in their last hour, and to a priest, Castiglioni, that he had betrayed innocent blood. This confession was not conveyed to the Government. The "Confraternity of Pity" dared not, the priest *would* not give the information. "I am here," the latter declared, "to take confessions, not depositions." Yet at the execution he commenced his exhortation with the strange words: "It is not always the guilty who die!" The inhabitants that day left the city, or shut themselves up in their houses; and it was afterward reported that a monk from Florence coming into the city, traversed its whole length without finding any one to inform him of the location of his convent!

These are horrors which it seems impossible could have occurred in our day. But, though now happily ended in the Æmelia and Romagna, they still continue in what remains of the Roman States. When we turn from the endless details of similar cases which are found in the "Governo Pontificio" to the more general accounts of the same transactions, we can readily imagine how many similar horrors are included under the cold statistics.

The Court of Rome, in the ten years after its

restoration, consigned from its little States more persons to punishment and death than all the other States of Europe together—if Austria be excluded.* And yet a Roman journal complains of its too great clemency. The Roman Government vindicated itself from that charge in the following words: "We propose to expose things in their true aspect, not regarding vague rumors, but stating facts. It is perhaps forgotten that in the provinces of Faenza and of Imola, in consequence of only two procedures, eighty-two individuals were shot, while ten others obtained commutation of similar punishment in the galleys, and thirty others were condemned to temporary or perpetual imprisonment." Surely this *is* a triumphant refutation of too great lenity! Another judge at Ravenna, Cardinal Rivarola, condemned eight hundred persons at a single sentence! No wonder that the joy of the inhabitants of the Romagna and Æmelia seemed almost frantic when they escaped from the Papal sway!

Surely there was never anything in the world like this priestly government—so shameless, so stupid, so illogical in its cruelty! What other government on the face of the earth would permit such records as the following to be made: "Censura.—In view of the present report and the *absence of proof* upon which to proceed equitably

---

* *I lutti*, p. xxxviii.

in a judicial process in the case of Giovanni Ricci, it is ordered that the arrested shall be *retained in prison for correction* for eight days, with the usual prison fare, and one day he shall have only bread and water.—The Governor of the District, Bevilacqua." It seems as if the Government punished persons for the disappointment of not finding them guilty. It seems to say to them, "You rogues, if you are not guilty you ought to be; and because you will otherwise make us obnoxious for having arrested you, we will make you smart for your inconvenient innocence!"

Here is another precious document from a Cardinal Secretary of State:

"Sig. Cardinale Commissario Strordinario of Bologna. The injuries and threats against a carabiniere on account of which L. A. was arrested, *not having been proved*, and in view of other circumstances, and of the imprisonment already long which he has suffered, the sanctity of our Lord *has benignantly deigned to condescend to release him from prison* with the injunction, however, that he shall receive a formal injunction to live well hereafter, coupled with the other condition which your Eminence will feel it to be necessary to add, that a *penalty of public labor for five years* will be inflicted upon him, for any offense which he may commit, independently of greater penalties provided by law in the cases of other criminals. BERNETTI."

The world may be challenged for such another document outside of the Roman Archives! It goes to the heart of the Roman authorities to release a man, though perfectly innocent, who *has been accused* of having wounded and insulted one of those dear carabinieri! But inasmuch as the provokingly innocent wretch has already been imprisoned for some time, the sanctity of our Lord graciously condescends to release him from prison; but he must be admonished, just as if he had been guilty, to live well hereafter, and if he should not, then over and above the other penalties provided by the law, he shall labor for five years on the public works—as his punishment *for having been accused* of having injured a carabiniere!

"The Council of Censure," whose proceedings were for the most part destroyed, was an instrument of tyranny such as has had no equal since the days of the Venitian Council of Ten. This tribunal, created in all the provinces, had jurisdiction over all the employees of the Government, and could at once remove them by proceedings, in which they were governed by no law, and for reasons which seemed to themselves satisfactory. What an instrument of corruption this—the threat of dismissal held over the heads of those the support of whose families depended upon the pittance which they received from Government. What a means of tempting or coercing wives and daughters—to whom the choice of starvation or of sin might be proposed! It was a suitable thing that a bigoted Spaniard, Monsignor De Avellá, should be placed at the head of the Censura. To the honor of the Romans it should be recorded that it was difficult to get any citizens to serve in this hateful office.

The reasons for which persons were ejected from office and thrown penniless upon the world are often supremely absurd. From a multitude of them gathered from various decrees, we copy the following:

"For having voted for the Constitution—for excessive loquacity—for having been one of the persons who in the time of the Republic raised a tree of liberty in the piazza—because he read with a loud voice the public journal, *varying his voice* when he read anything injurious to the Pontifical Government and against the priests—because he is not decisive enough for the Pontifical Government, etc., etc., etc."

With one more record from this mass of documents I close this painful chapter. The Governor of Faenza, a city of the province of Ravenna, addressed a letter to Mons. Bedini, in which these remarkable expressions occur:

"I have just come from a special examination of the prisons. Grief overwhelms my heart. Without counting other prisoners in other prisons, I find in one, ninety-one. Very few are under indictments. Some of them are the subjects of Austria; others are amenable to the *sacra consulta.* Many of them are imprisoned from precaution, without examination, without indictment, and perhaps without even suspicion —and these groan in captivity, some for months, some for years, and some for tens of years. This is an angry wound, and is the chief origin of that evil temper which prevails against authority, and of hatred against the Government. Crime is not restrained by striking at it thus in the mass; the people are not by this means drawn in love toward their august sovereign.

"By the last sanguinary acts of the late Governor and Gonfaloniere, three individuals were arrested by the mandate of the prosecutor, and these were only examined, and, as I know personally, were without fault. By order of Monsignor the delegate, twelve others were arrested for precaution. The outcry is universal. It will be necessary that firm and vigorous, but just measures, should be adopted in regard to them. But I declare to you that I do not know how to dry the tears of a hundred families, who mourn over the imprisonment of fathers, husbands, and sons, and which themselves languish in want and wretchedness, but by abandoning the arrest.

"Finally, turning my regards to the Cancellaria, I find there a still more painful scene. There are processes pending there of four or five years' standing, to the number of four hundred and fifty."

Such is the picture of one small city of one

province! If an enemy of the Roman Government had stated these facts, there would have been a loud outcry of denial. They were made by a comparatively humane official, who did not suppose that they would ever see the light.

But enough. Dreary and painful page after page of the same kind of records could be written. The mind refuses to take in such a mass of misery, or to believe that such transactions are possible in our day and in a Christian land.

It may be thought that these persecutions were the result of the impulse of revenge when the banished Papacy was first restored. Alas! the City of Rome and the States that remain to Rome are undergoing now, as they have been ever since the restoration, the same experience. If Victor Emmanuel shall ever get possession of the archives of the Vatican, a book written without and within with woes will then be opened. When the Court of Rome, on the eve of the battle of Solferino, looked for the destruction of the Franco-Italian army, many arrests were made in Fermo, in Jesi, in Ancona; consternation spread through the cities of the Roman States, and no one felt secure of rising free in the morning. The telegram was anxiously plied at the Vatican, and it was known through Rome that the Holy Father had ominously whispered that the moment approached for the punishment of the partisans of revolutions.

Napoleon III. is much censured for the good

which he has not done in Italy. But when one remembers what evils he has prevented, and what habitations of cruelty have been broken up, through the influences set in motion by the victories of Magenta and Solferino, he will bless him as the first if not the greatest of the benefactors of Italy. Napoleon is much blamed for not leaving Rome and allowing Victor Emmanuel to come in; but the perilous question to be settled is,—If he should leave could Francis Joseph be kept out? It is bad enough to have a house inhabited by one evil spirit, but it is worse to allow that spirit to go forth and bring in seven other spirits more evil than itself.

CHAPTER X.

ROME AND BRIGANDAGE.

THESE words are often connected. It is very generally believed that the Pope and the Papal Government encourage brigandage in the Kingdom of Italy. It is a very serious imputation to bring against a Christian bishop. Can it be true? Our readers will have no doubt upon this point when they shall have perused the following pages.

Since Naples has passed into the hands of Victor Emmanuel, brigandage of the most frightful and atrocious sort has raged along the frontier. No region can be conceived better adapted for the purpose. On the one side of the valley which runs from Frascati and spreads out into the lovely plain of Capua, between it and the sea, is a range of wild, barren mountains; and on the other side, in the Abruzzi, there is a still wilder, loftier, and more extensive range, stretching toward the Adriatic. From both ranges, bands of brigands swoop like vultures into the valley and into the villages on the slopes of the mountains, and rob and murder and levy contributions, and bind many by terror and interest to silence or connivance, and then retire with bread and wine and booty to rest and revel. It is just on and near the border of the Papal and Italian territories that these mountains are most wild and savage and best suited to the purposes of sudden attacks, and retreats to inaccessible fastnesses.

It so happens that on three separate occasions I have been on the Papal borders on the south and west, and on the Italian border on the north —on the very edges of the scenes of brigandage and of conflict with the Italian troops,—but never on the range that runs between the valley and the sea. With the exception of the Papal border south of Subiaco, which is extremely picturesque and lovely, they are stern and savage regions; they are either thickly wooded or bare and rugged. The western range is wild and desolate to the last degree. I passed over it at a more northern point than has been of late years the scene of brigandage. As, however, I wound all day in and out among the vertebræ of this backbone, as it is familiarly called, of Italy, in a drizzling rain, and rested at night in a lonely *locanda* in the very heart of the mountains, I thought I had never seen anything so sinister and dreary. I had been somewhat startled by the suggestion of the old man, who drove my little one-horse carriage over the mountains, that my baggage would be more secure if I placed it by my side than if it were strapped behind. But he assured me that there had been *very few* incursions of brigandage in that quarter since it had become part of the Italian Kingdom; it raged farther to the south and west. But he remembered—he was a very old man—that in the time of the first Napoleon, after his conquest of the country, it had been carried on in this region with indiscriminating and savage ferocity. When a boy—he can never forget it—he saw three hundred brigands shot by order of Napoleon. Since that period there has been scarcely any brigandage in that region.

On another occasion I made an excursion to Frosinone and Alatri on the Papal border, and to San Germano, Monte Casino, and Santa Maria on the Italian border. Alatri is near Sora, the neighborhood of which has been the very center of brigand intrigues and atrocities. The whole region is very interesting. In Alatri are found the best preserved and most massive Pelasgic walls in Italy. Near by is Arpino, the birthplace of Cicero. In the same neighborhood are the birthplaces of Sylla, Juvenal, and Varro. The scenery of this region is wild and picturesque, but not savage. At the time of my visit, in the middle of May, there had been an unusual activity and daring on the part of the brigands, and also on the part of the army sent to extirpate them as well as on the part of the local national guards. The latter body, hitherto so inert and inefficient, either through sympathy or fear, or both, had recently been reorganized, and seemed emulous to rival the army in energy and zeal. The consequence was that many captures had been made. San Germano and Santa Maria (old Capua) were the stations to which brigands were brought from the ranges of the mountains on either side of the valley. The recent trial of Ciprano and Gola had been published, and their ferocity and brutality, extending even to the crime of cannibalism, had sent a thrill of horror through all Italy, albeit long familiar with the atrocities of the brigands, and made it impossible for the most devoted partisans of Francis II. to claim a military or political character for these assassins. While walking in the street in Santa Maria, I saw a young brigand brought in by the soldiers and marched into the prison. He seemed surprisingly unconcerned. The next morning my friend walked out before breakfast, and beyond the walls he came unexpectedly upon a scene which, it seems, had been of late very frequently enacted in that place. Two files of soldiers were drawn up in the field; a carriage with two priests and a condemned brigand came upon the ground; the adjutant read the record of the crimes of which he had been convicted,—twelve murders and several other atrocities; and then, kneeling with his back to the soldiers, he was pierced by many bullets, and dropped—dead!

It seems that, while my friend and I were visiting the famous old Benedictine monastery of Monte Casino, and enjoying the society and the hospitality of an intelligent Benedictine Father from the United States, who had seen no fellow-countryman within a year, a case of brigandage of the most daring character was enacted within two miles of the monastery, and in the open day. I afterward saw an account of it in Naples. The story reads more like a romance of a hundred years ago than an incident of our day, which transpired within four miles of the railroad which transports crowds of tourists from Rome to Naples. A band of mounted brigands dashed down the mountains and seized an Italian gentleman, a proprietor, driving on the road. They demanded a ransom of 40,000 ducats. His relatives, unable or unwilling to do more, offered 10,000. They refused, and made the usual threat (alas, too often executed!) of sending to them one of his ears or hands if the money should not be sent within a given time. They promised to make the effort, and in the mean time devised an eminently Italian scheme for his rescue. An imprisoned brigand, who knew the band and its haunts, was employed to put himself at the head of forty supposititious brigands, who were soldiers of the army or of the National Guard, to go into the mountains and fraternize with his old friends, under the pretense that he had escaped and raised a new band, and at a propitious moment to make a rush and rescue the prisoner. The scheme succeeded. After the supposed new band had been with the party for three days, they took an opportunity when the prisoner was poorly guarded, and seized him and some of his guards, and returned in triumph to San Germano. The brigand who conducted the enterprise was released, and I believe admitted into the army.

But with all this has the Pope and the Papal Government anything to do? Before considering that question it may be well to show how easily the ex-King Francis II. *might* wield this instrument if he were inclined, or if he conceived it to be for his interest.

The great mass of the inhabitants of this wild mountain region come directly under the influence of King Francis for a large portion of the year. All the way from Rieti to Gaeta, with the exception of a few intervals, the country consists of enormous masses of volcanic rock, hard as flint. No fruit trees, no vines, no arable land,—how is it possible for the wretched inhabitants of these mountain wildernesses to live? They can wring no bread and press no wine out of those flint hills. Consequently they have been accustomed to emigrate *en masse* to the Pontifical territory and cultivate the Campagna which stretches from eighty and ninety miles in length to from twenty to forty miles in breadth. Besides this Campagna, valleys run up from it between the

Alban, Sabine, and Volscian hills, into which they also migrate. There they remain from early spring until October. They then return to their cabins in companies, each company being under the direction of a superintendent appointed by the proprietors of the land, or the "country merchants," who cultivate large tracts, which they rent for a term of years from the Roman princes. Each of these superintendents is authorized to look after these laborers during the winter, and to supply their wants and engage them for the following year. From their necessities they are frequently compelled to draw their scanty pay for a whole season in advance. This is not slavery indeed, but is it not essential serfdom? Could anything be conceived more convenient for King Francis than this arrangement, which enables him so readily to confer with so many of his still faithful and loving subjects, though in bondage under the hated Government of Victor Emmanuel? Could any arrangement put this population more completely under the direct control, if not of King Francis himself, yet of his bosom friends, the Roman princes, the Pope, and Antonelli?

It seems, then, clear that if Francis wishes to engage these men in brigandage, he has an excellent opportunity. And when one comes to know the condition of these poor creatures, he does not wonder that recruits for the wild, adventurous life of the mountains, with the promise of booty, the release from crushing toils in the pestilential Campagna, and with opportunities for obtaining abundance of food and wine, and for revel and license, could easily be secured. They are extremely poor, ignorant, and degraded. They are subjected to excessive toil, scanty food, and frequent disease. A harder lot than theirs can scarcely be conceived. As during the harvest I often traced them with my glass from the Alban hills, in large troops, scattered over the wide Campagna, I could not but feel that they had reason to envy the "dumb driven cattle," fat and sleek, and proof against all malaria, which were toiling with them. Indeed, the cattle are better housed and cared for than they are!

I had once an opportunity to observe and ascertain something of their situation while on the Campagna, which I would readily have avoided. As the whole incident was characteristic, and illustrates my present topic, and has, moreover, its amusing side, I venture to narrate it at a little length.

My excellent friend, Mr. Brown, the vice-consul of the United States at Rome, and a young friend, took the occasion of a Roman festa-day to visit with me the old Etruscan city of Cære. My passport was in his office, but as he could not find it, and time pressed, he concluded to throw himself on his official character on my behalf, and try whether he could thus pass me on the railroad. The gendarme made no objections, and we went joyfully on our way, and spent a most interesting day among the tombs. On our return we walked ten miles to Palo, a station on the railway, about half way between Rome and Civita Vecchia, expecting to take the six o'clock return train. But, lo! the official influence of my friend did not extend as far as Palo! The stolid gendarme doggedly refused to let me go. His logic was simple, and, to him, conclusive: "Three persons and two passports. Ergo, the two can go and the one cannot." He planted himself on that logical rock, and he could not be dislodged. My friend and I attempted several styles—the severely argumentative, the declamatory, the pathetic, the solemn, the minatory. Mr. Brown even brought out the majestic American eagle, but it made no more impression than if it had been a sparrow: "Two passports and three persons. Two can go; one must remain." Luther did not stand more firmly on his theses at Worms than this faithful official stood on this formula. It was all in vain to reason or expostulate or plead. My friend's distress was amusing. He would not leave me. The cars came, my young friend got in, and Mr. Brown and I were left, half amused and half disconsolate, at that lonely station, twenty miles from Rome, at the approach of night, on the wild and desolate and unwholesome Campagna.

What to do? It proved to be a more awkward

situation than we at first supposed. We learned on inquiry that there was not a single *locanda* or *osteria* at which a bed could be obtained on the whole line of the road from Rome to Civita Vecchia—forty-four miles. There was none of any kind within less than eight miles. We knew there was none at Cære. Moreover, it might not be safe for us at that hour to be traversing this lonely road. It would certainly expose us to malaria and the fever. What to do? There was an immense *tenûta*—a sort of headquarters, or large farm-house, with its barns and out-houses not far off, and surely we could get shelter and lodging there. Our informant did not know. There was no one in it but a priest and his servant, and he had but one bed. It seems that this great establishment, which could have been made to accommodate a hundred persons, had been long unoccupied except by a priest who was employed to perform mass for the laborers and to prepare them for death, and bury them when dead; and that even he deserted it in August, September, and October, and only made hasty visits on Sundays during those months, and returned to Rome before the fatal sunset! It had one furnished suite of rooms for the great country merchant who farmed all the estates in this neighborhood, and spent one week there in the healthiest season. But it was inexorably closed; and the suggestion of having it thrown open for us, which we subsequently made to the priest, seemed to fill him with horror and disgust. He would as soon have thrown open to us the gates of Paradise! We felt, however, that we could surely get shelter somewhere among those buildings, if not in the house, at least in a barn. But the priest was not in. He was out hunting quails with a friend from Rome.

We sat down on the steps of the little chapel connected with the *tenûta* to wait for his worship the priest. The laborers were returning with their oxen and horses and mules, which were all comfortably housed, and then they departed—we could not see whither. We supposed that they would occupy this vast empty house, or some of the large out-houses, but not one of them remained. They lingered awhile in the court-yard, where the servant of the priest gave them each a little wine, played dominos a few moments, and then glided away. It was a singular scene. In no respect did they seem to us superior to our slaves, in themselves or in their conditions. Not until it was fairly dark did the priest return. He wore a linen blouse, stained with the blood of quails, and looked exceedingly like a butcher. Our reception was not gracious. "Of course we could come in, but he had no bed for us." He swung his bag of quails over his shoulder, and we followed him up the dark passage into a room which was at once his dining-room, sitting-room, and kitchen. No Irish laborer in New York has one more bare and filthy! It seemed incredible that a priest, and *Archiprete*, too, as he afterward proved to be, could live in this fashion. He went directly to his cupboard and helped himself and friend to a large draught of wine, but offered none to us. My official friend saw "*the situation*," and diplomatically and incidentally let it appear that we expected to pay for our entertainment. Either that suggestion or the wine made our host more gracious. He stirred about to prepare supper. His servant assisted, but he cooked—alas! no quails, but only an omelette with unsavory herbs. The seventy-two quails were to be sold at Rome at five bajocci each! Nothing but a brave and strong appetite could have run the gauntlet of that cooking and that supper. Our host and his friend were no Pharisees—they ate with unwashed hands. I do not in the least exaggerate. No Irish laborer in our cities have a more squalid home. I hope few of them have so poor a supper. Such is the life of an Archiprete on the Campagna.

It was after the supper that we learned from the priest many particulars concerning the laborers on the Campagna. The great country merchant farmed a tract of the Campagna, stretching in one direction, toward the lake Bracciano, ten miles. He employed these laborers by the hundreds. There were more than a thousand in his pay. They were from the mountain region of Naples, which I have described, and from the

Sabine and Alban hills. Their wages were about twenty cents a day. They slept—where they chose! Some of the more provident brought with them little tents. Others crept into the round straw huts constructed for the cattle on the Campagna and slept there—the cattle, of course, having the best place. Others—many others—slept in the old tombs and in the substructions of the ruined Roman villas which abound on the Campagna. When we suggested that they should be admitted into this large unoccupied *tenûta*, or at least into the adjoining barns, the suggestion that these creatures should occupy respectable barns, and above all a *tenûta* in which a priest lived, struck him as almost as profane and audacious as our proposal to occupy the apartment of the majestic country merchant. I have no doubt he considered it a striking illustration of the want of reverence in the Protestant mind. "But how do these people live?" "What do they eat?" "Do they ever have meat?" At the latter question he was as much surprised as if we had asked him if they lived upon ambrosia. They lived upon bread and *polenta*. *Polenta* is the same as our Indian-meal. *Polenta* was the staple and bread was the luxury. The bread was brought from Bracciano or Rome, the one twelve and the other twenty miles distant. On Sundays, some of the hardier members of a party walk this distance, buy bread, put it in a sack, or string the loaves together like beads, sleep upon the piazzas in the noon, and toward evening swing the bread upon their shoulders, and return to resume their toil at three or four o'clock in the morning. Such is that population of Contadini in the Papal and Neapolitan States which the Pope and the priests would persuade us are almost Arcadian in the simplicity, ease, and innocence of their lives. In such a life there can be nothing but squalor, degradation, and vile and brutal passions. From such a population it is easy to see how readily brigands could be made, especially when these poor creatures were made to feel that by it they were serving both their God and King.

The priest afterward discovered that he had another bed. But such a bed! I will not describe it. In the morning, with our pay in his pocket, he endeavored to persuade the gendarme to allow me to go in the railroad to Rome. In vain! we delicately suggested to the priest—*a scudo!* In vain! He was incorruptible. He evidently had an impression that I was a dangerous person. I was compelled to walk to Rome in a melting sirocco day, was stopped at the gate, and detained at the guard-house until Mr. Brown could prove that I was nothing but a harmless American citizen, and had a passport! It was knowledge rather dearly bought, but I had learned how the Contadini live upon the Campagna.

To foster brigandage in the Neapolitan States

has always been the policy of the dethroned Neapolitan princes. It is indeed a stupid, brutal, suicidal policy,—but all the more likely for that reason to be adopted by a Bourbon, and especially by this Francis, who is *the Bourbonest* of the tribe. No doubt his object would be to organize a nucleus of reaction on the frontier, which might assume a quasi-military form, and which, he might hope, would ultimately spread into a general revolt and replace him upon the throne. If this scheme should fail, he would still be able, by fostering brigandage, to represent to foreign powers that the kingdom of Naples was in a disturbed and dissatisfied condition, and would never be happy until it should receive again its own sweet king. This is the use which is made of this state of things by the journals in Rome. They chronicle all these disorders in what they still call the "Kingdom of the two Sicilies," as evidences of the dissatisfaction of the people and of the inability of the new government to maintain the public peace. It is a circumstance which in no degree disturbs this father of his people, that it is his own subjects whom this atrocious policy subjects to pillage and mutilation, torture and murder.

In another chapter I will adduce direct proofs of the complicity of Francis and of the Papal Government in this awful crime.

CHAPTER XI.

ROME AND BRIGANDAGE.

IMMEDIATELY after the conquest of the kingdom of Naples, brigandage, for political purposes, was organized at Rome. The materials for chiefs and for subordinate officers were found in abundance in the old Neapolitan army,—which it is now generally admitted was too hastily disbanded, and thrown without resources upon the country by the Italian Government,—and in that body of Neapolitan troops which escaped from Gaeta to the Pontifical territory, and were disbanded by Francis at Velletri and Albano. From these were formed the nuclei of various bands. They were organized on a large scale, with a view to the occupation of the northern frontier of the Neapolitan territory.

The Italian Parliament sent a committee of inquiry into the matter of brigandage to Naples and to the frontier, who have made, through their chairman, Massari, a voluminous report upon the subject. I have read this document since my arrival in this country, and I find that it demonstrates abundantly and superabundantly both the agency of the King of Naples, and the complicity of the Papal Government, in this infamous business. It refers to proofs of the fact without number, similar to those which it produces,—which are contained in the military and police archives of Naples and Gaeta.

From this document of 200 pages, filled with proofs of the complicity of the Papal Government in this business, I translate the following passage:

"It is said that the asylum granted in Rome to Francis II. has had for its motive an impulse of gratitude, and that Pius IX. has wished to return the hospitality extended to him in Gaeta in 1848 and 1849. It may be so. Let it be granted that no political considerations have entered into this proceeding, and that it arises wholly from a sentiment of gratitude. What then? This sentiment—should it impose silence upon that of justice, of humanity, of charity? Abusing the hospitality of the Holy Father, Francis II. has rendered himself unworthy of it, and hence it should be withdrawn. This has not been done; and tolerance of the abuse has finally resolved itself into incontestable complicity. But facts prove that the connivance and complicity of the Pontifical Government with brigandage are not limited to the regions which we have described, but that there is a deliberate and conscious connivance with it—an active, constant, and most effective co-operation. Francis II. was said constantly at Sora to be the *pivot* of brigandage; but the Pontifical Government was openly its *support*.

"The root of brigandage," says the Senator Ferrigini, Advocate General of the Court of Cassation at Naples "is at Rome. Until this shall be unearthed, brigandage will not be extirpated." "From Rome," says the Senator Niutti, president of the same court, "comes the principal support of brigandage." "The greatest incitement to it," says the illustrious Luigi Settembrini, "comes from Rome, from whence even more than the money comes the idea that it and the King of the two Sicilies are its prime movers and supports."

"Facts demonstrate (continues the report) that these authoritative opinions are founded in truth. At Rome there is a regular enrollment of a band as of an army which prepares for conflict with an enemy. The Convents of Trisulti and Casimari are notorious receptacles of brigands and are their chosen headquarters. In 1861, Monsignore Montieri, Bishop of the Diocese of Sora, now deceased, had taken a chamber in the Convent of Casimari, and there, with the assistance of the Father Abbot of the monastery and of several legitimist foreigners, organized that band of brigands, headed by De Christen, who were followed and overcome by the troops commanded by a brave colleague, General Maurizio de Sonnaz. The Pontifical police naturally adopt every imaginable precaution to disguise their complicity with these miscreants. But their cunning, their caution, their astuteness are neutralized by facts. Bands are organized upon the Roman territory without molestation or interference. Tristany lays in supplies of bread and other food from the Roman territory with no opposition on the part of the Roman authorities. In the month of March, 1862, there were sent daily from Veroli one hundred and twenty-one rations of bread to the brigands assembled in the Convent of Trisulti, and no obstacles were interposed to this daily operation. Two natives of Selva de Sora lived at Veroli, and acted as guides to Tristany and the Pontifical police. The provinces of Frosinone and Velletri are those in which the bands are most frequently formed; none of the Contadini of these two provinces join them; they are foreign adventurers, generally worthless and wretched fellows from the Neapolitan provinces. Those who compose the band of Tristany are, for the most part, clothed in a military habit; and those who act as officers receive distinct military titles. The Pontifical police have no eye to see these preparations for hostility, and allow them tranquilly to complete their arrangements, without giving them the least disturbance.

"At the end of the summer of 1861, the band headed by Chiavone, often defeated and as often reorganized, assumed formidable proportions. It was divided into eight companies of fifty men each, and enrolled its officers with the titles which belong to a military organization. Among them were Spanish adventurers, French, Swiss, Irish, and the Belgian Traziuy. This band ranged unimpeded along the frontier of Sora, between S. Francesca and Casimare, with advance posts and videttes; and it never suffered any molestation up to the time when beaten by our troops in the fights at Imola and San Govanni Incarico, it resolved to pass the frontier on the 11th of November, 1861.

"Whenever the brigands have abandoned the frontier and have been met and defeated by our troops, they have always been able to recruit and reorganize by passing over into the Roman territory. At the Campo di Fiori and at the piazza Montanara in Rome there are persons notoriously employed to recruit the bands of brigands. They select and find their recruits among the Contadini of the Alrazzo Aquilana, who have fled to avoid the levy of the Italian Government, or to escape the punishment of their crimes. The Pontifical Government assists them with arms and money, and adopts every sort of artifice to avoid being detected. At one time, for instance, it furnishes several hundreds of military coats; and the Minister of War gives notice of a public sale by auction of these coats. A French priest presents himself at the auction and professes to buy them. Then he consigns them to those for whom they are intended. The Bourbon Committees of Alatri, of Frosinone of Ceccano, of Velletri, of Pratica, bestir themselves to aid the brigands in every possible way. On the Committee of Frosinone there is a Judge, a Chancellor of the Bishop, two Canons and the Curate. On that of Ceccano is a person who is attached to the household of Cardinal Antonelli. On that of Velletri there are several Canons. On that of Pratica, the Archiprete who sometimes accompanies the brigands in person. At the Abbey of the Passionists in Ceccano reside a Pontifical gendarme and two others who serve as guides to these murderous miscreants."

Page after page of such distinct specifications could be quoted from this authentic document. No serious attempt has ever been made to confute its undeniable testimonies.

A more recent elaborate work upon this subject, "Il Brigantaggio alla frontiera Pontificia dal, 1860 al 1863, del Conte Alessandro Bianco di Saint-Jorioz," an officer who was long employed in this difficult and repulsive service, and enjoyed the best opportunities for gaining correct information, is replete with the results of his own observation, and with facts gathered in the course of his wide and varied journeyings and expeditions. The work has been received with great favor in Italy, and is very damaging to the parties who have been engaged in this most nefarious business. After reading this work, it is impossible to disbelieve in the direct agency of both the ex-King and the Pope in the Neapolitan brigandage. It is a crime which deserves the execration of the world. Wars of guilty ambition are not unfrequent; but they always profess to promote the glory and prosperity of the nations in whose behalf they are waged, and are not without their pleas and promises in furtherance of the general good. But a system of pillaging, terrifying, torturing, and murdering one's own subjects, for the purpose of making a dead lie seem to be alive, which could be of no avail even if it were, is an infamy which only a Bomba or a Bombino (the nickname of Francis) could commit, and which only a Pope smitten with Bourbonic blindness and infatuation could bless and foster.

No effort of course would be spared, by the parties involved in this crime, to keep all proofs of it from the public eye. But murder will out. The enterprise was on too large a scale, and involved too many persons and too many interests, to make it possible that it should be kept from the Argus-eyed National Committee at Rome. Those who are familiar with the city will remember the Campo di Fiori and the Piazza Montenara. They will recollect what crowds of Contadini are accustomed to throng there on festas and Sundays, and how characteristic and alive these piazzas are on such occasions. But they probably did not suspect that they were *marts of murder*,—that brigands and robbers were there enrolled in the service of the ex-King of Naples. Yet this is what the National Committee charge, and charge with specifications of persons and times and places. They point out by name the individuals who are agents in this affair. Relying upon such information, as well as upon that which he has collected from the archives of Gaeta and from individuals, and challenging denial, the author makes such distinct specifications as the following. If they are not true, he should be delivered up to trial for as atrocious slanders upon private and public characters as were ever uttered. But there is no probability that he will be called for or disturbed:

"The brigands are publicly recruited in Rome by the druggist Vagnozzi, in Campo di Fiori, and by a certain Picarilli, ex-sergeant in the ex-army of the ex-King, and captain in the band of Chiavone; by the Abbe Ricci, and the priest Gonella, formerly Sacristan of Santa Restituta, in Sora, who was named Colonel by the ex-King, Francis II., and took command of a band of brigands which unsuccessfully attacked Acqua Santa; and by many others whose names it is difficult to ascertain. These brigands, united and enrolled in bands in the Piazza Montenara in Rome, are afterward assigned to various captains, and by them paid, clothed, and accompanied to the frontier."

The author then proceeds to give the names of those who acted as guides to these parties to the frontier, and the names of persons in various places on the Italian frontier who aided them,—many of whom were subsequently convicted and condemned for the crime of complicity with the brigands. How largely the Roman Government lent itself to this wholesale organized pillage and murder appears from the following record:

"In the hospital of the Commune at Ciprano there is a part used as barracks, occupied by twelve gendarmi of the Papal cavalry, and fifty brigands (20th February, 1862). Toward Fabraterra, the brigands occupy another barrack. Others, also, are in like manner occupied at Campolungo, toward Monte San Giovanni, by brigands. A man by the name of Battaglia has the care of them and pays them."

At that period the efforts to organize a band so large as that it should seem like a small army, had reached their highest point of success. There is no more reason to doubt the general correctness of the information which the Italian military authorities possessed of the organization and numbers and movements of the brigands, than there is of the usual information collected by armies of the movements of their enemies. The information is obtained by the same methods,—by the employment of spies and scouts. On this principle the following telegram from Captain Gregorio Ximines, of the 43d Infantry, of February 28th, from Isoletta, should be accepted in the same manner as are all other military messages:

"After the departure from Rome of about 2000 brigands, followed by another the day before yesterday (26th February, 1862), to-day I have some information as to the distribution of these forces. Yesterday (27th of February) two hundred from Pofi and from Ripi joined them, those from Ripi proceeding in the direction of Casimari, those from Pofi hiding in the retreats of Ceccano, the property of the Passionist Brothers. On this side (of the frontier) other columns may be also on the march in little bands, to be united at a designated point. About 600 departed this morning from Velletri for Fondi, where, in two or three days, the whole number may be found in line. A Swiss and a Spaniard, whose names I do not know, joined them yesterday at Trisulti."

On the 2d of March, 1862, Chiavone (the commander-in-chief of all the brigands) wrote to the Comandante of the Papal Gendarmi at Frosinone that he should provide for the passage of three hundred brigands coming from Terracina, and the Comandante answered that he would do so, but that it was necessary *to beware of the French soldiers!*

Among the discoveries made by the National Committee was that of a "plan of reaction," devised at Rome by the Bourbon committees, presided over by the ex-generals of Francis, Vial and Clary. It was sent to Colonel Lopez, at Sora, in September, 1861. The whole scheme can be seen in "Il Brigantaggio" (pp. 244, 245). It provides for the formation of five bands, and for four officers of direction at Rome, Velletri, Agnani, and in the Convent of Scifelli. It provides for a secret police of espionage, and regulates the rank of the officers, and assigns to the several bands their respective fields of operation.

In order to show how such information as is given in this work has been obtained, and to prove that it is authentic and reliable, I translate one account of a secret mission of an agent of the Italian Government, and one intercepted official document of a comandante of Papal gendarmes:

"In August, 1862, a certain Battista Achille, called Battistone, a shrewd and enterprising young man, who had already rendered various confidential services to the general commanding the military division of Chieti, and who was rewarded with the post of the Keeper of the Prisons at Pescara, was engaged in a secret service, under the direction of the Major-General Cav. Reccagni, in Lancianese, and there came in contact with another young man, Gorgio Acqui, employed by Raffaele di Tagliacozzo, in the pay of the Reactionists. Insinuating himself cautiously into his confidence, he learned from him that he often went to Rome, to convey information, and to bring back instructions, and that if he (Battistone) desired it, he should be introduced to King Francis. Having obtained permission and money from the general, he went to Rome with Gorgio, and on his return gave the following account of his journey. In consideration of the good services already rendered by Battistone, and his subsequent fidelity, his depositions are worthy of being believed.

"When he reached Rome he was introduced to D. Paolo Resta da Tagliacozzo, by whom Battistone had been formerly known as a maker of toys. Resta, one of the most confidential reactionary instruments of the ex-King, told him that the King was at that time in Albano, and would not return within ten days, but assured him that he himself had full authority to act on behalf of his master. In consequence of this, Battistone declared that his aversion to the new government had determined him in favor of the old; and receiving encouragement and promises of assistance at the future certain restoration of the old government, he was conducted by him to the Monte Cavallo, that he might see the numerous disbanded soldiers and deserters from the Italian army who held themselves in readiness for action. 'We could have,' he said, 'many more, but his Majesty, although he is the richest sovereign in the world, does not wish to waste his money, as, at the decisive moment, a large amount of it will be required. Moreover, already a large number of the old army who are in the new, are friends of the King; and it is better that they should live, in the mean time, at the expense of the usurping government, and remain where they can render better service to his Majesty.'"

Battistone saw full five hundred of these disbanded soldiers,* among whom he recognized the seven grenadiers who had deserted from Rieti on the 16th of September. (This information was subsequently confirmed.) Resta knew that a meditated general attack upon Lanciano within a few days had been deferred, in consequence of the presence of regular troops at that place. This, however, would soon be effected through directions to a Pontifical captain, who was at the head of a numerous band in the Abruzzi. (We had in fact, at that time, information of the captain of a band whose uniform was different from others, and who wore decorations.) From Monte Cavallo, Resta, saying that he was about to visit the Archbishop of Chieti, left him for a time, and put him in charge of a certain Paolino Ventura da Carsoli, whose office was that of paymaster to these disbanded soldiers. He inquired if Battistone knew a certain D. Raffaele Torano da Popoli, officer of the National Guard,

* A friend of mine in Rome informed me that he was told by a high official of the Papal Government, at the time when the frequent robberies and murders last winter excited so much apprehension, that there were 1100 disbanded soldiers of the ex-King of Naples at that time in the city, and most of them without occupation or means of support.

and hearing that he did, said: "Salute him from me, and tell him that I shall shoot him first, and then Camillo d'Aquila."

At this point Resta reappeared, and took him in a carriage and returned to the Pallazzo Farness. As they rode, he asked Battistone if he desired to remain in Rome; and the latter declaring that he could serve his King better in a field of action, Resta added: "Matters are now in such train that there can be no doubt of the result. We are about to clothe more than two thousand in the guise of French Zouaves, and while the Reactionists attack Avezanno, to which the forces of Tagliacozzo and Ciccolano will be joined, the way will be opened by them to the entrance of his Majesty into his kingdom. You must return, and confer with the Contadini in your neighborhood, assuring them that his Majesty will recompense with gold and protection as many as prove faithful. I will inform you by letter of the precise day of the movement, which will be between the 28th and 29th of August. I will then write you where you are to receive money, in order to distribute it in the coffee-houses. Be faithful; spoil and murder as many of the Piedmontese as possible. We have written the same things also to Signore Romeo at Pescara (the same who surrendered the fortress of Pescara in 1860), and if you meet him you may safely confer with him, for he hopes to retake the fort, and writes that the comandante of the fort has already an understanding with him. (He alludes probably to the second-lieutenant, Dupretis, already convicted as a partisan of the reactionary party.) If you have need of any counsel in any region where there are *patri*, you may trust them all, except those Cappuchini who wear a moustache. Do not doubt that when we get to Naples his Majesty will make you rich." (pp. 245–248.)

I have copied the whole of this account, with all details and names in full, because it has every internal mark of genuineness and probability.

These projects, indeed, proved abortive. The author adds: "So much pertinacity, so much sacrifice of money, such unconquerable fervor in an impracticable undertaking, such subtlety in the use of means, such capacity of insinuations, such a genius for intrigue, such astuteness in the adaptation of means, in manners, in blandishments, in promises,—all were employed always in the same fruitless efforts, and with the same inefficient operations, attempts, movements, and designs. To invade a wild, empty country; to commit robberies and crimes; to rush like Cossacks upon innocent persons and unprotected villages; to burn and plunder; to enjoy the puerile satisfaction of crying '*Viva Francesco II!*' and then to leap back like goats into the mountains,—these were the conceptions of the committee and of the ringleaders at Rome; and to this excessive poverty of military ideas and of strategetical designs, are due the wretched results obtained by the Reactionists after so much expenditure of activity and of money."

In the night of the 30th of May, 1862, ten brigands presented themselves to Fontini, Comandante of the Pontifical Gendarmi in Torre tre Ponte, situated on the Appian Way, about eighteen miles from Terracina, who demanded means of transport to Ceccano, the place of gathering for their band. The comandante consented. This is history. The proof of it is in the following document, the original of which was sent by the Italian military authority, by whom it was intercepted, *to the general commanding the French forces in Rome.*

The letter is addressed to his captain, Signore Cav. Fabo, at Vellatri.

"Illustrious Signore Captain:—I make known to you by this present writing, that yesterday evening there presented themselves to this detachment the officers of the Sicilian troops, whose names are herewith written, who go to join the Spanish column in the mountains of Ceccano; and hence, I have thought that I should give them a reception for this day also, inasmuch as the guide has not joined them whom they are expecting to accompany them."

Then follow the names of a captain, a lieutenant, two sub-lieutenants, two standard-bearers, and one medical officer. Then the letter continues:

"I have felt that I should retain them, more especially as by doing so, I should be able *to save them from encountering the French column.* Torre tre Ponte, 13 May, 1862. The commander of the detachment. S. FONTINI."

This precious document shows the singular and anomalous position of the French. The forces of the Emperor protect the Pope from his subjects. The forces of the Pope protect the brigands from the French!

I think no one can doubt, after reading the above pages, the complicity of the Pope with the brigandage of Francis. But, indeed, one who resides in, or ever visits Rome, and knows the character of the parties, and their history, and their hereditary and traditional policy, does not need any specific proofs. It seems proved by these facts, and by all that he hears and sees around him. The perfect accord between Francis and the Pope, their identical views of policy, their belief that liberty is sin and despotism duty, the exultant tones of the journals at the prevalence of brigandage, the conversation of the partisans of the Pope and Francis, the swarms of self-exiled, sympathizing priests and partisans of Francis, the agents of reaction in Rome, and the high favor which they enjoy, the knowledge of individual histories of brigands which he hears, and the stories which are told to him if he travels upon the frontiers,—all these make the complicity of the Papal Government with this awful crime a thing felt and seen and known, rather than a thing that needs formal proof.

And it is a thing so atrocious that there is no word hot enough and sharp enough in the whole vocabulary of indignation to be hurled against those by whom it is fostered and protected. And he who sanctions and promotes this thing is called his "Holiness," and "the Holiness of our Lord!" It may be safely said that there is no Christian sovereign now in Europe, who would not scorn to adopt such means to recover a throne, even if they were certain to succeed, except King Francis; and there is no other sovereign, except the one who professes to be at the same time the Vicar of Christ, who would not look upon it with loathing. For if, at the beginning, this brigandage might seem to promise to be the nucleus of a political and military reaction which would ultimately replace King Francis upon the throne; if it is conceivable that in the proverbially Bourbonic ignorance of the real state of things in this period of the world, the ex-King might for a time have flattered himself that he was waging war, and not organizing the assassination and robbery of his subjects, the time for that delusion has long since passed. He allows this awful system of crime to go on, in order that he may keep up the mere seeming and the pretense of what he has an absolute demonstration is untrue,—of a general and irrepressible dissatisfaction with the present government and a desire for the restoration of the old. And so long as this system continues, Francis is responsible for it,—the blood of his subjects cries against him. For he has but to intimate to the Pope that this warfare is useless and should cease—to withdraw his own countenance from it—to request the Papal Government not to foster but to repress it—to obtain, through the Pope, the co-operation of the French and Italian military authorities in connected and combined plans of operation, upon the mountains, and not one month would pass before this brigandage would be extirpated! And if Francis were not steeped in Bourbonic stupidity, he would see that his present course is arraying the civilized world against him, as a monster utterly unfit to occupy any Christian throne.

Indeed it tasks our faith to believe that he ever expected with such instruments to advance his pretensions to the throne. We have seen that brigandage is indigenous in Italy—that it arises from the poverty, ignorance, and brutality of the people in the wild mountain regions—that its chief recruits are to be found among the poor, half-starved Contadini, who migrate to and from Naples and the Campagna and the adjoining territory of the Papal States. Now it was from brigands already in the field, and from such recruits as these, that Francis was to organize a band of champions of legitimacy, and of prescriptive tyrannies and wrongs. It seems incredible that he could ever have believed that he was doing anything more than fostering, enlarging, and sanctifying the atrocious system of robbery and murder which had long been the scourge of his dominions. For notwithstanding that the "plan of reaction" seems to have contemplated regularly commissioned officers as in an army, and notwithstanding that the plan was devised by high ex-officers of the Neapolitan army, it does not appear that a single respectable officer was ever connected with these marauding and murdering bands; notwithstanding that loyalty and patriotism were loudly invoked, there was but one of the three leaders, and he a Spaniard (Borjis), who seemed to have been animated by a genuine but mistaken spirit of chivalrous loyalty to "throne and altar." The remainder were mere vulgar robbers and murderers. The common brigandage of the country was employed as a fraudulent instrument of pretended military and political objects. These wretches plied their old vocation, under the benediction of the Pope, and with the pay of Francis added to their plunder. They had no new duty to perform except to cry "*Viva Francesco!*" and to murder and plunder, particularly the Syndics of the villages into which they made irruptions, and to pull down the pictures of Victor Emmanuel. No doubt they were pleased to be converted, without a change, into paid and holy crusaders The military organization was a farce. The captains and lieutenants and standard-bearers were at the same time the rank and file. They were all officers, except a few of the newly-recruited Contadini. The leader of the whole band, Chiavone, was an ignorant and brutal but cunning Bourbon soldier, who plundered Francis on the one hand and his subjects on the other; and who so revolted the brigands themselves by his plundering of them, that he lost at last all authority with his followers, and all influence in every direction. Since the summer of 1862 this system of brigandage has been increasing in its atrocity, as it has been narrowed in its field. And now it may be truly said that, under the fostering care and protection of the Pope, it has reached a height of horror in its character, such as in all the ages of Italy it never reached before. The trial of Gola and Ciprano and their companions, which the *Osservatore Romano* was compelled by the French authority at Rome to publish in full, exhibits such a picture of revolting and wanton and ferocious cruelty as in our age has nowhere else been witnessed. And thus this Pio Nono, whose throne, when he first ascended it, was enthusiastically upheld by the most noble, pure, gifted, and patriotic spirits of the age,—who was hailed with rapture as the Regenerator of Rome and Italy, and as the Preserver, because the reformer of the periled Papacy,—whose beautiful presence and sweet voice and glorious words and corresponding deeds shed hope and joy and blessing all around, and converted all the days of happy Rome into festas,—this Pope and King of hearts will have, when he shall rest upon his dishonored bier, for his chief, if not his only mourners—Francis and Antonelli and the brigands!

CHAPTER XII.

NAPOLEON III. AND ROME.

THE relations of Napoleon III. to the Government of the Pope have been singular and varied. His first act as a man was to appear in arms, a rebel against the Government of the Pope, and to escape with difficulty from its power. Possibly, the Pope would prefer now to have him in one of the dungeons of St. Angelo, rather than to have that fortress manned by his soldiers, and himself occupying the most splendid and powerful throne in Europe.

A second time Napoleon escaped the vigilance of the Papal police, who were in eager watch for him. When he escaped from Ham, the Papal Government believed that he was again about to enter the Roman States with a political design. The police were strictly enjoined to watch for and seize him. Instructions were issued that he should be "arrested and closely confined." The authorities were in a fever to secure this "*sogetto.*" The word is not a complimentary one, and is difficult to translate without the use of some such slang expression as "bad subject," or "hard case." They thought that he had been tracked. The higher police authority at Bologna writes to an inferior at Porretta, and says: "It has come to our knowledge, that on the night of the 21st (June, 1846), a young stranger laden with arms and money, who took lodgings at the hotel of Luigi Ferrari, under a feigned name, was recognized by an English lady as the son of Jerome Bonaparte." This stranger sent a letter to a member of the Bonaparte family in Bologna, the Count Camarata, who came to Porretta at eleven A.M. on the 22d. The stranger met the Count a mile from town, and they walked in together. They afterward set off for Tuscany, having a Tuscan subject for their guide. Then the official at Porretta is rebuked for his remissness, because it is reported that the stranger was Louis Napoleon, the "*sogetto*" of whom they were in search.

It proved however that the stranger was not Louis Napoleon, but his cousin, the son of Jerome. At a later date the Government had obtained a precise description of the Prince, which was transmitted to the police-agent at Porretta. The description had been sent through the agency of the Legation of the Grand Duke of Tuscany in Paris, and is as follows:

"Personal marks of Prince Louis Napoleon Bonaparte. Age, 38 years. Height, a metre and sixty-six centimetres. Hair, chestnut. Eyebrows, ditto. Forehead, middling. Eyes, gray and small. Nose, big. Mouth, middling. Lips, thick. Beard, brown. Moustaches, fair. Chin, pointed. Visage, oval. Complexion, pale. Special characteristics are,—head stuck down between the shoulders—shoulders broad—back round—some gray hair."*

This must be pleasant reading at the Vatican, now that it is known to be in the library of the Tuileries!

The next prominent relation of Louis Napoleon to the Papal Government was when, as President of the French Republic, he sent his army to Rome, under General Oudinot, and destroyed the Roman Republic, and reinstated the Pope. It would seem as if this were a service to endear the "*sogetto*" to his Holiness. But it placed him under a painful obligation. He would have preferred that this service should have been rendered by the younger and more beloved son of the Church—the Joseph of his heart—Francis Joseph. He preferred the aid of thoroughly Catholic and retrograde Austria to enlightened and progressive France. It was a singular relation which Louis Napoleon then sustained, and has since sustained, to the Papal Government. In one aspect protector, and in another protected—sustaining the Pope and yet angry with him for his stupid and obstinate resistance to all reform—sustained by the Pope, who was angry with him for his presumption in suggesting reforms and interfering with his internal administration—Napoleon's position toward the Pope has been one of anomaly, humilia-

* Documents, part I., 55–63.

tion, and of apparent injustice to the Roman States which can have no other explanation or vindication but that, bad as the present state of things is, it would have been much worse but for his interference. Of this fact there can be no doubt.

The next singular chapter in the history of his relations to the Pope is that of Solferino and the treaty of Villa Franca, and of the events which followed. That the eldest son of the Church should have beaten back the younger son, in the interests of that excommunicated outcast, Victor Emmanuel, and that he should have allowed that impious robber to have laid hands upon some of the most precious States of the Church, those are crimes for which his impracticable scheme of confederated Italy, with a Pope at the head, furnishes no compensation. Louis Napoleon is now as cordially, though not as openly, detested by the Government of Rome as Victor Emmanuel. The priests of Rome speak of him with frightful bitterness.

Hence the Emperor occupies the position of protecting the Pope against his own subjects—against Victor Emmanuel, to whom he gave Lombardy—against the earnest, impatient, passionate desire of all Italy to constitute Rome the capital of the kingdom of Italy—and against the desires and convictions of the liberal part of his own subjects, of Europe, and of the world. To explain such a proceeding on the part of one who courts the glory of inaugurating in Europe the era of monarchies based on the will of the people, is a difficult task. It is the subject of many theories, conjectures, and explanations. By some persons he is thought to have had no policy, and to have been brought through a complication of expedients, in the place of a policy, to a dead lock, in which motion in any direction is impossible. Others believe that he is forced to protect the Pope from the single consideration of the safety of his own throne and dynasty. Others suppose his Roman policy is dictated by the desire to obtain supremacy over Austria in the affairs of Europe. Others regard it as really in the interest of the kingdom of Italy, which would be likely to be overwhelmed in a single-handed conflict with Austria. Others believe that it is dynastic ambition—the hope still entertained that Rome shall remain, whatever its form of government, at first under the protection, and afterward under the direct sway of that Imperial France, which is ultimately to absorb all Europe. Whether any of these conjectures, or several of them combined, explain the present position of Napoleon, the result, so far as the feelings of the Court of Rome are concerned, is the same. He is detested by the Pope, and is himself irritated by him, yet he upholds him, though often insulted by him, and often rebukes him, only to be rebuked in return in the tone of an Hildebrand or an Innocent III.

We find a curious illustration of the anomalous

position of the Emperor in reference to the Papal Government, in the fact that his own production, "The Napoleonic Ideas," has been made the object of the *surveillance* of the Pontifical police, since he ascended the throne, and at the very moment when his army was protecting the Pope at Rome. In 1852 an agent of the police addressed the illustrious Rev. Rector of the University of Bologna, and reviser of books at the custom-house, in reference to a book then circulating at Bologna, entitled "Delle idee Napoleoniche; Pensieri del Principi Luigi Napoleone Bonaparte; prima versione Italiana," etc. He writes that some persons declare that this work contains sentiments hostile to the policy of the Pontifical States. He begs information and direction upon the subject. The Rev. Rector evidently wishes that the too zealous agent of the police had not touched the matter. He admits that he had permitted the booksellers Rocchi and Romanogli to sell the book, but with "*the express injunction to sell it only to unexceptionable persons, and under their responsibility.*" The Rev. Rector evidently feels the awkwardness of pronouncing direct censure, and of forbidding the circulation of a work by the eldest son of the Church. He declines to hazard a judgment on a work which treats of the past, and forecasts the future. He then inquires whether there is any proof that this is really the production of Louis Napoleon. Does it contain the real thoughts of the President of

France? If so, do they agree with the present thoughts of the Emperor of the French? He professes himself incompetent to penetrate these difficult questions. And so the matter remains as it was. The booksellers were permitted to dispose of it—but only to *unexceptionable persons*. It may be conjectured that they found all who wished it unexceptionable!

It is believed that Napoleon III. cherishes all the great "Napoleonic ideas" of his uncle, and aims at their ultimate realization by slower, safer, and less startling processes. Now it is known that, at one period of his career, the first Napoleon entertained the scheme of constituting Italy a confederation, under the Presidency of the Pope, which the third Napoleon proposed at a time, and under circumstances, which, if he were sincere, led persons to make a low estimate of his practical sagacity. If it were a bigoted attachment to a "Napoleonic idea" which led him to make this proposition, which nothing in the then condition of the Italian mind, or in the state of the country seemed to render feasible, it is possible that another "Napoleonic idea" subsequently adopted, and which appears to the public for the first time in the recent publication of Documents by the Cavaliere Gennarelli, may also commend itself to his mind. Whether or no this may prove true, it will be interesting to see in this plan of the first Napoleon for the solution of the Roman Question, a considerable similarity to some of those recommended by the friends of united Italy.

The drafts of decrees from the archives of the first Napoleon came very directly into the hands of the Cavaliere Gennarelli, editor of the Government Documents, and are published by him in the "*Lutti dello Stato Romano.*" The manner in which he became possessed of them was this: In 1814 Austria took possession of the archives of the kingdom of Italy, but the more secret papers were secured by Napoleon's minister, Aldini. He left them by will to his secretary, Vincenzo Cristini, who committed them to the friend and relation of his principal, Gennarelli, who now for the first time (1860) brings them to the light.

From these documents it will plainly appear that the first Napoleon was persuaded of the incompatibility of the union of the temporal and spiritual power, and had resolved to withdraw the Roman States from Papal rule, and unite them, not to the Empire, but to other Italian provinces. If the third Napoleon should adopt this "Napoleonic idea," the unity of Italy might be delayed, but would ultimately be secured.

When Napoleon at Berlin issued the famous decrees for closing all the ports of Europe against English merchandise, he found that the Pope stubbornly refused. Napoleon addressed an angry remonstrance to the Cardinal Ambassador from the Holy See, to be transmitted to the Government at Rome. It was quite in vain. The authorities encouraged the people to evade and violate these decrees.

It was then that Napoleon devised the scheme of leaving to the Pope his spiritual supremacy and stripping him of temporal power. He communicated his design to his secretary, Aldini, and ordered him to present a report and draft decrees to put the plan in execution.

Aldini soon prepared them for the Emperor, as they now are published. Napoleon was then just on the point of hurrying to Spain, to recover the ground that had been lost there by his marshals, and he directed Aldini to transmit them to Murat, Imperial Secretary of State, who would accompany him.

In the report of Aldini to the Emperor preceding the decrees, he makes, among others, the following statements. He declares that Crescentius governed Rome for many years under the title of Patrician or Consul; that the Emperor Otho confirmed him in that title, and made him swear fealty to him; that during all the period of the dominion of the Emperors over Rome, they, and not the Popes, exercised the temporal power; that afterward a Senator of Rome exercised the civil authority; and that it was not until the beginning of the fourteenth century that the office of the Senator became one of civil subordination to the Pope. The report concluded with recommending three decrees in reference to the three following points:

1. The nomination of a Senator and a determinate number of Conservators.

2. *The reunion to the Kingdom of Italy of the countries comprising the Roman States.*

3. Various dispositions relative to his Holiness.

Then follow the drafts of the decrees. Omitting a portion of the grand introductory verbiage, I copy some of the principal provisions of these decrees:

"Napoleon, by the grace of God and by the Constitution, Emperor of the French, King of Italy, Protector of the Confederation of the Kingdom,—

"To all those to whom these presents shall come, greeting:

"Wishing to restore to the Roman people *that form of government which in former times they enjoyed*, we have ordered and decreed and do order and decree as follows:

"Art. I. Rome is a free Imperial City.

"Art. II. The Palace of the Quirinal and its dependencies is declared an Imperial Palace.

"Art. V. A Senator and a Magistracy of forty Conservators form the Government of the city and its territories.

"Art. VI. The Executive power is vested in a Senator, the Legislative in the Magistracy of Conservators; the Senator initiates laws. The office of Senator is for life; that of Conservator for four years.

"Art. IX. The Senator is always appointed by ourselves and our successors. For this present time we reserve also the right to appoint the Magistracy of Conservators. Hereafter, when they must be replaced, the Senator fills up vacancies from a double list presented to him by the Magistracy."

The next decree, with a similar introduction, has the following provisions:

"Art. I. All the districts composing the Roman States, with the exception of Rome and its territory as described in the first Roman Statute, are irrevocably and in perpetuity united to our Kingdom of Italy.

"Art. II. Possession of these districts will be formally taken on —— day, and the arms of the Kingdom will be set up.

"Art. III. On the same day the Code Napoleon will be published."

A third decree names Prince Borgese Senator, and then follows the decree entitled "Measures with regard to his Holiness:"

"Considering our First Roman Statute, we have decreed and do decree as follows:

"Art. I. The Church and Square of St. Peter's, the Palace of the Vatican, and that of the Holy Office, with their dependencies, freely belong to his Holiness.

"Art. II. The Chapter and the Building Committee of St. Peter's have preserved to them all their property, under such an administration as the Pope shall be pleased to appoint. His Holiness shall receive an annual revenue of a million of Italian livres, and shall preserve all the honor which he has enjoyed in the past."

These are certainly interesting documents in reference to this unsettled Roman Question. Napoleon, in the heat of the Spanish war, wrote to Aldini, then in Milan, to observe things narrowly at Rome, and to learn whether the time had come to put these decrees into operation. The answer of Aldini contains expressions in reference to the hopes and wishes of the Romans.

"The Pope, who has never enjoyed in Rome the public favor, has yet succeeded recently in interesting some fanatics, who call his obstinacy heroic resolution, and expect every day a miracle in his favor.

"With the exception of a few rich men who fear in the change of the Government the destruction of their privileges and the increase of taxation, *all classes agree in desiring a new order of things*, and all long for the moment when it shall come.

"I ought not to dissemble from you that this general disposition arises from two causes, viz.: the hope that they may receive regularly the interest of the public debt, which forms the support of a great number of families, *and the hope of seeing Rome become the capital of a great State, a hope which the Romans seem unable to relinquish.*"

Aldini then ventures to suggest some cautions

to his Imperial Master. He says that the English have exaggerated his want of success in Spain. Hence it will be better to delay the execution of these decrees until after a decisive victory. He moreover declares, in case his Majesty shall persist in assigning to Rome only a small territory, that this provision should wear the air of being only temporary, that the citizens may still indulge their hopes of being the capital of a great kingdom.

And finally, he feels bound to tell Napoleon that the Pope, "obstinately, and against the custom of his predecessors," persists in living in the Quirinal Palace, and protests that he will never leave it, and has had some of the entrances of it walled up. No doubt some spies had advised him of the purpose of Napoleon.

The Emperor followed the counsel of Aldini, and temporized. Afterward, having conquered Austria at Wagram, he believed the time was ripe for this project, and he proposed to increase the Pope's stipend to two millions. But after the protest of Pius VII., and the excommunication launched against himself, he yielded to anger, and annexed Rome to France, and made the Pope a prisoner.

The purpose of the first Napoleon was to unite the Roman States to the other States of Italy, and to confine the power of the Pope to spirituals, and to limit him to the occupancy of the Vatican and St. Peter's, and what is now called the Borgo, and was formerly known as the Leonine City. This portion constitutes about half of what is known as the Trastavere.

Now if Napoleon III. should adopt a similar idea of limiting the Pope to the Vatican and St. Peter's *in the interest of the King of Italy*, the Roman Question would soon be happily settled. But although we grant that the opinion of one who is not admitted into the *arcana* of European politics, on this obscure question, is of little value, we cannot resist the conviction that Napoleon still clings to the old "Napoleonic idea" of bringing the power of the Papacy, whatever may be its extent, and whether purely spiritual or mixed, in aid and support of the Empire. It is not probable that he indulges the hope that the grand vision of the renewal of the Empire of Charlemagne, which dazzled the first Napoleon, will be realized in his own person; but it is quite possible that he has the conviction, that the French civilization and the French language and French thought, and the superiority of French administration, will gradually, in connection with occasional French conquests, bring all Europe, by a willing annexation or absorption (like that of Savoy and Nice, which are known to have desired the transfer) into the Empire; and that then a second Napoleonic Charlemagne, not swaying Europe by conquest, but by the wills of consentient nations, shall be crowned at Rome, by a Pope whose universal spiritual supremacy shall at once uphold and be upheld by the temporal power of the new Cæsar of the Nations. We do not believe that the present policy of the Emperor of the French can be comprehended, except upon the theory that he is revolving vast designs, and laying deep and broad in his present policy the foundations of a future gigantic empire, constructed not like the Empire of Charlemagne, of ill-cemented feudal fragments, nor like that of the first Napoleon of heterogeneous nationalities, held together by the mere pressure of military power, but of nations homogeneous in civilization and assimilated in manners, and approximating to each other in the administration of justice through the wide-spread influence of the Code Napoleon, and penetrated with that sentiment and that gratification of being part and parcel of a magnificent empire, which made the boast, "I am a Roman citizen!" the proudest prerogative of the ancient world, from the confines of Britain to the remotest regions of the East. We do not believe that either the character or policy or designs of Napoleon can be understood except upon the supposition, that in connection with his astuteness and practical wisdom in the detail of administration, there is also something dreamy and vast and theoretical in his nature, which, running beyond the present possibilities of things, finds expression in such schemes as that of confederated Italy under the presidency of the Pope, and of a national congress in which Prussia should be expected to be humane, and Austria unselfish.

Hence, we can find no other explanation of his tenacious hold on Rome than in some unrelinquished Napoleonic dream of a future ascendency in the center of Italy, with a view to still more vast results in the future. This impression seems to derive countenance from the following facts:

His evident unwillingness that Victor Emmanuel should have any other portion of Italy united to his kingdom than that which *he* turned over to him by the Treaty of Villa Franca.

That this reluctance was not a comedy played between himself and the Government of Turin, is evident from the fact of Count Cavour's real indignation—of his profound depression, and of his undisguised reprehension of the Emperor as having been false to his promises, and false to the cause of Italy.

The unnecessarily long delay of his army in Italy—and his scarcely disguised desire of having a Napoleon placed over the Government of Tuscany—and the exertion of all his power, short of actual war, to prevent the lesser States of Italy from becoming absorbed in Sardinia.

The discontent which he evinced at the revolution of Naples, and the half-support which he granted to its beleagured King.

The same diplomatic opposition which he

showed to the annexation of the Æmelia and Romagna to the kingdom of Italy.

Hence, we cannot but surmise that, over and above the Emperor's determination to keep Austria out of Rome, and his sincere desire to exert his influence for some amelioration to its dreadfully oppressed population, there is also the reluctance to relinquish a vast and cherished hope of empire, which the spontaneous uprising of the great Italian nation must have sadly shaken, but to which he clings with his characteristic calm tenacity, and which he may suppose future European complications may still make possible.

To the question therefore,—"When will Napoleon withdraw his troops from Rome?"—I believe the true answer to be, "Not until he is compelled to do so by the pressure of some events—like that, for instance, of the rescue of Venice from Austria by Victor Emmanuel—such as would subject him to the execration of the civilized world if he should refuse."

The recent arrangement between France and Italy, by which it is understood that the capital of Italy is to be transferred to Florence, and that in two years Napoleon will withdraw his troops from Rome, may seem to conflict with this statement. So far as Napoleon is involved in this arrangement, we believe that he has come into it most reluctantly, and only because he could no longer retain his present position at Rome with self-respect, and with a due reference to the reputation which he covets. We regard the movement as the victory of Italian statesmanship, unity, patriotism, patience, and firmness, over Napoleonic ideas and Napoleonic policy. As to the abandonment of Rome by the French troops, two years yet remain before that is to take place. We cherish the conviction that this too will be accomplished; but that it will cause a mighty pang to the Imperial heart, and that the pen which is to sign that decree will be long held over it suspended—we have no doubt. But that which constitutes the most hopeful augury in this movement is, that it has been made quite irrespective of the feelings or wishes or remonstrances of the Pope. He may thunder "*non possumus*" as loudly as he will, but whereas the phrase once meant "*we will not,*" it will mean hereafter "*we cannot help ourselves.*"

CHAPTER XIII.

THE ISSUE, THE SITUATION, AND THE SOLUTION.

THAT the government of the Pope is heartily detested by all the people of the Roman States—that it is sustained solely by foreign force—that emancipation from it would be as rapturously welcomed by them as it was by the inhabitants of Bologna, Perugia, Ravenna, and Ancona, when they were incorporated into the kingdom of Italy, needs no proof. None but the blindest partisans of the Pope deny the fact.

But many persons suppose that this issue between the Pope and his subjects is recent. On the contrary, it is a thousand years old. During all that period, at intervals, the Romans have struggled against the temporal power of the Pope. They have never accepted it otherwise than as a necessity, except when adherence to the Pontiff was the rally of Italian patriotism, against German or French or Spanish invasions.

The French historians deny that Pepin, when he rescued the Bishop of Rome from the domination of the Iconoclastic Emperors of Constantinople, whose seat was at Ravenna, conferred upon *him* the temporal government of Rome, of

Ravenna, and of the Pentapolis. They contend that he retained the government for himself under the title of the Patrician of Rome. They declare that the Pope, under cover of certain donations for the benefit of the Church, subsequently claimed civil jurisdiction over the provinces in which they were situated.

Charlemagne was crowned Emperor at Rome by Leo III. He gave many benefices and estates to the Church; but where is the proof that he relinquished his own temporal sovereignty? From Aix-la-Chapelle he continued to govern and collect taxes from the Roman States, as from all the other portions of his dominions, and bequeathed them to his son Louis le Debonnaire. His successors pursued the same line of policy.

From the beginning of the ninth to the eleventh century, there was a constant struggle between the Popes and the nobles for supremacy, in which the nobles, represented usually by the family of the Dukes of Tusculum, generally prevailed.

The German Emperors renewed that strife, and until the fourteenth century, the Roman people were on the side of the Popes only when and because resistance to the Emperors became a struggle against foreign domination.

During the absence of the Popes at Avignon, the Senators of Rome exercised virtual sovereignty. The spirit of the Roman people found its expression in the effort of Rienzi to restore an absolute municipal independence of Pope and Emperor.

It was not until the Cardinals, after the death of Martin V., A.D. 1447, organized and *butressed* the Papal power that it became firmly established.

Since then, until the period of the French revolution, the Roman States, knowing that the great powers of Europe were leagued to support the Pope's temporal power, have made few efforts to resist and overcome it.

But, since the restoration of 1815, the Roman States have impatiently borne the Papal yoke, and have constantly made known to the Popes and to the world, that if left to themselves they would immediately throw off the hated and oppressive temporal power.

That issue, vaguely involved in the struggles of a thousand years' duration, has now become distinctly defined. The history of the Papacy, since the restoration in 1815, and especially the events of the last four years, have clearly revealed that issue to Pope and people. Each party, admonished by long experience, understands at this time, more clearly than ever before, what it aims at, what it should cling to, and what it must secure.

I will strive briefly to indicate how that issue has been evolved, since 1815, what it is, and what is now the relative position of the parties.

I.

At the restoration of the Papacy in 1815, it was so guaranteed by all the powers of Europe, that it had an opportunity freely to adopt such a line of policy as it should judge best and wisest. If by its long disasters it had learned new lessons of improved administration, of reforms adapted to the progress of society, of wise concessions which strengthen governments, by bringing to them their best supports, the confidence and affection of the people, there was no obstacle to their practical realization. It was hoped that in the school of adversity where Pius VII. had learned so well the lessons of heroic and Christian patience, he had also learned some lessons of practical wisdom.

But he proved to be as weak upon the throne as he had been firm in prison and exile. He gave himself up to the extreme clerical party. Their opinions were another name for their resentments. All that was new was hated and proscribed. It was associated with their suffering and persecution. Disappointment and reaction were inevitable. The secret associations of the Carbonari and young Italy, having for their objects the overthrow of the Pope's temporal power, and the independence and emancipation of Italy, spread over the Roman States. The clerical sect of the Sanfedisti (Holy believers) counterworked them. It was a bitter war of local and fruitless revolutionary outbreaks, of secret intrigues, and of conspiracies and assassinations.

After the revolution of 1821, in Naples and Piedmont, had been crushed by Austrian and

French intervention, the Governments of France and Austria earnestly recommended to the Pope reforms in the Papal administration. They hinted to him that his Government was a scandal in the eyes of the nations, and compromised all the respectable despotisms of Europe. In vain; "*Non possumus.*"

The successor of Pius, Leo XII. (1823–1829), with even more bigotry and bitterness, pursued the same line of policy, and at his death, the people were more discontented, and the liberals more enraged, than at his accession.

Pius VIII., who reigned but little more than a year, was a tool of Austria and of the Sanfedisti.

The death of his successor, Gregory XVI., in 1846, closed the first era of the new trial of the Papacy on the old system, which looked back to the middle age as the golden age, regarded despotism as profitable godliness, bigotry as the first of duties, and all progress and innovation as devices of the devil. What was the result?

The liberals were panting for an opportunity for vengeance, and the Sanfedisti, drunk with power, had abandoned all moderation.

Commerce was exceedingly depressed, and high restrictive duties had organized smuggling into a system as extensive as the regular trade.

The native troops were few and poor, and badly disciplined and paid, while the foreign regiments, better organized and rewarded, were a heavy burden upon the treasury, and hated by the people.

The police vexed the liberals and were keen in the scent of heretics, but allowed bandits to desolate the country, and were notoriously inefficient in arresting thieves and murderers.

The contributions and taxes were very heavy and unequally distributed.

The development of public wealth was repressed by laws which forbid improvements, such as the introduction of gas and railroads, enjoyed by other States.

The administration of justice was so complicated that right became tangled and strangled in a net-work of civil and canonical enactments, often contradictory, and always difficult to be understood and reconciled.

A debt of 37,000,000 of scudi and an annual deficit of half a million.

The career of arms dishonored and closed to the Roman youth, and closed equally diplomacy, politics, and magistracy, which were absorbed by the ecclesiastics.

A rigid censorship of the press, and, consequently, no free play to intellectual life.

Thousands of citizens *warned*, and, consequently, unable to hold any offices of profit or of honor.

Such are some of the prominent specifications of the indictment which impartial history brings against the Papacy, after a new trial of thirty years of its character and capacities under circumstances of peculiar advantage.

It taught the Roman people that it was the essential and unalterable nature of the Papal and priestly power to be despotic, to be repressive of all progress, to keep the people depressed, ignorant, inert, and in the rear of all the civilized and Christian communities in the world.

Hence, abandoning all hope of modification or reformation of the Government of the Pope, they directed themselves to the destruction of the temporal power, by associations, some of which contemplated united Republican Italy; some, Italy united under a constitutional monarchy; and others, only the independence and the Constitutional Government of the Roman States. These were the convictions and aims of a large majority of the Romans, although the Papacy has never failed to have many bigoted adherents among them.

II.

A new thing appeared in the world—a reforming Pope—a Pope who took the initiative in relaxing the restrictions of the Roman people; in admitting them to a participation in the Government, and in setting forward many schemes of municipal, social, and governmental reform. This proceeding awakened, stimulated, and sanctified popular movements and demonstrations in every country in Europe. It may be questioned whether it was not the *primum mobile* of the revolutions which took place in every great European nation in 1848.

That the movement was individual, spontaneous, and sincere on the part of Pius IX. can scarcely admit of doubt. At first, a gay young man of noble birth, then, wholly changed, an earnest, single-minded, godly ecclesiastic, diligent in every position in which he was placed, he at length reached the cardinalate with a high reputation for purity and zeal. Elected Pope, as unexpectedly to himself as to the world, he entered upon office with few trammels, and free to follow his own convictions. Having been a practical rather than a political ecclesiastic, he evidently did not know, at the commencement of his reign, that the system was stronger than any individual Pope, unless, indeed, he were a liberal Hildebrand, of giant power and equal will; and he seemed honestly to suppose that he could both accomplish and place bounds to the reformation of the Papacy. But while he was utterly unequal to the task, there was much in him to inspire hope and popular enthusiasm. In the vigor of life, with an eminently beautiful and noble person, of which one of his admirers says, that "there is nothing more glorious than his presence except that of the Holy Sacrament;" with a sweet and rich voice and exquisite elocution; with a history most honorable for zeal and benevolence, he was hailed by the Romans and by Europe in his first sincere efforts at reconciling the Papacy with the prevailing aspirations for liberty and progress, with a rapture of admiration and affection. For several months his life was a perpetual ovation. But he had no fixed policy; he was no statesman; he had no firmness; he soon became bewildered between the warnings and threats of the partisans of the old system on the one hand, and the claims and the growing irresistible progress of the innovators on the other. Soon his real character appeared.

Prompt to suggest but dilatory to perform; feeble in intellect but confident in his own judgment; benevolent, but vain and greedy of popular applause; obstinate in adhering to his purposes while they lasted, and yet often changing them suddenly and capriciously; believing himself superior to all influence and dictation, and yet easily managed by those who flattered his fancied independence; loving to excite transports of popular hope which he was afraid to fulfill,—such was Pius IX. at the beginning of his reign.

His effort to connect with the spiritual and temporal power of the Papacy popular and constitutional institutions, was soon seen to be a failure. The Pope, still retaining his absolute authority, wished the people to accept certain liberties and immunities as his *gifts*. He desired of his own will to specify them, to set bounds to them, and also to be gratefully and rapturously regarded as a generous master, who had spontaneously turned over some of his *own rights* to the people. But the people would not so regard them. They counted them to be their own rights, given by God, unlawfully filched from them for ages, and now, with tardy justice, restored. Of course misunderstandings speedily ensued. The people assumed more rights than the Pope had designed to give. The Pope became alarmed. Austria threatened and rebuked him, and occupied Ferrara. From that period the Pope was dragged on reluctantly by the enthusiastic and unanimous national feeling in the way of reform. He consented, with a bad grace, to the constitution and to the expulsion of the Jesuits. When national independence made war with Austria indispensable, the Pope retired to Gaeta, and the Romans, advancing in the line of popular progress, proclaimed that the temporal power of the Pope was at an end, and organized the Republic.

From that moment the Pope repented in sackcloth and ashes of his liberal sins, reconciled himself to Austria and Spain and the extreme Papal party, took Antonelli as his chief counselor, and has become as narrow-minded, bigoted, intolerant, and obstinate in his vindication of the high, old Hildebrandic claims for the Papacy, and in resistance of all amelioration in his government as he had previously proved himself vacillating, vain, and incompetent as a reformer. Since his restoration he has acted upon the maxims of his predecessors in the Papacy since 1815, and never has the true Papal theory of the absolute authority of the Pope, in temporals and spirituals, been more completely and rigorously executed.

III.

And now the issue between the Pope and the Roman people is distinctly made. It is simple, intelligible, and patent to all the world.

The Pope and the partisans of the Papal power are now fully and finally convinced, that to yield anything to the people as their own right, or as a concession, will be fatal to the existence of the Papacy. They are persuaded that a small reform creates a dangerous and inextinguishable thirst for more. They believe that the only safety for the Papacy, and the only temporal and spiritual salvation of the people, lies in an absolute double despotism of the throne and the altar. They contend that it is a blessed and paternal and sacred domination, and that it is only felt like the divine government itself, to be grievous when it is resisted.

The people are persuaded that the above is the conviction of the present Pope and Papal Government, and, moreover, that it results inevitably from the first principles of the Papal system. Logically and historically it has been proved to them that the Papacy cannot continue to be itself unless in temporals and spirituals it is absolutely despotic.

Hence they will never again be deluded as in the first days of Pius IX. with the dream that the Pope may connect a constitutional temporal government with the administration of the spiritual supremacy as it is understood and wielded by the Papacy. They have answered for themselves the question asked by the author of "The Pope and Congress"—"How can the chief of a church which excommunicates heretics be the chief of a state which protects liberty of conscience?" They will, hereafter, believe no promises of reform made under the pressure of fear of themselves, or of deference to the Emperor who carried the Papacy back into Rome upon the bayonets that were reeking with the blood of Romans. They will be satisfied with no concessions; for experience has proved to them that they are always temporary and illusive, and often treacherous.

The Papacy says, "We must exist, and hence there must be no liberty."

The people say, "We must have constitutional liberty, and hence the temporal power of the Papacy must cease."

Such is the issue. It is between the people and the temporal power of the Pope. It is not between the people and the spiritual supremacy. Some persons may believe that the two powers are inseparably conjoined, and that the one cannot be abdicated and the other retained; and that, therefore, both should be at once destroyed. But this is not the present issue. It may be hereafter. At present, thousands of Romans make no question of, but rather magnify, the Pope's spiritual supremacy, and believe that it is damaged and weakened by association with the temporal power, who are consequently earnest and enthusiastic for the destruction of the latter.

The Pope says, with that bland smile and that sweet voice for which he is celebrated, "My dear, poor, infatuated children, come and rest in security and peace under my triple power. My temporal scepter shall protect you as citizens; my pastoral crook shall guide you in the ways of sacred peace; and my keys shall open to you the gates of paradise." And the poor, dear, infatuated children answer: "Ah, my father! that scepter has been used as a bludgeon to bastinade us; that crook is pointed with temporal penalties and is dripping with our blood; and those keys—we are not quite so sure that they open paradise as we are that they lock the cells of San Michele and the dungeons of Paliano!"

And what is to be the end? It would be rash to prophesy. The question is one of exceeding complications. I find that those who have resided long in Europe, and studied the question most profoundly, are the most loathe to commit themselves to a decisive judgment as to the solution, or the time and means of its accomplishment. One can see what are some of the prominent forces which enter into this struggle, but he can by no means precisely estimate their power, nor can he be sure but that there are other and hidden powers which are greater than any of which he is aware, and which will prove in the end decisive.

IV.

On the side of the Pope are: The present possession of absolute power, thoroughly organized, with agents and instruments skillful and experienced,—many of them unprincipled and remorseless, and all of them committed by interest and safety to the preservation of the Government as it is.

The support and sympathy of the princes and many of their dependents; of the employees of the Government, and of some of the relatives of the priests; and of large numbers of ignorant Contadini of the Campagna and the mountains.

The *reserved hold* which the Papacy is found, in times of crisis and of trouble, still to have, from religious and hereditary feelings and associations, on the minds of those whose convictions are decidedly adverse to the temporal power. Many persons who would contend earnestly against the temporal power while the Pope exercised it at Rome, would have fearful and superstitious misgivings when they should see the Holy Father in exile at Gaeta; and would tremble when they should hear his voice of appeal, rebuke, and excommunication. This is a state of mind which it is difficult for a Protestant and Anglo-Saxon to comprehend; but it is real, and it always has been, and is always calculated upon as one of the great elements of the Papal power in times of difficulty and disaster.

Add to these the thorough sympathy and support of the great Catholic powers; and especially of Austria and Spain, who have always been ready to uphold and restore the Pope by fleets and armies.

But above all, and perhaps more effective than all besides, is the presence of the French army, the sure support and guarantee, while it continues, of the preservation of the Pope's temporal power. When we add to the mere fact of that presence, which is a pledge of the whole power of the Empire in support of the Papacy, the *words* uttered by Napoleon on his return from the battle of Solferino, and never since revoked, we seem to have an absolute security, so far as human force can give it, that the Pope's power will not be disturbed while the Emperor shall live, or his policy prevail. His memorable declaration was, "I hope that a new era of glory will begin for the Church on the day when every one shall share with me the conviction that the temporal power of the Pope is not contrary to the liberty and independence of Italy."

As we see that this protection is the most powerful support of the Papacy, so can we discern some great reasons for its continuance. It satisfies the strong partisans of the Pope in France; and thus rallies them to the support of the Imperial dynasty. It secures the preponderance of France over Austria in the counsels of Europe.

Whether there be deeper and ulterior reasons in the mind of the Emperor—whether, when he announced that Italy should be rid of Austrians from the Alps to the Adriatic, he meant Northern Italy for Victor Emmanuel and Central Italy, including Tuscany, for a Bonaparte, and Rome, with its Pope under his protection, for himself; whether, loath to relinquish such a scheme, he still hopes for its realization; or whether he believes all Italy, united under a Constitutional Government, would not be a good and edifying neighbor to France, held under a tight Imperial rule, and would stand in the way of her great ulterior destiny; or whether it be that Victor Emmanuel has not another Savoy and Nice to exchange for Rome: whether one or all of these reasons are in the mind of Napoleon to confirm his present purpose of retaining the French army as the support of the Papal throne,—who can tell?

However this may be, we should not fail to mention as a circumstance which strengthens the Pope's position, that notwithstanding the very many times that he has been beaten, driven away, and his power apparently at an end, he has still reappeared with all his old pretensions, and with the complete restoration of his power.

On the other side—the side of the Roman people—there are forces of prodigious power, though, at present, some of them are chained and imprisoned.

There is the intense hatred of the Papal Government, and the burning desire to become the capital of the kingdom of Italy on the part of the vast majority in numbers, intelligence, activity, and power of the Roman population. It is as vain to repress its manifestations as it would be to shut up the fires of Vesuvius. When it is not pouring from the crater of revolution, it is shaking the soil on which society reposes, and rumbling in the caverns of conspiracy, and gleaming out in jets of patriotic fire from the crevices which it makes for itself, and which no despotism can close. It is impossible that one who knows anything of the state of feeling in Rome can seriously deny this fact.

There is the enthusiastic, and yet calm and patient, determination of a great United Kingdom of 22,000,000 of inhabitants, that sooner or later Rome, occupying the very moral and local center of that Kingdom, *shall* be its capital. The people are intelligent, united, resolute, and ready for the most patriotic sacrifices for this great object. Their king is one of the first soldiers of the day; their marshals have no superiors in military capacity; their army numbers nearly 500,000 men in the vigor of life, and possessed with that patriotic passion, which, when guided by military discipline and knowledge, doubles an army's effective force. There is a patriotic surrender of individual convictions, whether for a United or Confederate Republic, and a hearty rally around the Constitutional throne of Victor Emmanuel.

There are all around the remnant of the Roman States which is left to the Pope, those who were formerly under the Papal bondage, the contrast of whose liberty, prosperity, and joy, constantly stimulates their brethren still in bonds to desire to join them; and who constitute their sleepless and energetic allies, ready to counsel and aid them in preparation for that coming deliverance which both parties confidently expect.

There is, moreover, the dissatisfaction if not irritation of the great protector of the Pope, the Emperor of the French, at the ingratitude of the Papacy for the immense services which he has rendered to it, and its obstinate and haughty refusal to listen to his counsels to save and consolidate his power by introducing ameliorations and reforms in his administration. If the policy or kindness of the Emperor had not mastered his just indignation, he would long since have left the Papacy to its fate.

There is also a growing obloquy attaching itself to the name of the Emperor because of his Italian policy, under which he may not long be content to rest.

And a reason which it would seem would weigh heavily with the Pope if he were not infatuated—it is obvious that all Italy is becoming not only alienated but bitterly hostile to the Papacy, because of its desperate tenacity in clinging to worldly power. He is fast losing his spiritual hold on Italy by holding on to the mere tatters of the old robe which covered power, while the power itself has fled. The Pope contends that the possession of his principate is essential to his exercise of spiritual supremacy, while all the world sees that he is fast destroying his spiritual influence by clinging to the mere shadow of temporal power. Will he not at length see this, and conciliate Italy, at least for a time, by welcoming Victor Emmanuel to Rome?

And lastly, I am not certain but that it should be regarded as the most hopeful of the elements which enter into this issue—the fact that the Pope is stubbornly resolute not to attempt to save his spiritual, at the sacrifice of his temporal power. Many persons, friends and enemies of the Pope, believe that he would strengthen and preserve his spiritual power over all the Church by ceasing to be the king of a petty nation. The Pope does not think so. The temporal power originally sprang from the roots of the spiritual supremacy; but the old decayed original trunk has long been propped up by the offshoot, and if that support should be withdrawn, it would immediately fall a rotten ruin, to the ground. This is evidently the Papal conviction. I believe it is just. A true spiritual power, not of this world, such as Christ gave to his Church, would indeed be strengthened by casting off all connection with a worldly kingdom. But the Pope's idea and claim of spiritual power is that men should be coerced into the faith, and punished, imprisoned, tortured, and destroyed for heresy. *Such* spiritual power could be upheld only by his own possession of temporal power. He knows that Victor Emmanuel would not exert it in his behalf. He knows that heresies would be rampant and unpunished at Rome. He knows that his little kingdom is almost the last refuge where this system, pure and simple, still prevails. No one but the Queen of Spain will now obey his behests to punish and imprison men for reading the Bible. He is therefore logical in determining that his temporal and spiritual power shall stand or fall together. And this may be ultimately well for the cause of the complete emancipation of United Italy from the Papal power, and the complete separation of Church and State. It may be well for the future of Rome and Italy that the poor old Pope, crying and cursing at the same time, should continue to fulminate his uncommonly tedious allocutions against Victor Emmanuel, and against all progress and reform. United Italy may at length say to him: "If you are so obstinate in the resolution that both your temporal and spiritual supremacy shall stand or fall together, we will destroy them both, and at the same time that we install a just king in the Quirinal, we will put a Christian Bishop in the place of an Anti-Christian Pope in the Vatican!"

We have forborne to prophesy, but we cannot but hope that this blessed consummation is nigh at hand.

CHAPTER XIV.

INTOLERANCE TOWARD JEWS AND PROTESTANTS AT ROME.

THERE are Romanists in this country who claim that the Pope sets a beautiful example of toleration in Rome. If, however, he does so, it is in direct opposition to what he announces to be his solemn duty. But is it indeed true that his charity thus overcomes his principles? The instances referred to are, his toleration of the Jews, and his permission to the English to hold services without, and to Americans to hold services within the walls.

Toleration of the Jews! Alas! that this bitter mockery should be added to the dreadful persecutions, ages long, which they have endured from the Pope in Rome. The bulls of the Popes in the ages all along constantly claim that they are directly authorized to inflict the divine judgments pronounced upon them for the crucifixion of the Saviour!

In another work, "St. Paul in Rome," I have entered somewhat fully into a description of the present condition of Jews in Rome. I will here confine myself to making a few extracts from a paper presented to me, at my request, by an intelligent Jew in Rome, concerning the present condition of his people in that city. It will be seen that he writes in the English language, with some degree of constraint, though with grammatical correctnesss.

"The Jews have always been considered in Rome in the light of things wholly at the mercy of those who governed them, and who had the power of imposing pecuniary exactions, casual or permanent, personal loans, and acts of servility; to confine them to close, unhealthy quarters; to subject them to the double jurisdiction of both the civil and ecclesiastical authorities; to impede by every kind of vexatious obstacle the exercise of their industry; to expel them from several towns and boroughs belonging to the State; to interdict their applying for aid or protection to the constituted authorities in any contingency; to compel them forcibly to listen to sermons composed purposely to convert them; to prohibit them from acting as servants to Christians, or from employing Christian servants for themselves; finally, to segregate them from all fellowship or society, so as to render their lives wearisome and miserable."

Such are the disabilities which always have been imposed upon the Jews. That they have not diminished, but have rather increased during the last half century, would appear from the fact that the population has diminished since 1812 from about 12,000 to 4000. The paper of my Jewish friend ends thus:

"The state of uncertainty consequent on the obscurity and instability of the laws, the frequency of the 'interregnum' (vacant see), the different views of the successor of the Pontiff, and the private interests of those who surround him, have had the effect of deciding those Jews who, with much labor and difficulty, had gathered together a patrimony sufficient to enable them to live quietly elsewhere, to emigrate to other countries. Instances of such expatriation have occurred even very lately, whenever new tribulations threatened to annoy the Roman Jews. We will not speak here of many rich Jewish families expatriated from the marches, from Ferrara, and other communities; we shall confine ourselves to Rome alone.

"After the re-establishment of the Pontifical Government in 1814, several Roman Jews emigrated, who, during the dominion of the French, had been the objects of universal respect.

"Others followed their example after the publication of the rigorous orders by Leo XII. in 1824 and 1825.

"Others again were led to take the same step in consequence of the unfavorable disposition manifested toward the Jews by the Government in 1850, and at present some are known to be about to quit this city, their intentions being well understood.

"The above-mentioned emigrants all have refuge in the Lombardo-Venetian States and in Tuscany, where they have generally made investments of capital in real estate, and where they exercise creditably banking and other important business. Such emigration may seem a matter of indifference to others, but it cannot be so regarded by the class of men to which they (the emigrants) belong, for the excessive number of poor (3000 in a population of 4000 individuals) increases in the same proportion as the diminished means of providing for them; and to those persons of more limited means who are obliged by their position to stay where they are, the weight has become insupportable.

"Such emigrations, more forced than voluntary, produce also the greatest disorder in the administration of the affairs of the Jewish community, depriving the population of its best support, as the most affluent families are those which emigrate. Thus the forced contributions, the expenses of worship, the alms and help to the infirm, etc. instituted without the existence of any fund established to provide for the poor, now fall entirely on individuals of limited means who have it not in their power to increase their own contributions so as to meet the deficiency caused by the loss of those payments of taxes, etc. formerly paid by the members of the community who have expatriated themselves.

"To the great misfortune of the Jews, deprived as they are of every other resource, they must devote themselves to traffic in all its various ramifications, and their subtlety is put to the utmost trial to gain a livelihood, to support the indigent, relieve the sick, and to encounter the expenses inherent to their condition. Yet bankruptcies rarely occur among them; the number of persons imprisoned is very small, and those all for slight offenses, none for murder or assassination, for forgery or felony, or for any great crimes; and this can be proved by a reference to the registers of the criminal tribunals.

"Notwithstanding this, the Jews are pointed at as beings altogether depraved, confined like criminals, and exposed or subjected to a moral torture and a cruel punishment,—that is, they are treated with contempt, with disdain, and the most active and industrious are rewarded by the hatred generated by envy."

Such is the toleration extended to the Jews! Permission to live in suffering, disability, persecution, and contempt!

As to the toleration of the services of the English Church at Rome, it may be said to be a bitter necessity. Rome could not *exist* without the money expended by the ten or fifteen thousand English visitors that resort to it every winter and sojourn there for a longer or shorter period. They would not thus throng to it without this permission. The English Government would stretch all her power and influence to force this concession. Even as it is, the permission is given with circumstances of indignity which justly raise the haughty Briton's wrath. It is not generally known, as we know directly from one of the officials of the English congregation at Rome, that no *permission* has ever been granted to the English to hold their services outside of the Porto del Popolo. The affair is simply *ignored.* It is not a matter of treaty or of expressly granted privilege. Rome has a convenient way of not seeing sins or inconsistency, if they drop *scudi* at her feet. But no more is granted, even in this ungracious way, than is just sufficient to secure the English visitors and their gold. The service is not permitted within the walls. When the Government heard—it was an unfounded rumor—that the trustees were about to give something of an external churchlike aspect to the old warehouse which they occupy, they were warned that it would not be permitted. This is the extent of their toleration. It is permitted as a profitable nuisance—nothing more.

We know some facts which fully confirm this statement. In the summer of 1862, the assistant of that church spent the hot months at Rocca del Papa, a lovely position, about twenty miles back of Rome, on the Alban hills. Our own place of sojourn was distant from his but six miles, at Albano. With him and around him was gathered a little group of English and

American families, consisting in all of less than twenty persons. The chaplain was accustomed to hold a morning service, without a sermon, in the apartment of an American lady. Nothing could be more quiet and less demonstrative. Yet as soon as it was discovered by the *Gens d'armes* it was broken up. Perhaps it was betrayed by the excessive loyalty of the padrone. He had been a poor and humble citizen. One summer evening, the Pope, making an excursion from Castle Gondolpho, was overtaken by a violent storm, and compelled to spend the night at his humble home. But the Pope cannot sleep under the roof of an untitled citizen. Hence he made the poor man a Roman noble before going to bed—and slept with a good conscience. It was all so precisely like St. Peter's method! It *was*, indeed, dreadful that Protestant services should be held in the apartment that the Pope had once occupied. That desecration may have had something to do with the breaking up of a heretical service so repugnant to this solemn event—commemorated in a marble tablet, and signalized by the gift, by the Pope, of his bust to the privileged host.

During the last winter the throng of English visitors was unusually great. Three separate services for three separate sets of worshipers did not accommodate the crowd that streamed out of the *Porto del Popolo* every Sunday. The celebrated Dean Alvord spent the winter in

Rome; and a strong effort was made by Odo Russell, the British diplomatic agent, seconded by the Government at home, to induce the Pope to permit him to hold services in the British Consulate. It was peremptorily and rudely refused. The Russian Ambassador had in like manner failed to obtain the permission of the Pope to erect a small chapel for the Greek Church in Rome. If such is the extent of the toleration granted to the indispensable, thoroughly heretical English, we may be sure that the Pope is never guilty of the *delirium* (see the last Encyclical) of permitting freedom of conscience to his own subjects. *Gens d'armes* guard the door of the English chapel to see that none of the faithful stray into those poisoned pastures. On one occasion a member of the Pope's guard, curious to see the English service, disguised himself in a civilian's garb and attempted to pass in, but the quick eye of the official at the door detected him and sent him back. The haughty scion of a princely house was compelled to submit and to leave the English lady whom he was escorting at the door. Two years previous, the Rev. Mr. Blood, an English clergyman whom I saw at Paris, was banished from Rome for circulating a narrative tract, in Italian, of a shipwreck, in which there was nothing controversial, but in which, it is true, there was included a distinct statement of the Gospel of free salvation through faith in Christ.

The case of American citizens is quite the same. It cannot be said that they are *permitted* to hold service within the walls; because it is the right of an ambassador to hold such service in his own apartment, which, however distasteful, cannot be refused. But it has been distinctly stated by Cardinal Antonelli, to one of our ambassadors, that it would be tolerated nowhere else within the walls. During the early part of winter, before the arrival of General King, the services were held for a time by the chaplain in his own apartment. He did not venture, however, to have any singing on those occasions, and always required his audience to go out and come in one by one. When he had reason to fear that the fact that he held this service was known, and that it might be broken up (for he occupied an apartment next to that of the now Cardinal Archbishop Manning), he thought it advisable to hold it—as he did—at the apartments of his parishioners, changing from one to another, until the arrival of the ambassador at the close of the year. Such is the toleration of the Pope to the citizens of a nation, in the midst of whom his own church and people have not only toleration, protection, and absolute equality before the laws, but often preference and aid. We deeply felt this gross injustice when in Rome. We thought, and think now, that it is a matter in behalf of which all civilized governments should interfere. If the Pope calls himself a king, then he should be made to conform to the usages of civilized and decent kings in relation to other powers. If he chooses, and is able, to prevent his subjects from reading any other books, or attending any other religious services, or holding any other opinions than those he dictates, this is a matter with which it does not become other powers to interfere. But it is insufferable that he should not permit the citizens of other countries to meet and worship while sojourning in his States, in accordance with their own convictions. It is an insult to which the nations should not submit. England and France and the United States should combine and *force* the Pope to cease this outrage against the rights and the comity of nations. There need be no fear of war on that behalf. France would not uphold him on that issue. Austria would not interfere. Even the Queen of Spain, and Maximilian of Mexico, would not send a dollar or a man for such an object. His own subjects, even the most bigoted, would rejoice. The Romans feel ashamed of the indignity and inhospitality to which strangers, on whom so much of their prosperity depends, are subjected. At least this injustice is enough. It is a little too much to add to it the claim on behalf of the Pope, that after enjoining intolerance as the most sacred of duties, he yet charitably sins by its violation.

CHAPTER XV.

INDULGENCES.

There is no doctrine of the Church of Rome upon which it is so difficult to obtain clear ideas as upon that of indulgences. In truth the Church has no definite system of doctrine on the subject. It is all a *muddle;* and its pecuniary interests are best served by keeping it in its present tangled and opaque condition.

In one respect, the practice of the Church in the sale of indulgences is not quite so bad as it was in the days of Tetzel. The Church does not so openly as then sell indulgences, or exemptions, for present, or prospective, or meditated sin. But in the sale of indulgences for the dead, the Church is not one whit behind what it was in the worst days of Leo.

Yet the present practice of indulgences is bad enough. The Pope assumes to set aside, for a consideration in money, not only canonical offenses and ecclesiastical discipline for the violation of the laws of the Church, but also of the law of God. The Church of Rome has set forth a table of consanguinity within which marriage is prohibited by *the law of God.* The table is made to extend to slight and remote relationships, apparently for no other purpose than to multiply the opportunities to extend dispensations, and to put the price into the Papal treasury. One would suppose that a claim upon the part of the Pope to dispense with the law of God would startle the most devout Romanist. But it does not do so. I was much struck with a case that came under my own observation.

Signore M—— was an Italian teacher who had been employed in my family. He was a widower of middle age, handsome, and with those beautifully courteous manners which are common to Italian gentlemen, and in which they have no superiors. He was also a superb singer, and was accustomed, with two or three other Italian gentlemen who were musical, kindly to come to my Tuesday evening receptions and regale my American friends and visitors, and others who called upon me at that time, with his really superior performances. I doubt not that some of my friends who read these lines will remember his spirited rendering of some portions of "*Figaro.*" On my return to Rome after the summer vacation, he called upon me in full dress, and beaming with satisfaction. He had just been married —and to his niece! Of course, I could not avoid looking and expressing my surprise. He spoke of the matter very freely and answered all my questions with great good nature. "Was it not difficult to get a dispensation from the Pope?"

"Oh, no! it required a delay of only about a month, in order that it might pass through the customary formalities." I asked how much it cost him. He replied that it cost 80 scudi to get the documents to present to the Vicar-General, and that the Vicar-General's fee was about the same amount. He was a good and devout Catholic. He discussed the subject with me in the evident full conviction that though it had been prohibited by God, the prohibition had been removed by the authority of the Pope; that it was right for the Pope to take money for the dispensation; and that he himself was fully acquitted in the forum of conscience of any wrong. The act had ceased to be wrong, and had become right, through the agency of the Pope. It was a new and startling thing for me to be actually in the presence of this state of mind, and to find that propositions which were self-evident to me could gain no assent from him. I would speak to him in this wise: "You admit that this thing is forbidden by the law of God, and that it is not an old ceremonial law, but one of moral and perpetual obligation. Now how can any man set aside God's law, and make that morally right which is morally wrong—and that not in the interests of pity and mercy toward others, but for the sake of pecuniary advantage to himself? How comes it that you can get this done for 160 scudi, whereas you say that if you were rich, or a prince, it would cost you from one to twenty thousand scudi?" He would answer me in this fashion: "It is true that this is forbidden by the law of God. But the Pope is divinely commissioned to execute the law of God. He has full authority—just as a human governor has over the laws of his kingdom—to execute them strictly, or to relax them according to his good pleasure, or from the promptings of his benevolence. This then is God's own relaxing of his laws—because God has put them into the hands of the Pope to administer them for him. That the price, or the consideration for such an exercise of benevolence, should vary with the wealth of the individual is perfectly natural and just. The Pope needs money to carry on the government of God in this world, and every man should contribute, when he receives a favor from God's Vicegerent, according to his ability." My friend was evidently and devoutly sincere. He mixed God and the Pope up in his mind in such a fashion, that any change or modification which the Pope might make in the law of God, was in his view God's own change or relaxation, *through him*. It was a very repulsive and Protestant view of God, which supposed that although He had expressly forbidden such a marriage, he would yet adhere to such a prohibition, and be so hard on a poor fellow who had fallen in love with an extremely pretty niece, as to forbid him to marry her! Such a harsh view of the character of God, as unfeeling and unsympathetic with man, he scouted with scorn!

Yet why should we wonder at this? At the canonization of the Japanese martyrs, the Pope lamented to the assembled prelates the decay of religion through the world. They answered him: "Thou art Peter and upon this rock Christ has built his Church, and the gates of hell shall not prevail against it. When thou speakest, we hear St. Peter, and *when thou commandest, we obey Christ.*" When the assembled prelates thus teach, it would surely be the height of presumption and blasphemy on the part of a poor teacher to doubt the Pope's power to allow him to marry a niece—especially considering that she is so uncommonly pretty!

But the most remarkable feature of the case to me was the fact that my friend has not the slightest reason for supposing that the case ever came to the Pope's knowledge. "Have you his signature? Do you know that it was brought before him, and considered and decided by him? Do you even believe that it was?" To all these questions my friend was constrained to reply in the negative. It was all done by the Pope's Vicar-General. To the Pope alone is committed this prerogative of relaxing and changing the law of God; and in probably ninety-nine cases in a hundred in which these dispensations are pronounced in his name, he knows nothing more of them than the Queen of England does of the thousand crimes which are prosecuted and decided in her name!

I have spoken of the difficulty of ascertaining what the present doctrine of indulgences is. This is particularly the case in reference to the doctrine of "plenary indulgences for the dead." Over innumerable churches and altars in Rome is placed the announcement that certain prayers and offerings will purchase "plenary indulgence for the living and the dead." And yet I have in vain endeavored to obtain a clear definition of what a *plenary* indulgence for the *dead* is. I do not mean that I have failed to get a definition of it which was reasonable and consistent; but I mean that I never received one that I could understand. I could not get at the meaning. I know what the Romanists mean by transubstantiation—but not what they mean by plenary indulgences for the dead. I asked a Roman friend to get for me from his confessor a simple and short statement of the doctrine. Neither my friend nor I could understand it. I asked an intelligent American priest in my parlor, in the presence of a group of friends, to explain it; assuring him that my purpose was not to cavil and object, but simply to understand. He set off famously and confidently on the general subject of indulgences for the dead—but upon the meaning and effect of the plenary indulgence he evidently knew nothing, and explained the matter into completer confusion than it had worn before; and after he left, the "variations of Protestants" as to what he *did* say, or *did* mean, were amusing.

I have asked Protestant clergymen who have spent years in Rome if they understood this dogma, and I have found them as completely in the dark as myself.

The general doctrine of the Roman Church on this subject is quite intelligible. It asserts that besides the eternal punishment denounced against sin, there are also temporal penalties attached to it, which are still due to the justice of God; and that these penalties may be inflicted in this world in part, and the remainder in purgatory hereafter. It teaches that to the Pope has been assigned power over souls in purgatory—in what is called in the modern phrase at Rome *la chiesa purgante*, the purifying church, to lessen or remove their pains. The Pope, in the exercise of this power, has granted indulgences to the suffering souls in purgatory, which they may enjoy through the prayers and offerings, and especially the masses (paid for) of the faithful. Certain prayers in certain churches, and at certain altars—certain offerings and masses shall purchase an exemption of a certain number of days, or months, or years of purgatory. They will shorten so much the period of the sufferings of those who dwell in that drear abode. These holy merits of the faithful shall be applied first to the souls of their relatives, next to those of their friends, and then to those of others who shall stand most in need.

Nothing is more remarkable than the magnificent profusion with which these indulgences for certain periods are given by the Pope. I have before me a manual of the "Pia Confraternita di Maria Santissima assunto in Cielo," in which so many indulgences are provided that if all the faithful at Rome would turn out on some specially favored day and diligently devote themselves to prayers and masses all the day, they could run the account up to billions of years of exemptions. I have been doing a little cyphering on the subject, and I have found a series of prayers called the *Corona*, which, if an earnest Catholic should repeat for ten hours, would give 20,000 years of release to some poor soul. If some statistical controversialist should take this matter in hand, he would be able to prove that, unless the period of purgatorial sufferings is billions upon billions of years, the souls of the departed must long ago have been *prayed out* of purgatory, and that it must be empty, and that there must be such a stock of meritorious prayers on hand in that void abode as to meet all the souls which shall approach it until the day of judgment, and waft them immediately to heaven!

And all this quite independent of *plenary* indulgences—which are just as profusely granted! What is a *plenary* indulgence? I asked my American friend how it came to pass that masses were constantly offered for the souls of those who had already, over and over again, received plenary indulgence—as was the case for instance with many of the Popes? How could it be plenary, if it needed to be renewed? He turned very red, and declared that the meaning was that it was *complete* for the *time* specified. "But do not most of your people understand by the word a complete release from purgatory, and an entrance into heaven?" "The Church," he replied, "was responsible for her doctrines and not for the misapprehensions of her children." But enough. An examination of this subject would lead us into a tangle of absurdities and contradictions into which we have no wish to enter. Suffice it to say that the whole doctrine is an appeal to the sympathies and superstitions of the people with a view to extract money from them; and that in her eagerness to stimulate offerings and devotions, the Church has committed herself with reckless and shameless disregard to even an appearance of consistency or probability. Before dismissing, however, the doctrinal question, I will copy from a manual* which was published at Rome for the purpose of furnishing prayers and directions for the relief of souls in purgatory, something which promises to be a satisfactory explanation upon the subject, but which utterly fails to assure the faithful on the point which is most important and fundamental, and always taken for granted—and that is the power

* Manuale della pia Confraternita di Maria Santissima assunto in Cielo, per suffragare le anime del purgatorio.

of the Pope to *effect* the liberation of a soul from purgatory.

The chapter is "a summary of some decisions of the Holy Congregation (or Committee) of indulgences." It thus opens: "In order to form a just idea of the value and effect of plenary indulgence, annexed to a privileged altar, *which liberates* a soul from purgatory, it is necessary to bear in mind the following decision of the Holy Congregation of indulgences, made to declare this important point. Its words are as follows: 'By the indulgence annexed to a privileged altar, if regard be had to the *intention* of the grantor (viz. the Pope), and the use of the power of the keys, we find that by plenary indulgence is to be understood the sudden liberation of a soul from all the pains of purgatory; if then regard be had *to the effect of the application of the same*, an indulgence should be understood to be of *such an extent as corresponds to the good pleasure and placability of the divine mercy!*'"

So then, after all, the Holy Congregation of indulgences, the highest authority upon this subject, decided in its session of July 28, 1840, that the Pope has only power to *pronounce* absolute indulgences, and to make them absolute only *in intention;* and that the effect of the Pope's intended action cannot be known, and that it depends upon the good pleasure and placability of God! But we turn from these absurdities of doctrine to those of practice.

CHAPTER XVI.

LAY CONFRATERNITIES.

THE Lay Confraternities of the Church of Rome are interesting and salutary institutions. They are founded on a right principle. They involve the acknowledgment of the duty of the people as well as of the priests, to render strictly religious and spiritual services to each other. They give the laity something to do. In a state where there are so few spheres of activity, aside from their professions and business, opened to them, this is an immense boon.

In every parish there are confraternities, connected with general associations, for various benovelent and ecclesiastical objects. There are confraternities for burying the dead, for releasing souls from purgatory through prayers and masses and offerings, for collecting alms for the prisoners, for visiting hospitals, for the restoration and consecration of shrines and holy places, for keeping in order the vestments and paraphernalia of crosses and banners for public processions, and for various other purposes. These associations are greatly favored and fostered by the priests. They absorb an activity and interest which might find vent in mischievous and revolutionary schemes.

I am told that many patriotic Romans are very zealous in them as the best method of escaping suspicion. On the other hand, they are said to be great instruments of influence and espionage in the hands of the priests, who have over them an absolute control. The more bigoted members of these associations act as spies for the priesthood and the police. In seeking to enroll members, they learn who are cool and who are ardent in the interests of the Church. They learn, or they surmise, the sentiments of those to whom they apply, or who are associated with them. The parish priests are careful, of course, to place the most devoted sons of the Church in positions of trust and honor. Thus the leading members are imbued with a priestly spirit. Many others, in order to escape suspicion, profess to be equally devoted. While, therefore, the work of these associations is often benevolent, and must tend to keep alive a fraternal spirit, and to develop the ethical element of religion, and is thus far salutary and comforting to the Roman people, they are yet capable of being made instruments of priestly domination.

There are three of these confraternities of which I will give a little account: 1. the *Sacconi;* 2. the "*Confraternita de Giovanni Decollato;*" and 3. the "*Confraternita dei Morti.*"

Every visitor at Rome has been startled by the apparition in the Corso of a strange being, clothed in a coarse linen sack, which entirely covers him from head to foot, with only two openings for his eyes, with a heavy rope around his loins, and dangling to his heels, and with rude sandals on his stockingless feet. He walks rapidly from door to door, rattles his tin money box for alms, asks no questions, pauses not for a moment, has rather a peremptory than a supplicating gait, and gives you the impression of one who is pushing through an unwelcome task with nervous energy. If you catch a sight of his hand you will see it to be soft and white, and possibly flashing with a diamond which he forgot to lay aside when he assumed his rough covering. He is one of the *Sacconi*. Every Friday he is compelled by the rules of his order to go out and collect alms for the poor. It is a society composed of patricians and persons high in office. That long, bare-legged, hideous-looking object may be the cardinal whose stately bearing and splendid robes you admired in the functions at St. Peter's on the day before. The object of the association is to benefit themselves and the poor by this voluntary humility, these good works, these self-imposed penances. One of their principal duties is to check and reprove profanity. As they make their rounds they enter into wine-shops, where they overhear the name of God or of the saints taken in vain.

They throw themselves upon their knees, exclaiming, "Praised be the Lord!" "Let the holy and dreadful name of God be blessed and praised!" Then humbly and solemnly they exhibit the evil of profanity, declare that God is present, and hears and sees all that is done, and has prepared a very warm place in purgatory for blasphemers; and if they are reviled and derided they answer in meekness, and leave behind them words of love.

On the afternoon of a warm summer day I was strolling near the Basilica Santa Croce, when I saw a procession of these *Sacconi* approaching. They were making the round of the Basilicas, and devoting the day to praying at privileged altars for the release of souls from purgatory. It was the first time that I had ever seen any considerable number of them together; indeed they are rarely so seen. It was odd, picturesque, impressive, weird almost, to see and hear this collection of solemn headless sacks, moving and chanting in a wild, fitful way, up the road. There were not more than three or four persons beside myself near them. Before they entered into the church they were permitted to pause in the shadow of the convent wall and drink from the fountain and cool themselves. When they lowered their hideous visors, they presented a collection of faces that had no appearance of mortification. They were, evidently, elegant gentlemen, who took good care of their whiskers and moustaches. While they rested and chatted, there was a most ludicrous contrast between their faces and manners on the one hand, and their sacks and sandals and their late ultra-monkish aspect on the other; and when again they put on their sacred character it seemed incredible that those silent, sanctimonious, awfully eremetical-looking beings, who seemed just to have stepped out of the fourth century and the deserts and caves of Egypt, could be the pleasant and comfortable-looking gentlemen whom I had seen chatting with each other, in free and easy way, a few moments before. But, a *presto!* the ranks were formed, they filed into the church, they chanted a most mournful dirge before a privileged altar, they seemed to be wrought up to a high pitch of devotional fervor, and, all at once, at a signal from their leader, they all prostrated themselves at length on the marble floor, with their faces downward, as if in an agony of silent prayer, and remained, amid a stillness which could be felt, for some minutes, and then rose and marched off rapidly to finish the devotions of the day at the Basilica of San Lorenzo. The scene was very impressive, and when they disappeared behind an angle of the wall of Rome, I seemed to have had a medieval dream.

The Confraternita de Giovanni decollato dates from the Pontificate of Innocent VIII., toward the close of the fifteenth century. Its object is to furnish consolation to those who are condemned to death, to be with them at the last moment, to bury their bodies, and to pray and furnish masses for their souls. On the day preceding the execution they place printed placards over all the city, in which they exhort the faithful to pray to God for the happy transition of the soul of the condemned to the other world. On the night of the execution, five or six of the brothers of this fraternity, together with a priest and a chaplain of the prisons, assemble in a neighboring church. There they pray for God's assistance to enable them rightly to discharge their painful mission; they agree upon their respective duties, and then, two by two, preceded by lanterns and in silence, they proceed to the prison of the condemned.

Entered into the chapel of the prison, which bears the name of the Chapel of Consolation, they clothe themselves with a black sack, bound with a cord, and give themselves to prayer. At the designated moment the jailors bring the prisoner, with his hands bound, and conduct him before the chapel, where a notary reads aloud the sentence of death. As he passes the threshold of the chapel, two of the brothers meet him, embrace him, and holding in their hands an image of the Saviour crucified, or of the *mater dolorosa*, they render him every kindness in their power. He thus prepares himself for the confession and the viaticum. After this he makes his will if he desires, asks pardon of all whom he has wronged, and assists at his last mass.

While these proceedings take place at the prison, the other members of the fraternity assemble in the Church of San Giovanni decollato (near the Forum), and at sunrise proceed, two by two, covered with their black sacks, and preceded by an enormous black cross, toward the prison, and when the prisoner mounts the tumbril the whole procession moves toward the place of execution. The brothers selected for that purpose stand by him to the last moment, holding up their images, and addressing to him words of cheer and consolation. After the execution they take possession of his body, consign it to the grave with the accustomed religious rites, and for several days provide that masses shall be said for the repose of his soul.

A bull of Benedict XIV. has added to the privileges conferred on this society the prerogative of pardoning every year one criminal condemned to death. After he has been selected, the pardon is conferred with some striking and characteristic ceremonies. The whole fraternity march in procession to the prison. A beadle precedes them, carrying in one hand a black baton, and in the other a tunic of red taffeta and a torch of white wax, which he is to present to the liberated prisoner. After the beadle follow two brothers with lanterns, and six others bearing lighted candles and a crucifix. The crucifix which serves on this occasion has upon its feet a garland of olive, gilded, which is to be placed upon the head of the elected prisoner. The prison is ornamented with draperies, and the space before it is strewn with box and flowers. When the procession arrives, and the liberated prisoner appears, he prostrates himself before the crucifix, and the beadle places the garland upon his brow, and the whole procession returns to the church and chants a Te Deum. After mass he dines with the chaplain, and is accompanied to his home amid the congratulation and applause of the people. The whole scene is very characteristic and national. It is said that the recent policy of the Government is to give less and less publicity to public executions and to the ceremonies above described. But they still take place, and whoever resides in Rome, and makes the acquaintance of an old citizen, will be able to learn where and when such executions occur. But the Roman journals will give him no information on the subject. From the Roman journals it would appear that the Pope was the chief shepherd in a happy Arcadia, where crimes are all unknown.

The Confraternity of the Dead was instituted toward the middle of the sixteenth century. Its object was to give honorable and Christian burial to the dead, especially to those who were carried off by the fevers of the Campagna, or who perished in the inundations of the Tiber. It is a society which has always been distinguished by the self-denying zeal and heroism with which it has discharged its painful duty. It has a high place in the regards of the citizens of Rome. Its members belong to the nobility and to the highest class of citizens. Their official costume is a black sack, sandals without stockings, and a cord for a girdle. They are permitted to travel, when on official duty, only on foot.

When any of them receives news that a dead body has been found in the fields or in the woods, he immediately communicates the news to his fellow-members. Those on whom the lot falls for this office, immediately put on their sack, and start upon the journey to the dead, whatever may be the hour, the season of the year, or the distance to be traversed. It is not unusual for them to go fifteen or twenty miles. Under Clement VIII., in consequence of an excessive inundation, they proceeded to the mouth of the Tiber and to Ostia, where they were engaged for several days and nights in recovering the dead bodies borne down by the current.

This fraternity have devoted much zeal to the object of securing masses for the relief of the souls of those whose bodies they recover. This seems now to be the primary, and its original single object to be now the secondary end they have in view. The means which they have taken to accomplish this object are so peculiar, and my visit to their church in the Via Gulia was such an unique experience, that I must make it the subject of a separate chapter.

CHAPTER XVII.

A CHAPEL OF DEAD MEN'S BONES.

IMMEDIATELY in the rear of the *Palazzo Farnase* runs the *via Gulia.* In the days of Leo X. it was the most splendid street in Rome. Some of the finest specimens of the older palatial and domestic architecture are still to be found there. Whoever has failed to ride or walk through it—and thousands of visitors never enter it—has missed seeing one of the most characteristic and suggestive portions of the city. As one strolls through the quiet street, under the stately old palaces of the cardinals, it is not a difficult feat of the imagination to repeople it with the quaint gay costumes and equipages of the time, which the art of Rome has made as familiar to the mind as those which belong to the present era, and to see again the plump, easy, and elegant Leo, or the keen-eyed, strong, imperious Julius II., as they live in the canvas of Raphael, passing, in all the magnificence of that gorgeous period of the Papacy, through that crowded and brilliant thoroughfare.

The street is still and sleepy now, but dignified and impressive. The Church of the "*Confrater-*

nita dei Morti," immediately in the rear of the palace of Francis II., has nothing in its external appearance or its interior to distinguish it from a hundred other handsome churches. It is not mentioned by Murray; and yet it contains something more remarkable than almost anything which the guide-books have described. I refer to the chapel below the church, and the services for the relief and repose of souls in purgatory which are performed there every year during the *Octave* or first eight days of November. As I saw the chapel in connection with the ceremonies performed there, I shall connect them in my description.

Through a covered entrance, at the side of the church, we proceeded with an eager group of devotees toward the steps which descend into the chapel. Over the door were death's head effigies, and the ubiquitous verse from Maccabees which constitutes Rome's Scriptural argument for prayers for the dead: "*Duodicim millia drachmas argenti misit Jerusolymam offeri pro peccatis mortuorum sacrificium:* 2 Macc. xii. 43." As we went down—down—we heard the rattle of money-boxes and loud appeals for pity on the poor souls in purgatory. On reaching the foot of the stairs we found four or five of the brothers, in their black sacks, with death-heads and cross-bones, and crosses worked in white upon them, vigorously rattling their boxes and making their appeals for the poor suffering souls in purgatory to each new-comer. To avoid unpleasant observation, my friend and I dropped a few baiocchi in the box. It was a strange and ghastly sight that presented itself. The chapel was about fifty feet long and half as broad. The walls were constructed wholly of human bones and skulls. The architecture was elaborate and elegant—in a far higher style of art, if I may so express myself, than the well-known cloister of a similar kind in the convent of the Cappucini. The pilasters were ornamented with little curved bones, in the style that prevailed in the days of Hadrian, and were in admirable taste. The bones and skulls in the walls were arranged in the picturesque architectonic forms which prevailed during the early Imperial era of Rome. The chandeliers depending from the ceiling, itself wrought into ogives of human bones, were finely fashioned from the smaller bones of the hands and feet. In each of the four arches there was an entire skeleton, which held in its fleshless hand some solemn appeal in behalf of the dead, or some startling warning to the living. Close by the foot of the stairs, at a table covered with black, and having a grinning skull in the middle, sat three brothers in black, one of whom received money, and two of whom gave receipts for masses that were to be said for souls. There seemed to be no uniform price—for I heard chaffering about it between the women and the salesman, just of the sort that one would hear at the stalls of meat or vegetables. I was strongly tempted to purchase a mass for some *living* friend, and thus repeat an experiment of the Rev. Mr. Seymour; but my friend, an older Roman than I, dissuaded me on the ground that it might lead to our ejection. The two clerks and the money-changer performed their functions in a very business way, in strong contrast to the lugubrious appeals of those who shook the boxes and made the baiocchi clink in a very importunate fashion. They had their quiet jokes, and their little subdued laughs in the face of the skeleton that grinned upon them from the table. That perpetual appeal for the dead, and that rattling of the money-boxes constantly reminded me of Tetzel and his loud cry. "As soon as the money clinks at the bottom of the box, a soul escapes from purgatory!"

At the other end of the room was an altar, separated by a heavy rail, at which three priests were saying masses with impetuous rapidity. The altar was composed entirely of human skulls. A large number of devotees were kneeling and joining in the service, or "assisting at the mass," as the phrase is. One sight particularly attracted my attention. On many of the skulls the name of the persons to whom they belonged, and the mode of their death and of their recovery, were inscribed. One of the brothers told me that these were often presented to the fraternity by the surviving relatives and friends as pious offerings for the adornment and solemnization of the chapel, and as evidences of their gratitude to the good brothers. Many of the common people prefer to see the bones of their friends consecrated to a pious use, and thus carefully preserved, rather than to have them thrust into those lime-pits where they are soon resolved into the great death-heap into which the dead are *kneaded* in the vaults of San Lorenzo. Before one of these skulls a respectable middle-aged woman was kneeling and praying in an agony of grief. She would occasionally kiss the smooth forehead with passionate affection, and then resume her prayer. No one but ourselves seemed to be surprised or particularly to notice these outbursts of love and sorrow. It was the skull of her husband! How odd it seemed! how touching, and yet how horrible too! I did not know how to feel about it—except to be sure that the whole exhibition was one which could have taken place nowhere but at Rome!

Passing out of a door near the rail of the altar, and ascending a few steps, we emerge into a truly beautiful apartment. It may be called a saloon, in which devotees rest after paying their devotions in the chapel. One can sit in the deep embrasure of the window, and look directly down into the Tiber. In this parlor of the dead, art has done its best to convert the horrible into the elegant. Like the chapel, it is made up wholly of dead men's bones—but there is no uncleanness. It is recherché and cheerful in its aspect, and no grim skulls and skeletons are there to interfere with the general effect.

But the most remarkable thing connected with this saloon is what we should call in our country "an exhibition of wax figures," in a deep recess as broad as the saloon itself. The Contadini and the common people gaze upon it with an admiration and awe which know no bounds. It is a representation of the scene described in the verse of the Maccabees already quoted, and consists of five wax figures, as large as life, in the ancient Roman costume. The King Judas stands in an attitude of regal majesty, giving directions to two soldiers, who have each a box of treasure, to take them to Jerusalem; and two other soldiers, in shining helmets, and exaggerated *wax-figury* martial attitudes, stand by as attendants of the King. I have before me as I write, a print of this wax-work proof of the doctrine of purgatory, and of prayers for the dead, which I bought upon the spot. It vividly recalls the absurd scene, which evidently produced a profound impression upon the minds of the people. Embody an idea, a doctrine, or a legend for the uneducated Italian, and then it is to him for evermore true. Did he not see it with his own eyes?

From the chapel we ascended to the church. It was crowded, and the smoke of candles and the clouds of incense made the air thick and sickening. An immense amount of mass-work was going on. Brothers of the fraternity were receiving money and giving receipts as below. A high mass was in the process of being chanted for one whose body rested in a coffin elevated upon a high, altar-like structure, around which were grouped about a dozen priests with lighted candles, who chanted lustily. Other masses were at the same time performed at other altars. The whole scene was a perfect Babel. All solemnity seemed lost in the rush and hurry of the crowd of holy business which pressed upon the weary-looking brothers and the priests.

I subsequently learned from my old Roman friend, who suggested to me to go to this service, and who had studied all the tricks of the priesthood with intense curiosity and bitter prejudice, some very curious facts with regard to the method which the priests adopt to discharge the obligation to say the innumerable masses which are paid for during the week. The receipts which are given for the masses which are to be said, are all numbered. I have one of them lying before me, which acknowledges that forty baiocchi have been received, for which two masses are due. It is a small slip of paper, printed, but with blanks left for the date and name and amount paid, which are filled up in writing. It is surmounted by a picture of the seal of the society, which is a skull and cross-bones, resting on hour-glasses, and surmounted by a cross, and circled with the motto "*In hoc signo vinces.*" The following is a copy of the document:

"Number 896. Venerabile Archiconfraternita di S. Maria dell' orazioni e morti di Roma; Received from Sig. Giacomo de Sextis, —— scudi, forty baj., of offerings for two masses to be said in our church. This 6th of Nov. 1863. The Deputy, C. Restori."

Now it seems that when the priests perform a mass which has been paid for, they are in the habit of adding, to the name of the person for whom it is offered, as many of the numbers of these receipts as they can run over in their minds without interrupting the continuity of the service. When a grand mass is offered in the church a large number of cases can thus be summarily disposed of. Now, my friend considers this to be unfair as a commercial transaction. He insists that as these people have paid for a whole mass, they are entitled to it, and that it is not fair to give them but a joint stock interest of only a tenth or twentieth part of that the whole of which has been paid for. But inexhaustible are the resources of pious ingenuity sharpened with anxiety for suffering souls in purgatory! I find in the "Manual" of this confraternity some of the decisions of the holy congregation for indulgences which sanction such proceedings on the part of the priests. It is not, therefore, a dishonesty, but a holy economical desire of the Church to save time, and to turn its spiritual treasures to the best account. Among these decisions of "the holy congregation of indulgences" is the following:

"No. 4. The priests who celebrate the holy mass for offerings received, *may, with the same communion, obtain a plenary indulgence for whoever demands a mass, and apply it for himself or for the dead.* In like manner the priests who celebrate for the dead and apply to them the plenary indulgence of a privileged altar, may, *in the same communion,* obtain another plenary indulgence for which a mass is necessary, and apply it to whomsoever they may please."

But the most astounding part of this proceeding remains to be told. At the end of the octave the priests of this church of the dead find themselves under an obligation to say such a number of masses as it is literally imposible for them to do if the whole staff should occupy every altar and do nothing else but mass-work day and night for the ensuing year. In this emergency they go to the Pope, and he graciously gives them a dispensation. Here again my friend contends that there is a cruel cheat inflicted upon the living and the dead. The masses have been paid for. The souls burning in purgatory are panting for release, or for the cooling efficacy and refreshment which come from this relief, which was publicly offered for sale, fairly purchased, and honestly paid for, and yet never given. And it is the Pope himself that inflicts this wrong. But my friend evidently does not understand the extent of the Pope's power. The Pope does not dispense them from performing this service; but by his plenary and miraculous power *makes it in fact to have been done*, or at least provides that the efficacy of acts never performed shall not be wanting! That this is the true explanation of the Pope's agency, and that it is not a violation of the contract, appears from another portion of the decisions of the holy congregation of indulgences.

"No. 11. It is to be observed, finally, that during the year of universal jubilee, commonly called the *Anno Santo*, all indulgences shall be suspended. Notwithstanding this, various Popes, in order not to deprive the souls in purgatory of the benefits of the offerings of the faithful, have decided that indulgences may be extended to *them* through the agency *of prayers!*" Here the Popes decree that prayers shall be just as efficacious as masses—shall perform the same function. He who can change prayers into masses, or make the one do the duty of the other by his word and will, can he not as well give to masses which have not been said, or have been said only in promise or intention, the same efficacy as to masses duly performed? Why not? What is a Pope good for if he cannot do things like these?

This manual is a wonderful little book. No one can conceive the heights and depths and lengths and breadths of absurdity and blasphemy and contradiction and degradation of Rome in connection with this doctrine, who does not study some such work as this. Among other things it contains devotional thoughts for each day in November, in connection with the dead, and the duty of praying and offering for them; and to these devotional meditations is added some wonderful history which shows the benefits of prayers and masses for the souls in purgatory. As a specimen of them I translate the *Esempio* attached to the meditations for the first of November.

"A conspicuous and rich Englishman passed into the other world. His son went to the *certosa* where his father was buried, and offered to the prior a great sum of silver and gold, praying him to make supplications for the soul of the dead. Then the good fathers, in full choir, with one voice, sang alone '*Requiescat in pace*,' to which the prior responded *Amen!* and then, doing nothing more except bowing their knee to the altar, they retired in silence to their several cells. Seeing this, the young man said in his heart,—'Alas! that such a sum of gold should be paid for this short prayer, "*requiescat in pace*."' Whence he gathered courage, and ingenuously and humbly made his complaints to the prior. 'So then, my father, your monks do so little as this for my father for the large sum of money which I have paid!' To whom the prudent superior answered,—'Do you think then, my dear sir, to compare the value of your offering in gold with the prayers, however brief, of my monks? Wait a little, and you shall see how much our prayers are superior to your offerings.'

"Then, having given orders that every monk should write upon a slip of paper in his cell the words *requiescat in pace*, and carry it in his hand, he produced a balance, in one side of which he placed the silver and the gold given by the young man, which, of course, weighed down the scale. Then kneeling, and invoking the divine aid, he said to the offerer, 'You shall now see what is the weight of the brief prayer *requiescat in pace*, written on these little bits of paper, which I shall place upon the other scale of the balance.' Oh, great prodigy! The mass of gold rose on high like the lightest down, and the pieces of paper, like the heaviest lead, precipitated the scale suddenly to the bottom!

"At this miracle all made the sign of the cross in their astonishment, and soon the fame of it spread, and gave great value to the prayers of that religious community. He who had made this offering was particularly impressed, and with tears in his eyes demanded pardon for his little faith, and afterward had engraved in large letters upon a precious stone the words *requiescat in pace* upon the tomb of his father, and considered it certain that these few words had insured the perfect liberation of the soul of his parent from the pains of purgatory."

A charming story! The moral so simple and edifying! Little praying by the priests and much money for it by the people!

CHAPTER XVIII.

FLAGELLATION.

It is not generally known that the *ceremony*—shall I call it?—of flagellation is practiced in one of the churches of Rome on every Saturday evening during Lent. I was informed of the fact by an earnest Prussian Protestant, who has a singular fancy for collecting the instruments of penance and mortification which are in use among the Romanists of our day. It is painful to think that it is just the most conscientious and pure who suffer most from these self-inflicted pains. My friend has an odd collection of hair-belts, and shoes with sharp points upon the inner sole, and leathern scourges with knots, and other devices for punishing one's self into holiness.

Following the direction of my friend, I found myself in a little church in the via Cara Vita near the Corso at six o'clock in the evening. The lamps had just been lighted upon the Corso. I seemed to be the second person in the church. One dim lamp was burning on the altar. Shortly after two more were lighted before the image of the Virgin. Gradually persons came in and moved like shadows in the dim uncertain light.

A large black cross was placed against the chancel, and most of the persons who came in kissed it, and then prostrated themselves with their faces on the marble pavement of the church. After the lapse of half an hour, there seemed to be between fifty and seventy-five men within the church. No women are admitted. A priest entered and read a litany to the Virgin. Another followed and chanted magnificently some hymn or psalm of praise. During this performance a man moved around among the kneeling worshipers, with a string of leathern thongs upon his arm —arranged in a way to remind me of the railroad checks on leathern straps which are seen on the arms of our railroad baggage-masters—and offered them to all, except those who like myself had taken seats on the raised benches against the walls of the church. I was evidently the solitary Protestant spectator of the scene. I strained my eyes in the dim light to see what precisely the thongs were. They all had, or seemed to have, one large knot at the end and a little loop for a handle. After the hymn ceased —*presto!*—the lights were at once extinguished, and the blackest darkness prevailed. There was no hint of light anywhere, except as one looked up to the altar he could see a dim rim of inferior darkness, behind a lantern which inclosed the one unextinguished light. After a pause of what may be called black silence, the voice of the priest was heard in tones slow, solemn, and sepulchral. He commenced, in that utter darkness, a confession and supplication to the Virgin, which grew every moment more passionate in its avowals of sin, and more vehement in its pleadings for pardon. His voice, which was at first plaintive, became choked with real or feigned emotion. He confessed sins of the most aggravated character on behalf of the worshipers. He confessed the awful sins of Romans against themselves, against each other, against the church, and against the Pope. He continued in this strain for perhaps fifteen minutes in a prayer evidently extempore, and which resembled not a little such as are heard at our camp meetings, and which became sublime in its vehemence and passion. The effect of such a performance, under these circumstances, on the sensitive and excitable minds of Italians, many of whom had perhaps resorted to the church under the pressure of intolerable self-reproach for sin, can well be imagined. Certainly that solemn and impressive voice in that dark place, now vibrating and now broken with intense emotion, was well calculated to produce a profound impression. When the prayer ceased, the flagellation began. There was a loud noise from the blows. Some of them I confess sounded marvelously as if they were inflicted upon the marble pavement of the church. Whether any of them could have produced much pain through the thick coats and cloaks which are worn at this season, may well admit of doubt.

But the sincerity of some of them could not well be called in question. My next neighbor laid it on his back with a rapidity and energy truly edifying, but a little alarming, lest in some access of penitent enthusiasm his cord should take too wide a sweep and hit me—who felt altogether unworthy of exercising so exalted a style of penitence. But I dared not move on the other side, lest another brother who was applying his scourge in that quarter might make some eccentric devotional deviation in my direction. I was the more uncomfortable too in finding myself so close to such earnest devotees, when I was sure that they were not so near me when the darkness set in, and I remembered the warning of an old Roman friend as to the pocket-picking which often attends this act of excessive devotion. Fortunately I had left my purse and watch at home. But nothing occurred to annoy me, and the big knot continued to come down with that peculiar *thunk* with which the ears of the school-boys of my generation were familiar, upon the shoulders of my penitent neighbor. He was too busy or too much out of breath to sing; but from every part of the church, while this lashing was in progress, there arose such pealing litanies, mingling with the noise of the flagellation, that the effect was exceedingly exciting and altogether peculiar. This mingled noise of the lashing and chanting continued about ten minutes, and ceased suddenly at the ringing of a bell at the altar. Then again—*presto!* like the shifting of a scene in a theater—the altar was lighted, the doors were unlocked, and the ceremony closed. How much of reality there was in it is known only unto God. But this at least may be said of it—that it is not one of the ceremonies gotten up for Protestants; for it is not even mentioned in the Diario Romano, and very few persons who visit Rome are aware of it.

In the following year I went with two newcomers—clerical friends—to see, or rather *hear*, again, this strange performance. But the programme was entirely changed. An old Roman friend subsequently informed me that it was dropped, because it was frequented by such thieves and cut-throats that it was not considered safe; and that it had already been the scene of theft and robbery. Instead of tragedy there was comedy. Two priests took their seats upon an open platform and began to discuss some of the fundamental doctrines of Christianity and of the church. The objector stated his doubts and difficulties with great freedom, but with equal vagueness and want of point. The respondent answered him with much ingenuity, and with such wit and sarcasm, as made the discomfited objector confess himself defeated and convinced, and called forth laughter and expressions of applause from the audience. They became very warm and animated—they professed to be indignant at each other's sentiments—they interrupted each other constantly and loudly—they rose from their seats and gestured energetically—and altogether *acted* very well. I was told by the same old friend that this custom prevailed formerly to a great extent, but that it is now almost extinct. It is a relic and specimen of that scenic and histrionic mode of presenting facts and dogmas which is so congenial to the genius of the Romish system.

CHAPTER XIX.

THE SACRED IMAGE OF THE SANCTA SANCTORUM.

EVERY one has heard of the *scala santa* at Rome, and of Luther's hearing a voice—"the just shall live by faith"—as he toiled up on them upon his knees. It is set forth upon the authority of the Church that these holy stairs were brought to Rome under the protection of the Empress Helena, about the year 326, and placed in the chapel connected with the Lateran Basilica, called the *Sancta Sanctorum.* Great religious privileges were connected with acts of devotion on these holy steps, mounted often by our blessed Lord in the last hours of his life. Leo the IV. in 850, and Pascal the II. in 1100, granted nine years' indulgence for each of the twenty-eight steps of the aforesaid holy stairs, once in the Pretor's house of Pontius Pilate, when mounted on the knees with devout prayers and meditations on the passion of our Lord. Pius VII. in 1817 renewed this indulgence, and declared that it might be applied to souls in purgatory. An active person can then in ten minutes abbreviate the term of the suffering of a soul in purgatory 252 years. If he should spend five hours a day at this holy work, he would shorten those sufferings each day 7560 years! Surely, unless the duration of the pains of purgatory are interminable, no pious person who visits Rome should allow the soul of a relative to remain there, when he can cut down the term of his suffering, by a month's devotion, 226,800 years; and by continuing at the same pious work for one year, can diminish it 2,721,600 years! Are the pains of purgatory likely to continue much longer than this? We cannot tell—for Rome is never specific in its statements on this head.

There is still another priceless treasure in the chapel of the *Sancta Sanctorum*. It is the miraculous picture of the Saviour attributed to St. Luke. Murray's guide-book is in error in stating that it is said to be an exact likeness of our Lord at the age of twelve. I have an engraving, set forth by authority, which is a copy of the picture, and is called a "*vera effigies*" of the original, which represents a man in full maturity, and with an ample beard and mustache. Although the picture is rude, there is great power in the face; and I do not wonder that in contrast with that feeble and crushed type of the Saviour that prevails at Rome, this old vigorous Byzantine picture should produce a great impression on the minds of Romans. Indeed, the only representations of the Saviour which I saw in Rome, which have any dignity, strength, and divine manhood in them, are Byzantine. This miraculous image is very similar to the large Byzantine Mosaic of the Saviour in the apse of S. Maria Maggiore.

The wonderful and miraculous history of this picture is set forth in a printed document scattered profusely over Rome at the time of the exposition of the picture, entitled "origine della S. Imagine," and concluding with the words "*Con permesso.*" The account given of it is that the Disciples, and especially the Virgin, wishing to have a faithful picture of the Saviour three days after his ascension, requested St. Luke to paint it. St. Luke drew an outline of the picture —and lo! in the morning it was found to have been colored and completed by the hands of angels! During the siege of Jerusalem it was carried to Pella, and subsequently to Constantinople. In the seventh century it was taken away from the Iconoclasts of Constantinople by the persecuted bishop of that see. Not knowing how else to save it, the bishop tied a description of the picture to it, and committed it to the sea. Traveling with a rapidity which far transcends that of a modern steamship, it passed over the waters, in a perpendicular position, to Ostia in twenty-four hours! I cannot refrain from translating at this point a portion of this authentic narrative, sanctioned and attested by the Church.

"Now, while the Pope reposed in the same night, in a divine dream he felt himself stimulated to the duty of going immediately to meet the Supreme King, who was thus approaching him. Early in the morning the High Priest ordered that the clergy should follow him with candles and censors, and should proceed along the banks of the Tiber to the sea; and having arrived at the point where they unite, he saw far off the sacred image coming rapidly toward the shore, and remaining until it approached nearer, he was overwhelmed with wonder, and inundated at once with joy and fear, and falling upon his knees, and resorting to prayer, adored it, and shed copious tears, and exclaimed: 'Oh! Lord, can it be that you will to lodge with us, all unworthy, and is it to the City of Rome that your journey is directed? Since you thus walk upon the waters, deign, we beseech you, to approach us, because we dare not assume to draw nigh to you, since as you walk upon the waters so your counsels are as the great deep.' These things said the Supreme Pontiff, moved thereto by an unswerving faith. Then the sacred picture suddenly rose from the waves, and flying through the air, came and placed itself in his hands. And who can ever sufficiently express the greatness of this miracle? And who can tell the excessive joy of the Pontiff, and of all the crowd of people who accompanied him, and indeed of all Rome? The Pontiff mounted upon a coach to the end that the picture might be seen of all, carried the sacred image in his hands, thus proceeding to the Sacred City, all the clergy and the people advancing with joyful songs of praise and hymns to the majesty of the Lord."

The remainder of the narrative describes briefly the history of the sacred image in the Holy City. It was for many years an object of immense veneration. It wrought many miracles. It was brought out and carried with a procession of all the Roman priesthood to S. Maria Maggiore only on occasion of the most momentous emergency in the fortunes of the Papacy. The last occasion of its exhibition was during that period of the French Revolution when it was at its height, and threatened to sweep away all religion in the abyss of Atheism. The Pope, judging that a crisis of almost equal peril to the Papacy had now arrived, determined that it should again be exposed for the veneration of the faithful and the salvation of the Church. In the judgment of the Papal Government no crisis of equal danger had occurred to the Papacy during the whole period which intervened from the French Revolution to the present time. The captivity of Pope Pius VII., and the capture of Rome, and the establishment of the Kingdom of Italy were not so injurious to the interests of the Papacy as the events of the last few years. It is a striking testimony to the importance of those events; and we believe that is no more than just.

Nothing was wanting to give the greatest possible *eclat* to this exposition. As it occurred before my return to Rome, I have availed myself of the description of a friend who witnessed it, and whose judgment upon the date of the picture is worth much more than my own would have been.

"Arriving at the Church of Sta. Giovanni Laterano some time before the hour (4 P.M.) named in the Proclamation for the starting of the procession, I found the doors closed, the picture having been removed to the church from the chapel called Sancta Sanctorum at the head of the Santa Scala, during the night previous. There were then few people in the piazza; gradually the number increased, and about 3 o'clock a French regiment, with its band playing a lively march, swept round to the front of the church and commenced forming 'the hedge' on each side of the intended route of the procession, to Sta. Maria Maggiore, about one mile. Some regiments of the Pope's troops, in addition, completed the line, the men standing at some distance apart. Gendarmes were of course plentifully sprinkled about. Various bodies of the clergy now began to arrive, and one after another entered the church. Whether the whole were able to find standing-room inside, I am unable to say. By 3½ a very large crowd had gathered in the piazza adjoining, and, wishing to see the arrangements along the line of march, I left before the hour of starting and walked toward

Sta. Maria. All along the road, which runs most of the way between the walls of vineyards and gardens, the people were gathered; in some places so densely that it was difficult to pass. The tops of the walls were in many places crowded with spectators. Reaching the Square in front of Sta. Maria by making a detour, I found it thronged with people on foot and in carriages, representing apparently all classes of the population of Rome and the neighboring country. Hawkers of medals, pictures, and books representing and describing the miraculous picture, mingled their cries with those of the usual venders of nick-nacks sold on public occasions, shouting 'Un baiocco, Un baicco pe'l Santo Salvatore, Un baiocco,' and similar inducements to buy. At length the drums in the distance announced the approach of the procession, which slowly made its way up the avenue, across the Square, and into the church. Those who have seen that of the Corpus Domini, can form a good idea of the arrangement. With the exception of two charitable confraternities connected with the custody of the painting, it was composed exclusively of the clergy. There was the same display of banners, padiglioni, lighted candles, and other paraphernalia. The whole clergy of Rome, regular and secular (about 5000 by census), were directed by the Proclamation to be present, and I presume most of them were. It was long before the picture, which was carried near the end of the procession, came in sight: when it appeared, all hats were taken off and the more devout fell on their knees and remained until it had passed. There was, however, less appearance of devotion in the multitude than I had expected, the majority of whom seemed to be drawn out more by curiosity and the Roman love of spectacle. The picture was borne aloft and erect upon the shoulders of members of the two Archiconfraternite to which its keeping is intrusted. This is said to have been its first exposure to the public view since the first French Revolution. It was incased in a gorgeous frame with open doors, richly sculptured in relievo and gilded; the painting itself is so covered by an ornamented screen, apparently of medieval work, that only the face could be dimly seen through the glass. From a careful later examination I should suppose it a production of the lowest period of Byzantine art, *i.e.* about the time that it is said to have made its extraordinary voyage to Rome. The frame and doors are of later and better workmanship. The procession was escorted by detachments of French and Papal troops.

"After remaining exposed on the great altar of Sta. Maria during the week, the painting was, with the same pomp and ceremony, carried back to San Giovanni Laterano to remain according to the first proclamation until Wednesday. Before that day, however, a second proclamation appeared, stating in substance that on account of the immense spiritual benefit already obtained by its exhibition, and to allow further opportunity to those who had been prevented from availing themselves of the privilege of visiting and adoring the thaumaturgic image, S. S. had graciously directed that it should remain on view until the following Sunday.

"During the two weeks, from early morning until sunset, the churches were thronged by worshipers, confessing and receiving the sacrament, and kneeling before the picture, and were visited at different times by all the so-called Archi-confraternities in procession with banners, candles, etc., and dressed in their strange costumes. The Pope and other high clerical and civic dignitaries, in great state, repeatedly visited the picture and presented to it their most elaborate devotions.

"During the last days, the press toward the picture, of people with rosaries, crosses, jewels, handkerchiefs, books, and other articles, kept two priests constantly employed in touching these to the glass in front by which a miraculous virtue was supposed to be imparted to them; and the soldiers could with difficulty keep the crowd back from the altar."

It seems wonderful that such a ceremony should be gravely proposed in our day as the last reserved and most potent of the resources of the Church, to arrest the evils of the times, and avert the wrath of God. But this is the ground taken by the Cardinal Vicar in his *invito sacro* appointing this performance. "This sacred effigy," he remarks, "is not to be removed from the place in which it has been deposited except in the most momentous and extraordinary circumstances, and when there is the most pressing necessity to satisfy the justice of God, and to obtain special grace for the people. Now, not many words are needed to persuade every one that in the unhappy times in which we live, in which, in addition to the languor of faith are added many positive iniquities, it is more than ever necessary to adopt extraordinary means to placate the wrath of God, justly angry with us, and to avert those scourges which our sins have deserved. And, indeed, already we have a foretaste of these castigations in the contagious disease which has fallen upon our cattle, which we should accept as immediately from the hand of God, without seeking for any secondary cause, as the chastisement of our rebellion against his laws."—"The obsequious homage, however, which we shall render to the revered image of the God-Man, the Saviour of men, will serve *as a compensation* for the outrages offered to his divine Person by the recent Publication of a sacrilegious pen."

The Vicar then laments the condition of poor Italy and Poland—both of them overrun by the enemies of the Papacy and of the faith, and anticipates an arrest to be laid upon the progress of evil over all the world by this propitiation of the Divine wrath through the exposition and worship of the sacred image.

Alas! the Pope has brought forth from his storehouse his most powerful instrument of regeneration, and *since then* Victor Emmanuel has made Florence his capital, Spain has recognized the Kingdom of Italy, Maximilian has proved undutiful, Francis Joseph indifferent, and Napoleon III. has designated the day for withdrawing his army from Rome! What now remains?

CHAPTER XX.

A VISIT TO LORETTO.

THE Casa Santa of Loretto, the house in which Christ was born, and the services and the wonders connected with it, are among the most marvelous and characteristic things *of* Rome, though not *in* Rome. My description of it shall consist of my diary as it was written upon the spot at the close of May, 1864.

"From the moment I entered Loretto I was made to feel that I was in the presence of a great money-making imposition. Prices of everything are ridiculously high. I asked for a newspaper, which at Ancona sells for a sous, and the price was a franc. I shuddered at the thought,—'Suppose my dinner should be in the same proportion!' The street is a bazaar for the sale of *Madonna things*,—rosaries, coronals, beads, crosses, and medals, which, when blessed by being touched by the plate of *terra cotta*, which was transported in the Casa Santa, become of inestimable value. The nice-looking women and girls who attend in these shops run out of them and importune strangers to buy their wares, after the fashion of the apprentice boys of London, as described in the Fortunes of Nigel. I have seen this done in no other city, and in reference to no other wares, except when exhibited in booths.

"As I entered the church at six o'clock last evening I came upon a striking scene. One of the only two sermons delivered here during the week occurs at this hour. A little, fat, young priest was bellowing like a bull of Bashan about Maria! Maria! Among the superlative adjectives constantly repeated I heard most frequently that of *bellissima*. How did he know that the Virgin was *bellissima?* The group to which he was preaching was very picturesque. It was a parterre of gently moving and shifting colors that would have charmed an artist. The costume of the men and women was unlike any that I had seen on the other side of the mountains. The women's dresses were very high waisted, with a small hoop extending the dress a little in front and not behind; and their head-dresses and little shawls were always of vivid colors. They seemed to have scarcely any jewelry, and in this respect are exceedingly unlike the Roman and Neapolitan women. The men wore a white smock shirt over their pants, which reached below their knees, with a red figured vest, over which the large white collar of their shirts rested in a Byronic manner. They have a fashion of trimming their hair very close, with the exception of a few little coquettish curls, which give a most remarkable expression to their clear, bronzed faces. More healthy-looking persons I have not seen in Italy. Brown and florid, their high colors in dress, red, yellow, and bright chestnut, harmonize well with their complexions. They were profoundly attentive to the stentorian little donkey that was braying at them. He importuned them, with the vehemence of a revival preacher, to come early next morning to the mass and matins. He represented that their absence would be a gross indignity to the Virgin, and would be regarded as such by her, and would be likely to bring upon them some misfortune. According to the usual custom, as the sermon was drawing toward the close, boys circulated among the audience, rattling contribution boxes for the offerings of the faithful. It is a proceeding which would be likely to disturb a Protestant preacher. I heard two of the Contadini discussing the sermon. One of them said, '*It hit well!*'

"This morning the church is the scene of the liveliest activity. Certainly among the people the most beautiful reverence prevails. There are no forestieri to give an air of secularity to the scene. Even the inevitable English woman, with her sketch-book and her brown bowl hat, has not yet made her appearance. That swell of chanting voices, as I write, how magnificent! It is not a choir of singers but a chapel full of big-lunged priests, made strong and hearty by pure air and good living, from whom this manly music comes. One might shut his eyes and suppose himself in the Cathedral of Milan, with St. Ambrose at the altar, so simple, massive, and majestic are these chants.

"It would certainly be difficult to have more religious work transacted in a church than is now going on here. Priests in the confessional; priests ministering at many altars; priests robing in the sacristy; priests robing at many of the wardrobes in the open church near the altars; priests seated behind counters selling consecrated rosaries and other sacred jewelry; richly-robed attendants and servitors looking like the flunkeys of the cardinals at Rome; red-capped, blue-capped, and yellow-capped officials flitting around; incense rising; worshipers kneeling and praying in all corners,—what a scene! There must be at least a hundred officials performing in some way. A constant stream of Contadini, mixed with soldiers and a few persons of the better class, are passing through the aisles and through the Santa Casa. In the height of the season, which this is not, the religious business done here must be immense!

"There is one thing that I do not understand. Of course, anything that has special reference to the Virgin, or any peculiar history or tradition, is kissed by these devout people. The bell-rope of the Casa, I know not why, seems to be an especial object of this devotion. But on one of the bronzed doors and on one of those at the entrance of the church, the favorite, and, indeed, the only figures kissed, are those of Adam as he is driven away from Paradise, and Cain as he is driven out from God, a vagabond over the earth. On what principle, or from what sentiment these figures have been selected for kissing, I cannot comprehend. Why should not somebody kiss Eve or some of the saints whose figures are close by? I wonder whether this can be a manifestation of that pity and sympathy for the guilty which is so striking a feature of Italian character, and which makes the extirpation of brigandage so difficult. Whatever may be the cause, poor Adam has been kissed into the most meager form, — destroyed by kindness! Cain has not fared much better. His extended arm is almost as thin as a wafer. I do not doubt that these kindly creatures when they do this, murmur *povero Adamo! povero Cain!* How queer it is,—yet how characteristic! I like them for it!

"The church is large and imposing, but has all the faults of the *Renaissance.* Many of its frescoes have been ruined by the damp. The mosaic copies, however, of some master-pieces will be found fresh so long as the church shall stand. The campanile, and the portico, and the piazza, designed by Bramante, form a fine ensemble. The whole group of buildings seen from below, crowning the hill, is striking. The angels who placed the Casa on this beautiful isolated elevation had an eye for picturesque effect.

"The history of the Casa is briefly this. That the house of Mary was preserved from the ravages of time and of the Mohammedans as by a miracle, is proved by reference to history. The Empress Helena saw it and built a church about it in the fourth century. St. Louis of France made a pilgrimage to it in A.D. 1252. But in 1291, in order to escape the ravages of the Saracens, the house was carried away by angels, first to Tessato, on the coast of Dalmatia; then in 1294 it was borne across the Adriatic, to the estate of a lady named Lauretta. Eight months later it moved a mile inland, to the estate of two brothers. As the brothers impiously quarreled about it, the angels finally perched it on its present breezy elevation.

"On this marvelous history four hundred writers have dissertated, and none more satisfactorily than the American Archbishop Kenrick. Forty-four Popes have pledged themselves, more or less distinctly, to the truth of the miracle. 'True, no accredited historians or other writers of the times nearest to the supposed event,' says Mr. Hemans, a devout Catholic, 'have mentioned the event.' It is true also, as shown by Dean Stanley in his Sinai and Palestine, that 'the walls of the so-called Virgin's house at Nazareth, inclosed within the church, agree neither in form nor dimensions with those at Loretto.' It is true, moreover, that Eastern houses never consist of a single chamber in the form of a parallelogram. But what of that? Roman faith is meritorious in proportion to the difficulties which it overcomes. When it believes the impossible and the contradictory then it is high in merit.

"I entered within the Casa and stood some time. It is difficult to avoid treading on the crowd of kneeling and prostrate worshipers in the uncertain light. The large silver lamps gave light enough to enable me to observe the contrast between the coarse stone walls and the splendid offerings that hang around it, and the gorgeous jewelry that bedizened the little black image of the Madonna and child above the altar. The place was so dim that I wished to remain until I could see the character of the structure and the style of the masonry. Yet though I waited long, and applied my eye-glass, it was difficult to see. But to me, somewhat familiar by my studies in Rome with the masonry of different periods, it looked like some portion of a medieval structure. This is made up frequently of small stones, irregular in shape and size, and yet laid along rudely in courses. There are several specimens of precisely the same sort of work in the middle-age ruins on the Roman Campagna. It seemed, too, to be composed of the same sort of stone as abounds in this neighborhood. With a crowd of kneeling worshipers all around, and a lynx-eyed soldier watching me, I could not examine it as closely as I desired. My belief is that it is one remaining room of a medieval castle perched upon this height. I have seen a dozen of which as plausible a house of the Virgin might be assumed.

"The revenue of the church from various gifts is estimated to be from 60,000 to 80,000 scudi a year. This is a large sum for Italy. The riches of the church in offerings, previous to the French spoliations, are estimated to have been 6,000,000 scudi. Everything of value was taken away at that period. But since then, magnificent offerings have been presented, and Loretto is again very rich, but less resplendent with gems and gold. My guide-book gives me a list of sixty-nine cabinets in which treasures are contained, and furnishes a complete catalogue of all the offerings. They are of every kind and of all values. They are contained in a sacristy larger than an ordinary church, adorned with frescoes of the Madonna's history, and with sybils and prophets, after the manner of the Sistine Chapel. Jeweled crosses, gold chalices, the necklaces of queens, breast-pins, watches, rings, even a suit of kingly clothes, everything in short that has excessive value in a small space, is here. More than three hundred vessels of porcelain, painted from the designs of Raphael, Michael Angelo, and Giulio Romano, have had an offer of a substitute by their weight in silver, and been refused.

Within the Casa the jewels on the Virgin's dress and crown, how priceless!

"The edifice of white marble which incloses the Casa and the sculptures and the bas-reliefs upon it are most admirable. The structure is unique. It is neither a tomb, nor a chapel, nor an oratory, and is yet intended to have some of the characteristics of each. The effect as a whole, and all the details, are in the highest style of art. No wonder! for they were designed by Bramante and executed by Sansovino.

"It was prepared in 1510, commenced under Leo X., continued under Clement VII., finished under Paul III., and exposed to view in 1536. The architecture is classic. A richly molded basement, Corinthian columns, a highly ornate frieze, crowned by a classic balustrade, all in white marble of the purest kind, and all perfectly preserved and perfectly clean, presents an ensemble which satisfies alike the eye and the mind. In the niches are the statues of the ten sybils and the ten principal prophets—the latter colossal—and bas-reliefs, illustrating the history of the Virgin, which are, beyond expression, beautiful! Where else is there anything so beautiful? Nothing in St. Peter's certainly in the way of bas-relief. The structure stands immediately below the dome. The effect of it, with its group of worshipers kneeling all around it, is unsurpassed in picturesque impressiveness and beauty. The light bathes it from the dome above, and gives to it strong lights and shades, and casts its broad bands of radiance over the kneeling Contadini under the arches, and makes their varied and vivid costumes glow like one of their own fields of red and yellow clover, sprinkled with blazing poppies. In the season of pilgrimage, when all its avenues are thronged, and when worshipers crowd together from Spain on the west to the opposite shore of the Adriatic on the east, and from the Tyrol on the north, there must be such opportunities for the study by artists of costumes and groupings and effects as are furnished in no other place in the world. The enthusiasm on such occasions is so strong, and the pressure so impetuous, that there would be loss of life but for the arrangements of the police.

In a little old guide-book about Loretto of the date 1765, I find a description of the Casa as it was before the French spoliations. Its interior must have been surpassingly gorgeous. The walls were lined with plates of silver. There were statues of solid silver and lamps of gold set with gems. The image of the Virgin, a little, ugly, black, wooden affair, sculptured, of course, by St. Luke, was adorned as no human queen in all her glory was ever arrayed. It must have been a very heaven to jewelers and milliners. I find, in the catalogue, long lists of statues and lamps, of solid silver, weighing from 100 to 250 pounds. Opening the catalogue at random, my eye rested on records such as these: "A regal crown, with 304 diamonds and 88 rubies, and a scepter, with 82 diamonds and 57 rubies, the whole of gold, the gift of Christina Alexandra, Queen of Sweden." And so the catalogue continues, page after page. I asked the priest who conducted me through this treasury to whom the duty of arranging and changing Mary's wardrobe was assigned? "To the priests, of course!" A dignified function!

I find, also, in this little book, that previous to the French Revolution there were twenty-three chaplains maintained at Loretto to say masses for the souls of illustrious persons,—kings, queens, and cardinals. The modern book does not say how many are still retained. But I suspect this must account for the immense staff of priests and the incessant masses.

I must not fail to record some of the terrible judgments that have fallen on those who have taken away the least fragment from the holy house. In 1585, a person from Palermo took away a stone from the wall. Alas! he was immediately taken ill! At every recurrence of the season at which he had committed the sacrilege, he suffered unspeakable torments of mind and body. At last he sent for the priest, confessed his crime, restored the stone, and after twenty years of tormenting suffering was perfectly restored. Another gentleman from Macerato went through the same process, except in his case the stone escaped from the cabinet in which he had locked it up, and placed itself in its old position and mortared itself in. There are several other similar stories, the moral of which is the danger of taking away any part of the sacred house.

There are other strange things in this little book. It declares that Mary was constituted "Mistress and directress of the Apostles." They met at this Casa after the Saviour's ascension, and received directions about their ministry. The Casa was converted into a chapel. The Apostles, and especially St. Peter, often said mass here. The original altar remains at which the prince of the Apostles officiated.

This was the house in which it is said that Christ was born, and yet all the interest is made to gather, not about Him, but about his mother!

CHAPTER XXI.

MORALS OF THE PRIESTHOOD.

It is common to hear sweeping assertions concerning the Roman Priesthood—especially at Rome. A hundred times, from those who know much and those who know nothing, I have heard the assertion—"These priests do not themselves believe the doctrines which they impose upon the people!" The former class reach this conclusion by a rash deduction from the partial data to which alone peculiar circumstances or their prejudices have directed their attention. The latter class adopt it from a greedy credulity of everything evil. But it is a superficial and unjust judgment. It is indeed wonderful that any thoughtful man can adopt the Romish system; but not so wonderful as it would be that every one who professed to adopt it should be insincere.

In like manner sweeping declarations are often made with regard to the morality of the priesthood. That they are all impure and licentious is an assertion which I have often heard. I believe this also to be a rash and unjust judgment. As I entered Rome with the conviction that such a judgment against the priesthood as a class was unjust, so I leave it with the conviction that there are high ecclesiastics not a few, of great purity, holiness, and zeal; and that among the working parish clergy there are many who are irreproachable, laborious, affectionate pastors, who accomplish all the good which a bad system will permit.

Yet I must allow that the longer I remained in Rome, and the more I knew of the priesthood, the more unfavorable my judgment of them, in this respect, became. I do not profess to have enjoyed any unusual facilities for information on this subject, nor to have made it a matter of special inquiry. It will be better for me, therefore, rather than to give an opinion, or even to form an opinion, as to the extent to which licentiousness prevails among the Roman priesthood, to state some of the facts from which a judgment upon this subject is to be formed.

One class of witnesses on this subject—and, indeed, on every other—should be thrown aside at once as worthless. I refer to hackmen and commissioners, and *id omne genus*, who, when they perceive that travelers are eager to hear disparaging stories of the priesthood, are generally willing to furnish a supply of them equal to the demand. It is possible that they may sometimes tell the truth; but it is certain that they often fabricate and falsify.

There is a very general conviction among Romans themselves of the prevalence of impurity among the priesthood. In proof of the fact that such is the conviction of the people, we have the statement of a French Jesuit, who has written an elaborate and able work in vindication of everything in modern Rome, and especially of the manners of the clergy. The title of his book is "Rome Vengée ou la unité sur les personnes and les Choses." After stating that it is not strange that revolutionists and unbelievers should slander the clergy, he adds: "But that Catholics should allow the apple of their eye to be wounded; that they should rejoice not only in real scandals, but in those that are chimerical; that they should listen to these horrors without covering their faces, and without expressions of indignation; that they should believe them and repeat them,—this is incredible, *but it is true.* I will say more: this fault, or rather this crime, is found not only among bad Christians, *but also among pious souls.* Without resorting to bad circles in a few hours one will hear opinions the most rash, the most false, the most ridiculous concerning the Roman clergy from the high prelates to the simple priests."

Now it is certain that no persons can know the character of the Roman clergy so well as the Roman people. If they all, the good equally with the bad, friends as well as foes, the "pious souls" as well as the "bad Christians" agree in an unfavorable opinion of the morals of the clergy, then the author has certainly a difficult thesis to sustain when he contends that they are in advance of all the clergy of the world in both piety and learning. It is strange, if this be so, that the Roman people should so unanimously labor under this misapprehension. The people of England and Scotland and of the United States entertain no such conviction with regard to their respective clergy.

As an evidence of the popular feeling on this subject, I may mention the remark made to me by a gentleman of Perugia with entire sincerity, and as a sort of apology for the clergy, to the effect that "if the priests were married, they would be no worse than other men." Pasquin is always sharp upon them. On one occasion, during the excitement which was created by the rumor that Garibaldi was about to come to Rome, when it was feared that there was to be an attack upon the priests, Pasquin wrote: "Beware, unhappy Romans! reflect that you may all become parricides!"

As a confirmation of this unfavorable impression, there are some notorious and glaring facts, which come to the knowledge of even most of the mere visitors to Rome. It is as well known that some of the most eminent Cardinals and Monsignori have mistresses and children, as it is that they have not wives. They will be pointed out to one in their carriages on the Corso. Now it is not strange, it is not even an evidence of a slanderous temper, if the inference be drawn that the same practice prevails among the lower ranks of the clergy. Inspiration has taught us to say —"like priest, like people!" It is an analogous inference—"Like prelates, like priests!"

Moreover, one who has intimate Roman friends will hear many stories of this kind, with all the details of time and place and name, of which he can no more doubt than he can of any other domestic histories which reach him direct from persons upon whose statements he perfectly relies. Some of them are harrowing and revolting. Some of them would furnish scenes for Mrs. Radcliff. Burials of new-born babes at midnight in the dark corners of cloisters—poisonings to escape detection—the priest found dead from a stiletto thrust, which is recorded as a sad evidence of political animosity, but which is in fact a husband's revenge, into which it is politic not too particularly to inquire,—such are the stories which run under the surface of society at Rome. When it is remembered that the crimes of priests are tried alone by secret ecclesiastical tribunals, and that the victims, and the friends of the victims of their guilt, are terrified into silence, and that the guilty priests may either be transferred to a prison for priests (one of which is situated not far from Civita Vecchia), or to a new field of labor, and that no publicity is given to such events by the press, and that the faithful are enjoined, for the honor of the Church, not to bruit them abroad, it will not seem surprising that these stories are whispered rather than spoken, and that the appearance of propriety is retained in cases which, in a land of free presses and free speech, would have convulsed society with horror.

Moreover, there are occasionally scandals in nunneries and monasteries of so large a kind that they cannot be disguised. They may excite exaggerated estimates of similar crimes in others which never come to light. The recent developments on this subject in Piedmont, however, have certainly been alarming. The Italian Government, pursuing a policy the opposite of the Papal, have published the evidence on which a convent of the "*Ignoranti*" near Turin—an order which devotes itself to the instruction of youth—was recently broken up, and its brothers subjected to imprisonment, after a trial in the civil court. The details filled Turin with horror. The head of the convent escaped. I was assured by an Italian gentleman, an advocate at Turin, that only enough evidence was brought forth to convict the brothers of the unnatural and horrible crime of these teachers committed against their pupils; and to satisfy the public of the entire justice of their sentence; but that he was cognizant of the fact that much more could have been adduced. It was said that if the head of the establishment had not fled he would have been in danger of having been torn to pieces. The facts which this trial disclosed led the Government to institute inquiries into other establishments of the same kind in Piedmont, and *five* others had been broken up on the same grounds. It has been a dreadful blow to the reputation of the clergy in that part of Italy. This order was unusually acceptable to the people. It was honored, because it was regarded as engaged in a useful and active function. The indignation against them, and the present distrust of all the priesthood, is excessive. I found my friends in Turin in no mood to accept my charitable judgment that a large portion of the priesthood were men of exemplary lives and earnest characters.

Without entering into details upon this subject, which would be unbecoming, I may yet indicate some of the causes which furnish peculiar facilities and temptations to the clergy of the Roman States to the indulgence of this vice of licentiousness.

It is not necessary to repeat the usual arguments which are adduced to show that the enforced celibacy of the clergy inevitably leads many of them into sin. In the effort to lift a body of men, many of whom are gross and ignorant and sensual in their constitution, *above* nature, instead of teaching them to lift nature to the level of spirit, of holiness, and of duty, the Romish Church does but teach them to *degrade* nature and to add to the worst crimes of sensuality those of hypocrisy and falsehood. If this were all, the evil were far less fearful than it is. When sensuality finds its victims *within* the family circle—when it comes in the garb of holiness—when it destroys or perverts the religious sentiment, and subjects the conscience to untold tortures—when it ruins the purity and peace of Christian households, and wrecks the happiness of loving hearts,—then, indeed, it is a sin whose devilishness no language can express. That there is that in the Romish system of celibacy, in connection with its doctrines in reference to penance and absolution, which has a tendency to foster this vice, has been too often and too conclusively shown to make it necessary that I should dwell upon the point.

But that which I wish particularly to notice is the fact that at Rome the government of the priests gives them peculiar facilities, and leads them into peculiar temptations in this respect. In addition to the power which the priesthood elsewhere exercises over the minds and consciences of men, it wields at Rome the immense power of the patronage of the State. Thousands of families are dependent upon them for their civil and social status, and for their daily bread. Those who hold office, or seek office, under the Government must secure the patronage of their parish priest, or of some other priest, who is connected with a Cardinal or Monsignore, or Bishop, or with some of the influential officials of these great personages. Now here is a fearful double power over men, and women, and households, which bad priests may in many cases abuse with impunity, and which may lead priests hitherto correct into temptations too powerful for them to resist. When the alternatives are presented to families, of secret dishonor with plenty, or personal purity with starvation, and perhaps with deadly persecution by spies and informers, —what wonder that many yield, and that shameful connections and more shameful connivances sometimes follow? It is precisely such cases as this that one hears of most frequently at Rome. It is not so often through the Confessional, or the Pastoral relation, as it is through the power of patronage, direct and indirect, wielded by the priesthood that this evil comes. Hence, too, the charges of depravity in this respect are much more general against the higher clergy who wield most of this power, and against those political priests who are connected with them, in subordinate offices, than against the working parish clergy and the poorer priests. It is not so much seduction as it is the pressure of power. It is the knowledge of this shameful abuse of the power of patronage which gives to the hatred of the Romans an intensity and bitterness against the priesthood which is felt in no other part of Europe.

There is a peculiar institution in Rome which is the boast of the priesthood as eminently conservative of morals. That I may not fail correctly to describe it, I will use the words of the author of Rome Vengée.

"A city which is most religious is necessarily

the most moral. To assert the contrary is more than an error, it is a stupid and silly paradox. Not only is piety the best safeguard of morality, but it suggests to Christian charity the most efficacious means of preserving it. In the case of many persons, for the want of objects of the first necessity, marriage becomes a forbidden fruit. In this perplexity the Devil suggests speedily the only means of tasting the fatal fruit in a method contrary to the divine law. When the heart speaks, often before reason, and indigence presents itself before a man and woman, and says—'Pause! go no farther!' what will human nature prompt? What a door is thus opened to the most frightful disorders!

"But in view of this state of things societies are formed, whose contributions, divided among young girls, the most worthy, go to the establishment of families, the first duty of which is the love of virtue. Without mentioning the numerous individual dotations of private charity which God alone can know, we can count at Rome every year at least 1200, either for marriage or for a religious profession.

"These young endowed girls form a corporation, and they have a particular costume in certain ceremonies of the Church. This costume consists of a black dress and a large white veil fastened to the hair, and falling to the shoulders, which gives rise to their name of the 'Amantate,' or persons covered with a mantle. Those who are destined to the monastery wear with this a crown, and a species of stomacher which hides the lower part of their face, and their veil is retained by many pins. The crown and the stomacher are emblems of their virginity consecrated to the Saviour; and the pins, a symbol, borrowed from the porcupine, signify that their innocence is defended against the assaults of the world, as this animal is defended by the quills with which he is bristling.

"It is necessary, above all, that these girls should enjoy an irreproachable reputation. Hence they must not be employed in certain occupations, which, though not evil in themselves, have a certain discredit, in consequence of the dissipation which is often connected with them. They must not be grape-harvesters, innkeepers, washwomen, or servants in a hotel. Moreover, they must be subjected to the oversight of some deputies chosen among the most pious and the most prudent, and after three years of trial, they are admitted to receive their dowry. Such a novitiate, at the most critical period of life, cannot but have a most happy influence upon public morals."

Such an institution as this, it would seem, must be a great and true charity. No doubt it is. In the present state of society at Rome, it doubtless rescues many worthy girls from poverty, and some no doubt from temptation and vice, and promotes the welfare and morality of the lower classes. And yet this account itself leads to some reflections, not so favorable to the general conclusions of the author as to the superior moral condition of Rome as he might suppose that it would be; and other informations with regard to this institution, not given by the author, lead to the conviction that it is by no means promotive of unmixed good.

I have heard it said that this institution is itself the greatest instrument, in the hands of the priesthood of Rome, for the seduction and corruption of woman. The author of Rome Vengée says nothing about the relation of priests to this institution. Like almost everything else at Rome, it is entirely under their control. The candidate for a dowry must be recommended by a priest. The funds are administered and distributed by priests. Now it is charged that there are cases, not a few, in which most unworthy girls, for vile purposes, are put among the endowed; and that worthy ones have their confidence in their priestly benefactors abused, and their position of dependence taken advantage of; and that they are disposed of in marriage to worthless persons, in order that guilty connections may continue, undetected and unpunished. Or another case may well be imagined in which both parties are hurried by temptation into guilt. A priest puts a poor worthy and attractive girl in his parish among the endowed. She is grateful, and he is gratified and happy to have been the instrument of giving her a prospect of happiness, comfort, and respectability in life. A relation is at once established between them, which would have in it no element of temptation if he were a married man. But with the natural channels for his affections which would have been opened in the family relation all closed up—in his loneliness and dreariness, and craving for affection, he finds the gratitude and confidence and love of this poor girl dear to him; and as the time of the termination of her relation to him, and dependence upon him, and of entire surrender to another, draws near, he finds himself agitated by contending feelings and passions. Then it is that evil may gain a victory in his heart, and he may fall into a sin which it will require many other sins to cover, and from which he may not have energy or principle enough to extricate himself. It is a fearful moral position to which the celibacy of the Romish clergy condemns them!

The fact that the charity of the Romans takes this form, is itself significant. It suggests that the state of society exists which makes an institution necessary, which is established in no other city, in order to preserve its young girls from guilt. The author of Rome Vengée, with the utmost *naïveté*, speaks as if the only alternative for poor girls were guilt or marriage. The writers of no other nation in the world would take this position. As the girls who are selected for dotations are the most worthy of the class from which they are taken, it seems strange to hear him speak of them as inevitably consigned to a life of vice, if provision is not made for them to marry. This is certainly not true of the same class in any other nation in the world—notwithstanding that the author of this book seems to take it for granted that it is. He writes: "Twelve hundred meritorious persons are thus endowed. Now suppose that even a third part of them pass into monasteries, there still remain eight hundred young girls who become the wives of brave workmen, and qualified to transmit to their children the heritage, doubly precious, of virtue painfully acquired. I imagine to myself, on the contrary, that this great number of dotations are not made, and that these girls, instead of being at Rome, are at Paris, or at London—God guard me from unfolding the scroll of their destiny!"

Now one cannot but inquire if the eight hundred best girls in Rome are only saved from ruin by having dotations for marriage, what becomes of the eight thousand or more, less exemplary girls who are not endowed? If we accept the logic of Mon. Gassiat, we must conclude that they are all ruined. But this we should be loathe to believe in its full extent. We rather suppose that in the warmth of his advocacy of the unusual purity of Rome, he has been betrayed into an exaggeration which logically concludes its unusual depravity.

The passage which I have quoted from "Rome Vengée" leads to another observation. The representation which it gives of the endowed girls, whose dress consists in part of a symbol of the porcupine, to denote their armed innocence, is a fair specimen of that constant and disgusting harping upon virginity, to which Rome is so addicted, and which is one of the most effectual of all methods of undermining that sweet virgin chastity whose chief charm is an innocent unconsciousness. Think of a number of girls, marching through the streets, parading and proclaiming to the world, by a symbolism of the porcupine, their proud consciousness of possessing, what belongs equally to all decent unmarried women! I believe in my heart that this incessant harping upon virginity, in connection with the Virgin Mary, and with the life of monasteries, is one of the most prolific of all the sources of corruption to the clergy and the monastic orders. If they would be content to *be* celibate and virgin, and cease their indecent and disgusting talk about it, they would be far purer, and the world relieved of an immense amount of sanctimonious twaddle which is but hypocritical prudery or pruriency disguised.

I have indicated the sources and agencies of the corruption of the priesthood; I have expressed incidentally my conviction that there is much of it at Rome; and yet I conclude as I commenced with the expression of my belief, that it is far from being universal or general; and my strong assurance that among the present Romish clergy there are many men, spiritual in heart, and pure in life, and laborious in duty. A different or a larger opportunity for knowledge upon the subject may lead others to a judgment more or less unfavorable.

CHAPTER XXII.

SICKNESS AND DEATH.

THE treatment of sick and dying and dead visitors and strangers in Rome is heartless and cruel in the extreme. The Romans have a childish terror of infectious diseases, and a superstitious horror of the dying and the dead. Even in the case of their own nearest and dearest relatives the same feelings are manifested. At the approach of death, all the family, except some friend or distant relative and the priest, abandon the house. The body is not permitted to remain in the house over night, but is carried to the church upon a gaudy bier, with a procession of priests and hired Cappucini and the members of some confraternity for burying the dead, clothed in black or gray sacks, with hideous masks of the same color and material, and lazily, fitfully, and out of tune, droning a funeral dirge. No relatives are in the procession. The body remains in the church before the altar, until near the dawn of day, when it is carried to the cemetery of San Lorenzo, and if the family are not sufficiently rich to purchase a separate burial place, it is thrust naked into one of those 365 lime-pits, one of which is opened every day in the year, to receive the dead, where a dozen or more bodies are soon mingled in one mass. Can anything more inhuman and barbarous be conceived? Can any perversion of "natural affection" more revolting be imagined? Protestants, and, indeed, all other civilized human beings, count it as one of their dearest privileges to surround their loved dying ones, and to convey expressions and evidences of affection to their last glimmer of consciousness, and to receive their last messages and sighs; and the memory of these ministrations is a blessing and comfort to survivors in all after-life. And who of us, when he thinks of death, does not desire, above all things, next to the presence of his Saviour, the presence of those dear ones whom the Saviour has given to his permitted and sanctified affection?

All these beautiful natural affections, shared and sanctioned and purified by the Saviour, are prevented by this dreadful system which fosters all our natural evil and thwarts and poisons all those inborn loves which are the most innocent and best part of us. It is not easy to account for the horror of a *dead body* which is so universal in Rome and Italy. It may arise from the fact that death, under the Romish system, is regarded simply as a transit to a tormented life, and from the thought that the body, like an accursed thing, is to be given up to ages of purgatorial fire.

The apologists for Rome and all its practices not only defend this monstrous custom, but claim that it is the expression of the highest style of sanctity. One of them, the author of Rome Vengée, writes of it in this wise: "If death is indeed the end of something, it is also, in another point of view, the beginning of all things. It is a moment of final decision, of fearful solemnity, in which *any distraction of thoughts may open an abyss of woe.* This is the reason why the chamber of the dying is, voluntarily or by force (*i.e.* by the priests), *made empty.* Father, mother, sister, son, daughter, are all removed. There remains but some distant relative, some friend, and the priest, *who is more tender than all parents and more faithful than all friends.*"

"I have heard," continues the author, "this custom much blamed. At the first view I admit that it seems very strange, but our surprise soon ceases. Without doubt it is much to be desired that nature, lifted above itself by religion, should be sufficiently strong to enable one to aid a dear departing one to die as he ought, and to point him to heaven, as did that heroic mother who said to her son, '*Nate! respice Cœlum!*' and this may sometimes take place in the families of the pious. But, in general, if we take men as they are, with their real or assumed sensibility, this sublime apostolate of the family fails just at the hour when it is most needed. Selfishness makes us think of what we are losing and not of that which the dying one may lose through us. Tears and sobs avail nothing for the life that is, and put all eternity in peril.

"Nature is not more strong at Rome than elsewhere, *but faith is more developed;* and if, perchance, it seems to sleep during life, it awakes more ardent at the view of death. It brings religion to seat herself by the pillow of the dying, and to watch over him with a solicitude more tender than that of human love, and to breathe for him purer prayer; and thus the soul, held no longer to the earth by human ties, gently detaches itself, and flies to the bosom of God!"

We need not pause to point out the fallacy of this passage. It is false in logic, and false to the standards of the Romish Church. It is an absolute heresy in the Church of Rome, to speak of souls, except of those which have been canonized as saints, as flying anywhere but into the terrific material fire of purgatory. That is described as a very different place from the bosom of God.

This abandonment of the dead was often, in former times, and is even now, in some cases, connected with the most revolting circumstances. The chamber of the dying man was stripped by his attendants of its most precious contents before he lost his consciousness. This was regarded as the just perquisite of those who rendered so abhorrent a service as that of waiting upon the dying and watching with the dead. It is similar to that of the executioner, who takes all that is upon the person of his victim. Many Popes have been utterly abandoned, and died alone, after having been robbed by their attendants of everything in their chamber. In the middle ages this custom sometimes proceeded so far as to degenerate into a sacking of the palace by the populace.

May none of my friends be dangerously ill in Rome! It is a most painful side of Roman character which is then exhibited. I love the Romans. The higher classes are winning, gentle, affectionate, and beautifully refined. The middle class are friendly and good-humored. The lowest class, I admit, are frightfully brutal. M. About finds in them—especially among those who live in the Trastevere—a sort of savage generosity and grandeur which he affects to admire. I confess that my observation and some experience of this class has left in my mind no element of admiration. It does not enhance my estimate of a ruffian that he looks picturesque, and wears a red vest and sash, and a conical hat with a feather in it. Napoleon used to say, "Scratch the polish off from a Russian, and you will find beneath a wild Tartar." We may say, "Come athwart the passions of the lower Romans, resist their extortions, rebuke them for their insolent and peremptory demands, and up springs the brigand." And a more horrible and cruel brute, with nothing to redeem his brutality, than an Italian brigand is not to be found on earth. And we are sorry to say that there are circumstances which will start up a similar exhibition of brutality and cruelty amid that genial and friendly middle class with which strangers are brought in contact in business and in hiring apartments, and who are found in ordinary circumstances to be kind and genial. Let a friend be dangerously ill, or dead, in the apartment which you have hired, and you will have, in addition to the anxiety and sorrow connected with such an event, a horror on your mind from witnessing and being subjected to one of the most painful and pitiable exhibitions of the weakness and cruelty of human nature that can be conceived. Your good-natured padrone will become rude and cold, and tell you how much his apartment will suffer from having had a sick person in it, and your round, sleek *padrona*, who has hitherto moved about as quietly and purred as softly as an old tabby-cat, will be transformed into a very tigress.

I attended many sick and some dying beds in Rome, and such revolting exhibitions of human nature in the same respectable classes I have certainly never known, as on these occasions. A childish terror, partly real and partly assumed, seizes upon the *padrone*. All pity is lost in real or pretended fear that the sickness will injure the reputation of his apartment. He makes his feigned or real terror subserve his interest, and gives you early to understand that he shall demand and insist upon increased compensation for the injury which you have inflicted upon his apartment, and the disgust and horror you have excited in his mind by suggesting the thought of ugly death to him. If the disease is of a kind which gives him the least opportunity to claim that it was contagious, then your situation is made as uncomfortable as possible. You will be treated as if you were guilty of an unpardonable outrage, and your hitherto fawning servant, whom you may have loaded with benefits, will begin to be insolent and to express his sorrow for the "*poor padrone*." I speak on this subject from painful experience. At a moment when you need to be calm you will be subjected to the most irritating and exciting annoyances. When you need and crave and expect the sympathy of those who have hitherto treated you with courtesy, you are subjected to insult and outrage.

Many instances of this kind occur to my memory, but I will limit myself to one. An elderly English lady, a widow of large wealth and equal benevolence, came to pass the winter in Rome with two maiden sisters. There she met a woman, who, several years before, had been her maid, but who, in the mean time, had married a householder in Rome, and had thus become a respectable *padrona*. Her apartment was roomy and central and well furnished, but in a dark, narrow, and filthy street, and directly over a court-yard in which were several stables. My friend and parishioner (for she was both) was so importuned by her former maid to take this apartment that from mere kindness of heart she yielded and gave up a cheerful home upon the Corso. It was a sacrifice made from pure benevolence, and one which would surprise all who did not know, as I did, her singular generosity and unselfishness of character. Of course she counted upon this one advantage from the change —that she would be sure of the gratitude and the assiduous attention of one who had been greatly favored by her and seemed attached to her. All went well, until on returning from a visit to Naples, she was taken suddenly and alarmingly ill. The change in the *padrona* was instantaneous. She wished to have her sick benefactress immediately removed. There was no effort made to keep up even the appearance of kindness and respect. Her sisters were treated as if they and she were guilty of the greatest outrage against poor, unprotected householders. They were told that a large additional remuneration would be expected whatever might be the result of the sickness. All this I would have considered incredible if I had not seen and heard it in my daily visits. It was with great difficulty that these ladies kept the knowledge of all these painful circumstances from their dying sister. If her consciousness had been more clear it would have been impossible. In a week she died.

Then, again, there was a new and greater excitement. The horror of having the dead body in the house for some days, although it was embalmed and cased in lead ready for transportation to England, was the occasion or the pretense of new outbreaks of cruelty and spite. The *padrona* insisted that it should be removed. The British consul was applied to for protection by the ladies, and succeeded in preventing its removal until her business agent should come from England. A more painful week than those ladies spent in the house with their dead sister and with these heartless wretches it is difficult to conceive. When the agent of the lady arrived, a demand of 300 scudi (more than $300) was made for the injury inflicted from these innocent sufferers, and he was actually compelled to pay as a compromise 150 scudi, rather than to be subjected to the delay and annoyance of a trial of the case.

In this case there was no pretense that the disease of which the lady died was contagious. It was a rapid fever. The compensation demanded was for injury done to the apartment by having a dead body deposited in it for several days.

CHAPTER XXIII.

SICKNESS AND DEATH.

My own experience of the manner in which the sick and dying are sometimes treated by Roman Padroni was very painful.

Among the visitors at Rome during the winter of 1863–64 was a young man, a student of divinity, a son of a dear clerical friend and classmate, who was threatened with consumption. He was a singularly pleasing, gentle, genial youth, whose affectionate disposition and cordial manners added greatly to the interest awakened by his evidently failing health. He occupied a chamber in a large house which was let out in single rooms, and which had become quite a gathering-place for gentlemen from the United States, who were studious of economy, and preferred quiet quarters. Here he enjoyed the society of friends, some of them clergymen, who became greatly attached to him, and comforted and cheered him alike by personal attention and religious ministrations. It was felt to be a privilege to render services to one so grateful, cheerful, and affectionate.

As the brief winter lapsed into the debilitating spring, it was evident to all who looked upon him that our young friend was failing. The great ceremonies of the year were over. The visitors at the apartment which he occupied had all departed, and left him alone. Under the pretext of wishing to répair the apartment—but in fact from the prevailing horror of having the death of a consumptive occur in it—the padrone advised him that it would be necessary to seek other quarters. He went to that great Caravanserai—the Minerva Hotel. There he was very low—confined to his bed. His room was small and dark, looking out on nothing but a blank wall a few feet from the window. Nothing could be more depressing and doleful. His physician advised me that he could not properly be cared for there, and that he would sink rapidly. Hence I determined to have him removed to my apartment, although I felt certain that my brutal and niggardly landlord would make me trouble.

It was a most cheerful apartment in the Via del Tritone, near the Piazza Barbarini. Five rooms were on the sunny side, and from their windows we looked out upon the greenery of the gardens of the Quirinal Palace. When my wife got our dear young friend out upon the balcony, with his feet wrapped in a shawl, and the sunshine bathing him, and the strange picturesque life of the Roman streets flowing below him, he declared, that in contrast with the Hotel Minerva, it was like entering Paradise. He lingered with us for a month, the most patient, cheerful, and pleasant of invalids, unconscious of his rapid failure, flattering himself with the hope of soon removing to Leghorn, and yet constantly growing in grace and in meetness for the better world, which he was so soon to enter. We had sent for his father without his knowledge, and did everything in our power to keep him up in the hope that he would arrive in time to see his son alive. But this consolation was denied him. His father did not reach Rome until he had been a week buried.

It was a sad satisfaction to minister to this dear young man. He became to us as a son. His tranquillity, his sweet and gentle gratitude were very touching and engaging. But it involved us in a most painful difficulty with the landlord. He raged as if we had been guilty of a cruel outrage. He denounced us as dishonestly taking into the apartment more than had been agreed upon; and as bringing into it wantonly and unnecessarily a dying consumptive, not a member of our own family, whose death in his apartment would injure its reputation, and make it difficult for him to rent it again. His abuse of me, publicly and loudly in the Banking House of Freeborn & Co., of which he was a partner, and to which I had recommended many of my countrymen, was savage and frightful. With the other worthy members of this house, from whom I received many courtesies, and to whom I became much attached, I have no fault to find, but this man is a disgrace to this otherwise respectable establishment.

Very soon after our young friend was settled in his home I was waited upon by one of the partners of the padrone who came to tell me of *his* grievances, and to propose an amicable compromise. The compromise proposed was that I should purchase all the furniture in the saloon—for my young friend spent most of his time there—and all the furniture of the bed-room which he occupied—and, *after his death*, pay the expense of the legal fumigations, and scrapings, and cleansings, which would be necessary for the disinfection of the room. The alternative was, that I should be subjected to legal proceedings, and to the heavy damages which a Roman court would assuredly render in such a case. There was something so inhuman, horrible, and vulture-like in thus hovering over this innocent dying young man for prey, that I was filled with indignation, and pronounced the whole proceeding infamous, and utterly refused to listen to any terms, and declared myself ready for legal proceedings. At the same time I declared that, if I had not been so outraged by the incessant abuse to which as I learned I was subjected by the landlord, and if he had waited with a decently restrained greediness until my young friend was cold before he pounced upon him, I might then, knowing the usual Roman feeling in reference to the contagious nature of consumption, have been willing to have made such compensation as was uusal in such cases. But under these circumstances I told him that I should resist to the utmost a claim which was at the best an inhuman extortion unworthy of a civilized people; and added that it might be a good opportunity to have it demonstrated whether indeed Roman law sanctioned such an outrage, or whether it was an old traditional imposition of landlords upon their tenants.

I will not dwell upon the painfulness of such a position, and upon the difficulty of keeping a knowledge of these circumstances from our young friend. Suffice it to say, that the poor youth grew worse from day to day, but was never confined to his bed, and rode out on the day of the night in which he died, and in one month from the time he joined us passed away, with expressions of resignation and of trust in the merits of the Redeemer.

Then began some painful experiences. I received a peremptory message that the dead body should not be permitted to rest in the house over night, but must be removed *to the shop of the undertaker;* and buried on the following morning in the English graveyard. I endeavored to resist this demand; but the Roman gentleman appointed by the Government to attend to the interment of Protestant foreigners, assured me that it would be useless. *Gens d'armes* would come to the apartment and enforce the removal. The attempt to retain the body—especially if it were successful—would much prejudice my cause when it should come on for trial. The superstitious horror of Romans at the thought of having a dead body remain in an inhabited apartment through the night, was excessive and universal. It was scarcely ever permitted. He told us of several cases which had recently occurred in which the members of high English families who were Protestants, had been compelled to acquiesce in the removal of the bodies of deceased friends in a similar way. Only a few evenings before, the body of Lady —— had been deposited over night in the lumber-room of a bookstore, because the coffin-maker's narrow shop could not afford proper accommodation.

It was with a heavy heart that I yielded to these representations. At eleven o'clock, six men, draped in black cotton coverings, came with the official manager of funerals, and the coffin, to prepare the body for the removal and the interment. After they had completed their work, they gathered around me for *drink-money*. I turned from them with loathing, and referred them to the official. The whole proceeding was unspeakably distressing and repulsive. That we should be compelled to put away the body of this dear young man, a child of God, worthy of all honor and affection, as if he were a polluted and accursed thing—that there was no place in which the body of a Protestant could be permitted to lie at night in Rome but in the shop of an undertaker—that the head of the Apostate Church of Rome, the Antichrist, should place this indignity upon one of the dear saints of God,—these things filled me with a blended passionate sorrow and indignation. When I walked those silent streets of Rome at twelve o'clock at night, the solitary attendant of that poor boy, so distant from his friends and country, and thought of his sweet home far away on the banks of the Connecticut, and of the troops of loving friends and fellow-students that would have honored his funeral there, and of all those ministrations of Christian affection which transform tumultuous sorrow into elevated peace, I could not restrain my emotion, and walked by the side of him, who seemed to be my own dishonored son, weeping and sobbing like a child. It was an hour which I never can forget, nor cease often to recall.

From this period the war with the padrone began with new vigor. He again sent me terms of compromise—200 scudi, about $215. I declined paying him anything, for I could not feel that in justice I owed him anything. In the first place, it is by no means a universal opinion of the Roman physicians that consumption, even in the worst form, is contagious. The modern school of physicians, for the most part, discard this opinion. If it is ever deemed contagious, it is in cases where the patient has been long confined to his bed. Our young friend had not been confined to his bed a day, and took a ride on the very day of his death. Moreover, my lawyer advised me that there was no Roman law to the effect that reparation must be made to the landlord in every case in which a consumptive dies in an apartment—that he is to be paid for all the furniture, and carpets, and bedding (which are professedly burnt, but are more frequently sold again to Jews and second-hand dealers), and for all the absurd replastering of the walls, and scraping of the floors, and doors, and wood-work, by which the landlord chooses to renew and improve his apartment. There are only general laws, as in every other country, by which a landlord may recover for injury done to the furniture, or to the *reputation* of an apartment. But it has been the policy of landlords, and hotel-keepers, and all their following, whose interests are connected with theirs, to represent it as undoubted Roman law that this remuneration is to be made, and that it is simpler and cheaper at once to make it, than to be compelled to make it and be subjected in addition to the expenses and annoyances of a lawsuit in a foreign land, where one is entirely at the mercy of strangers whose interests are all interlinked. But I was resolute to resist this series of outrages, not only for my own satisfaction, but for that of others. I was well known in Rome. The case would be public, and its result would be learned by many residents and visitors. I felt that it would be to some extent a public benefit and protection to my countrymen, strangers, and to others, if I should conquer. It seemed to me my duty to test the matter, and it was one which my indignation made me very ready to discharge.

My excellent and courteous lawyer, active and wide-awake, advised me that there *were* certain fumigations prescribed by authority which must be made—and these being made, he thought he could sustain the plea that everything had been done which the law required, in order to restore the apartment in as good condition and reputation as it was in when I took possession. But—we must be quick! The landlord's fumigators, if they should come first, must not be admitted. He hurried to the police department, obtained an order for four *Gens d'armes*, who were directed not to allow Sig. C.'s fumigators to enter the apartment if they should make the attempt. Sure enough, Sig. C.'s fumigators were first on the ground, but the police were at the foot of the stairs and sent them away. My admirable counselor, Sig. Cecconi (whom I commend to all Americans who may need legal counsel in Rome), was radiant at this preliminary and essential triumph.

When the fumigators came and proceeded to business, the whole proceeding struck me as wonderfully ludicrous and absurd. The operations could scarcely have been more thorough had it been an admitted case of the plague or of Asiatic cholera. Some of the bed-clothing was taken away to be burned. The mattresses were ripped open and their contents spread out to enjoy the fumigation, and were afterward made over. Most penetrating and stifling disinfecting agents were steaming in the tight-closed room for three days. I have the solemn sealed certificate of the authorized apothecary that everything had been done *en regle*, and according to the exigency of the case. And yet I received messages from my amiable landlord to the effect that the purification was wholly insufficient. The furniture should have been scraped and revarnished, the plastering should have been taken down and renewed, and the window-sashes scraped and painted anew! And all because a young man had died in the apartment of consumption!

It must be confessed that much of the popular superstition and fear upon this subject, especially among the lower classes, is genuine, and that it has been fostered by the opinions of many eminent physicians, and increased by the regulations which have been put forth by the authorities in respect to disinfection. At the same time it is also notoriously true, that landlords and hotel-keepers affect more terror on this subject than they feel, in order that they may extort the more *scudi* from their guests or tenants; and that the Romans themselves observe or neglect these regulations, in ordinary cases of consumption, according to their opinion and feeling upon the subject. One of them told me that if such a case as that of my young friend had occurred in his own family, he could have omitted all these disinfecting processes. But he owned his apartment and furniture, and no one could make anything out of him by moving in the matter! If, indeed, he had had a particularly timid or superstitious neighbor who threatened to enforce the regulation, he might then have been compelled to adopt some of the prescribed fumigations.

It seems incredible that the same regulations should be adopted in the case of consumptives as are prescribed in the *case of plague*—but I have the printed regulations, issued by authority, to that effect! They are entitled "Regulations approved by the *Sacra Consulta*, the Supreme Sanitary Magistracy, for the disinfection of the effects and chambers of consumptives" (dei Tisici). I translate some of these regulations. "4. Furniture of wood must be subjected to chloric fumigations and then polished anew. Frames of beds which are varnished, must be scraped and varnished again. Wooden furniture which is not desired to be retained, and the drapery frames of the bed, may be broken and thrown into a fire in a place apart and not public, or thrown into the Tiber." "6. Pictures in oil, after having been exposed to the fumigations of Morveau repeated for three days, ought to be scraped and *gummed* anew. Frescoes which merit preservation should be washed in water and in vinegar." "7. To disinfect the chamber of a consumptive during his life, the nitric fumigations of Smith should be used; and after death, the first three days, those of Guÿton Morveau, unfolding and exposing all the drapery, house linen, and clothing, and gathering together all the furniture of the deceased. Then the walls of the chamber should be scraped as well as the floor, the ceiling, the frames and sashes of the windows, and the doors; and, finally, the pavement [most of the floors are pavements of brick or a lava composition] should be washed with water and vinegar, and polished anew." "These regulations are, for the most part, used in all the Lazzaretti of Europe to disinfect goods suspected of the plague of the Levant, or of yellow fever, and hence they cannot be defective; *rather they are excessive for a disease of doubtful contagiousness, such as is pulmonary consumption.*"

Now it was on the latter clause that my apothecary and lawyer rested for the sufficiency of the fumigations, and up-ripping and burnings which they had adopted; while the landlord demanded that everything should be done according to the letter of the regulations adopted for the plague! Two or three weeks wore away in preliminary proceedings, and in various skirmishings, real or simulated, between the lawyers on either side. In the mean time I received various advices from parties apparently disinterested, after the usual subtle Italian fashion, to the effect that it was so unusual, and scarcely creditable a thing for a foreigner, and especially an ecclesiastic, to go to law in Rome, that it would be better for me to yield the point and pay the demand. I knew where these suggestions came from, and was quite unmoved. I fully share that strong trait common to an Englishman and an American—an intense dislike to being cheated. My will, and my principle, and my pledge were all enlisted, and I would not yield. After a time a message was sent to me—"Would I compromise on 150 scudi?" "No!" Shortly after—"On 100 scudi?" "No!" Again—"On 50 scudi?" "No!" I left Rome with the matter unsettled, and with directions to offer only so much as the inevitable additional expenses would be if it were carried to the court, and we were successful. Shortly after I reached Paris the matter was settled by paying Sig. C. 30 scudi! There were indeed other expenses, but nothing more went to my grasping padrone; and when his lawyer was paid, probably nothing was left to him but his wrath.

I enter into all these particulars to show that the whole system is one of mere plunder which could be broken up, if gentlemen would resolutely resist it; and if the national representatives at Rome would support them—as General King kindly supported me—in the vindication of their rights. It is a cruel and inhuman business. Broken-hearted relatives are in no mood of mind, at the moment of their loss, to question such claims. The resident physicians scarcely dare to aid the friends of their patients in exposing and resisting these extortions. I have known of cases at hotels where a claim of 500 scudi has been presented and enforced.

I had successfully resisted an outrage, but the whole matter left a sort of horror on my mind. The father of my young friend approved of my proceedings, and I need not add, would not allow me to suffer loss. That I should have been compelled to enter into such a contest, with my young friend dying under my eye, and after his death, while I occupied all alone (my family having departed for Switzerland) an apartment which had now so many painful and repulsive associations, was very distressing. It served to wean me from Rome, which had been so uniformly pleasant to me heretofore. I was impatient to be gone. I needed change. I was conscious of unfitness for society and for work. One cannot come in contact with such baseness and resist it even successfully, without a singular sensation of being degraded by it. Providentially the term of my service at Rome was drawing to a close. I left it with grateful recollections of the uniform and extreme kindness which I had received from the pleasant group of American residents at Rome. If it should have seemed to any of them that my departure was a little abrupt and unceremonious, I trust (if any of them should see these lines) that they will believe that it was due to this state of feeling; and receive the assurances of my regard, and of my grateful sense of unnumbered courtesies and kindnesses to me and mine.

CHAPTER XXIV.

A CHAPTER OF FRAGMENTS.

My book is growing beyond the bounds within which I promised it should be kept. I must omit many topics in order to have even a little space in which to speak of the social state of Rome. This chapter, therefore, shall be one of scraps and memoranda.

"Witnessed in the Church of S. Ignatio, on the 21st of June, a singular spectacle. All the children of the schools were gathered together and filled almost the entire vast area. Each of them addresses a letter to the saint, containing expressions of reverence and supplication. They are placed by a cardinal at the foot of the statue of the saint, to the number of five or six thousand. Although they are overlooked by their teachers, yet occasionally some mischievous anonymous epistles are foisted in, begging the saint to send Garibaldi as soon as possible to Rome, or entreating him to make their teacher somewhat less of a fool!"

"It seems that deformed beggars, by a recent order, are forbidden to ply their trade in the street. It will surely be an immense relief. I find that the licensed beggars who have their brass badges, are confined to certain localities except on Saturday, when they have a free range of the city. Every store has a pile of baijocci on the counter ready for the beggars on Saturday, and never have I seen a beggar treated harshly by a Roman."

"The journals are full of the processions and offerings made to the winking Madonna at Vico Varo. A friend tells me that some of my old friends, the Contadini of Sarasanesco, drew their tongues on the floor of the chapel from the door to the picture upon the altar. An artist gave me a plausible explanation of the supposed movement of the eyes. He says the canvas is loose, and the wind makes the picture move in little waves."

"I find that I have been in more than thirty towns in the neighborhood of Rome, which have a range of from 1000 to 6000 inhabitants. In not one of them, not even in Albano, the summer resort of many of the aristocracy of Rome, is there a book-store, or a book-stall, or a place where one can buy a newspaper. What a fact that is! Indeed, anything more dismal, dreary, degraded, dirty, dead,—and if there be any other unpleasant adjective beginning with *d*, that too,—than a Roman town, I do not believe is anywhere to be found short of Turkey."

"There are things in the Roman Ritual which I cannot believe are contained in the rituals of the Romish church in our country, especially in reference to baptism. There must occur some strange scenes in Roman homes if the directions of the ritual are carried out. The doctrine of the church is, 'No baptism, no salvation!' It is rigidly and logically applied. Hence no consideration of delicacy, or even of consistency of doctrine, must be allowed to interfere with the performance of the saving rite without which an immortal soul is consigned to hell. The doctrine of the church is that to the priesthood alone is consigned the administration of the sacraments; but in cases of peril of death to infants or adults it gives way to the other doctrine of 'No baptism, no salvation!' and it is expressly prescribed in such cases that the baptism may be administered by laymen, 'even by the excommunicated, by believer or unbeliever, Catholic or heretic, man or woman.' In the case of infants, provisions are made for baptism which it is difficult, with a due regard to delicacy, to explain, but which one should know who would learn the inexorable consistency with which Rome carries out this dogma. The child, half-born, if likely to die; the quick child taken from the womb of its dead mother,—these must be baptized. If even the yet unborn infant dies it is not permitted to be buried in consecrated ground. When a *lusus naturæ* is born, the question is to be considered, 'Is it one or two? With one or two souls?' and according to the answer there must be one or two baptisms. Nay, if there be a monster born, of which it is doubtful whether it is human, it is to be baptized with the formula, 'if thou art human,' etc. It never seems to occur to Rome that we can sometimes reason backward from conclusions to premises. She is strong in the conviction that if premises are true, no legitimate consequences from them can be absurd; but she does not seem to admit that if the conclusions *are* manifestly absurd, the premises must be false."

"There is another very singular office of the Roman church—that of absolving the excommunicated already dead. If the body is not buried it is to be beaten with a rod, and then absolved. If buried it is to be exhumed if it can conveniently be done, and the same ceremony is to be performed. If the exhumation is very difficult, then the tomb or the monument undergoes the castigation, and the absolution is pronounced."

"Heard to-day that, in imitation of the Virgin in Vico Varo, a picture in a small street not far from the Corso had begun to wink. Went with my friend B. to see it. There was quite a crowd. Some were kneeling, others gazing intently. The utmost reverence and silence prevailed. Went the next day, and the picture had been covered by order of the Pope. That Virgin must not be allowed to be miraculous. Virgins should know how to behave themselves better than to be winking in the crowded thoroughfares of Rome, where there are so many infidels and heretics who would deny the most palpable and energetic rolling up of the eyes. There are few heretics and unbelievers that would make a pilgrimage so far off as lonely Vico Varo is; and when the faithful reach there, exhausted with fatigue and with empty stomachs, and enter the chapel where there is a frenzy of devout excitement, it is much easier for the Virgin to wink, and for the worshipers to see it. I once asked a poor woman, 'Suppose she does wink? What of it? What good does it do? What does it mean? Why does she not speak?' She was puzzled, but afterward brought me triumphantly a sacred ballad, in which it was set forth that the Virgin rolled up her eyes because she was offended that so many people in Rome favored Renan and the revolutionists, and were not loyal to Papa!"

"A Roman friend overheard Mons. Manning extolling the free schools and colleges and libraries of Rome to one of those Puseyite Englishmen who, by one short step, so often pass into the Roman church. 'But,' said my friend, 'I could have shown him that it is a wretched education, and that there is very little of it, such as it is; for when the summer vacation of three months is deducted from it, there are also six and a half months more lost to instruction in fasts and festas and sacred ceremonials, so that there are but two and a half months of instruction, and those not consecutive.'

"These festas are the execration of the poor people in Rome. An artist told me that on the nights previous to festa days the poor cobbler who occupied the area of his apartment, always worked all night, and slept through the festa. The Pope will allow no work to be done on these days, and hence the very poor are driven to such shifts in order to put bread into their mouths."

"I was told to-day about the court 'del Spoglia.' It seems that priests are not permitted by law to embark, or put their money into any business. This court, 'del Spoglia,' takes cognizance of such cases. The law is constantly evaded. The priests carry on business through others. Cardinal Antonelli is the greatest business man, next to Torlonia, in Rome. But it is all through his brother. Now when the Roman Government has proof that a priest is so engaged, it does not interfere with him, but allows him to go on and make money, and then when he dies, breaks his will, because his property has been accumulated contrary to law, and appropriates it to herself. Truly the children of light are sometimes as wise in their generation as the children of this world."

"Signore —— gave me an account of his sickness since I saw him last, previous to leaving Rome for the summer. He was very ill of a fever. The doctor is obliged at a certain stage of the sickness, when the patient is in peril, to admonish him to send for a priest and confess. If he refuses to do so, the doctor is obliged to abandon him to his fate, and no other physician would dare to take charge of the case; and if he should die unconfessed, he would be buried in unconsecrated ground, and his property would be confiscated to the Church, on the ground that he had died a heretic. The relatives of Signore —— begged him to call a priest when the physician had advised him of his perilous state, for the purpose of saving them from the disgrace of having him buried in unconsecrated ground, and, no doubt, also with the view of succeeding to his little patrimony. He consented only on the condition that they would send for a certain priest,—his friend, and like-minded with himself in reference to many of the dogmas and practices of the Church. When the priest arrived, the room was cleared of all other persons. Signore —— told his friend, the priest, that he confessed *to God* in *his presence*, that he was a sinner, and relied wholly on the redemption of Christ for a full and free forgiveness. The priest assured him that this was the true doctrine, and that his confession was satisfactory, and he declared him to be forgiven, and made out his certificate in the usual form. But my friend recovered to tell me the story. In answer to my question whether there were many such priests in Rome, he answered that there were several that he knew that played double, but this was the only one of his acquaintance whom he would trust."

"A professor of the Propaganda, the Rev. Dr. S——, one of whose functions is evidently to manipulate Americans when they come to Rome, and especially to lead them into Romish dogmas *through the Catacombs*, to which he acts as cicerone and learned expositor to many parties of Americans and English, was lately caught in an absurd blunder. He is, indeed, a blundering Irishman, whose ignorance and assumption it is difficult to avoid injudiciously rebuking when he is engaged in this *propaganda* work. He was escorting a group of American and English people through the Catacombs, and had dwelt particularly upon the fact that a peculiar form of the cross—that one which was divinely revealed to Constantine — is never found on monuments earlier than toward the close of Constantine's reign. Subsequently he was enlarging upon a petition, which was a virtual prayer for the dead, on another tablet, which he contended belonged to the early part of the second century, and was, of course, showing how fallacious was the Protestant assertion that no prayers for the dead could be found earlier than the fourth century. My friend S—, who told me the story (a highly intelligent Independent English clergyman), saw in a corner of the tablet that precise form of the cross which the priest had truly declared never was met with previous to Constantine, and pointed it out, and asked him how he reconciled the fact with his theory, that the tablet was of the second century. The poor man turned very red in the face, and had not even presence of mind enough to say that it might have been put upon the tablet subsequently, but turned away with the deliciously absurd observation, 'that there were exceptions to all rules!'"

"The *number* of priests and monks and nuns, and the extent of ground covered by ecclesiastical buildings of various kinds, strikes me more and more every day. The number of these ecclesiastical persons properly belonging to Rome is about 7000. Since the establishment of the Kingdom of Italy about 3000 more have flocked in. Some of them are very poor. I have had respectable and well-dressed priests beg a few baijocci to buy bread. The number of Roman citizens is about 180,000. This makes one ecclesiastical person to every 18 of the laity, including women and children. A sufficient supply—enough to ruin them! I once said to my old Roman friend that it really seemed to me that the space covered by strictly ecclesiastical property within the walls of Rome must be half of its whole area. He replied that he did not doubt it, and that as he had some large maps he would amuse himself in making the estimate. He did make it, and assured me that *it covered two-thirds!* It will not seem at all improbable to one who thinks of its 380 churches, some of them like the Basilicas with large areas about them, the convents with their extensive gardens, the nunneries, and the Pope's three *parsonages*, the Vatican and the Lateran and the Quirinal, with their enormous adjuncts and gardens."

"The representations which the priests make to the Romans of the condition of Protestant nations is ludicrous from their grotesque exaggerations. They describe them as without religion, in a state of anarchy and wretchedness that is frightful. They contrast the prosperous, peaceful, and happy state of the Roman people with the degraded and oppressed and awfully polluted condition of the population of Great Britain and the United States. 'The Catechism of the Protestants,' a work put forth by Perrone, the foremost modern theologian of Rome, contains such representations as show how fully he calculates upon the absolute ignorance of the people. Here is a specimen:

"'Disciple. Protestantism seems to me then a perfect Babel.

"'Teacher. It would be a small matter if it were only a Babel, but the truth is it contains doctrines horrible in theory, immoral in practice, an outrage to God and man, ruinous to society, and contrary to good sense and modesty.

"'D. Can you prove the truth of these dreadful accusations?

"'T. Certainly, with the greatest ease. It is sufficient to open the works of Luther, of Zwingle, and of Calvin, to find it everywhere argued that God is the author of sin; that God forces a man to sin in order to punish him. You will find then that whoever has faith, however great may be the enormities which he commits, does not cease to please God; that the elect, howmuchsoever they may sin, cannot be damned; that good works are not necessary to salvation; that man by original sin has become a machine deprived of free will, etc.

"'D. These doctrines fill me with horror. Are they not in some respects worse than those of Pagans?

"'T. *Indeed they are. Neither the Pagans nor the Turks have ever adopted such impious doctrines.*'"

We look very ugly when we see ourselves *in a Roman mirror.*

CHAPTER XXV.

HABITS AND MANNERS.

We have been accustomed to think of the Italians as an idle people. The "*dolce far niente*," of which we hear so much, is synonymous, in our minds, with laziness. An acquaintance with the habits of the people must modify this notion, if not change it entirely.

The women of all ranks are very conscientious in the discharge of their duties. They all "look well to their households," and those of the middle and lower classes are actively industrious. Indeed a housekeeper from Boston or Baltimore must sometimes doubt whether in this matter her Italian sister is not more constantly employed than herself.

Certainly, one wearisome care comes upon her which is spared our own ladies, viz., the charge, to a great degree, of the clothing of her domestics. Her child's nurse expects her to provide every article of clothing that she wears, and to have it of good quality, and in great abundance. The wrought muslins and laces, and bright ribbons for summer use, and the gold-laced scarlet cloth boddice for winter are costly matters. Neither are the head-dresses insignificant items,—the large silver or gold filigree pin by which they are secured, costing alone from five to twenty dollars each.

The men-servants are no less troublesome. She must provide them all with a best suit of clothes, with livery—if it be used—and with gloves for table service as well as for out-door uses. Besides these expensive perquisites, every domestic is entitled to ten cents a day for wine and bread-money, in addition to other full board.

In view of all this, I think I may safely say that wages are no lower in Italy than with us, and that an American who keeps house there will soon learn to prefer his own customary high rates of money payments, to those involving so much of annoying care. I do but justice to Italian servants when I add, that we never saw one of them who would admit that all had been done for them that could have been expected! The system is bad,—very bad,—fostering a grasping as well as a dependent spirit in all who serve, from the cook who caters for your table, to the coachman who expects not only wages and broadcloth, but "buono mano" fees beside.

When, therefore, a well-rounded and handsome Italian lady sinks into her carriage to enjoy her afternoon drive, one who knows, sees in the perfect toilet of all parties inside and outside of the equipage, evidence of a vast deal of thought and care.

We did not find, either, that the men were any less industrious than those of most other lands. One would not find in their wine-shops or cafés more idlers than throng our own less innocent places of refreshment; and nowhere in Italy can one see such hosts of feeble-looking youths, and gross-looking lounging men as continually crowd the steps and sidewalks in front of our hotels.

The Italian of all classes rises early. He gets a cup or two of coffee and a large piece of bread any time between four o'clock and seven, according to his plan of work for the day. Between this time and his substantial and plentiful breakfast between ten and twelve o'clock, he works industriously. And afterward again, if he be a professional or literary man, until about three in the afternoon. The merchants, mechanics, and laborers rest from one to three hours in the middle of the day, and then resume labor until the evening.

The country people rise at about three o'clock in the morning,—sometimes indeed just after midnight, if the way to their fields be long—and work steadily, only stopping for wine and water and bread, until noon. Then comes the idleness which tourists see, the sleeping upon their carts, if in motion, or under them if not, or upon the rude benches inside or outside of their wine-shops. Those men have already done a fair day's work, in the cool of the morning, while we who rise at nine or ten are just ready for ours.

I recall, as I write, the despair of our family, when, after a day of settling down into a beautiful summer home in Albano, we were aroused at about two o'clock out of our soundest sleep, by the braying of donkeys passing under our windows, the shouting of their drivers, and the loud, prolonged, and most barbarous singing peculiar to the peasants of that whole region. I remember too our amazement upon finding that these were "indolent Italians" going to their day's work! We do not contend that the Italian does as much work in a given time as a German or a Scotchman, but we think, that according to his strength, and in view of the character of his climate, he does all that is possible.

There is a saying which one finds all over the continent which runs thus: "An Italian for a cook, a Frenchman for a companion, an Englishman for a friend, and a German for a husband," and like almost all similar sayings, it contains much truth in few words. Indifferent cooks are not tolerated in respectable Italian families. None, therefore, hire themselves as such, who do not understand their business. They are a very important element in the household. They buy everything needed in kitchen and pantry,—accounting to you, daily, for every penny spent; and the number of delicious courses that will follow each other upon your table, in view of the small outlay you are called upon to make, is amazing.

While at Albano, we were served in this capacity by a woman. She was a grandmother, had raised many children, was perhaps fifty-five years of age, and somewhat portly, but possessing singular beauty. Daily, when the dinner was nearly over, she would enter the room. A thin muslin lace-edged kerchief upon her still beautiful black hair, another crossed over her ample bosom, and a wide white apron, were the peculiarities of her costume. Moving statelily around the table, bowing and curtesying as she went, her face beaming with smiles, she would ask whether the dinner was satisfactory. To the invariable affirmative, she would as invariably answer, "Ah, I am glad, but it shall be much better to-morrow." Then the "padrone" (or master) must offer her a glass of wine and water, which she would drink with "many thanks, Master Mine," and, after a last curtesy, the little ceremony ended. Of course, every one had something to say to the good soul as she would make her progress around the table, and we were delighted with the custom, so quaint, so foreign, and so pretty. We did not find the same thing among the cooks who are hired by foreigners in Rome. It is probably confined to the country or only in use among the Italians themselves.

Englishmen, accustomed to the fiery wines and liquors used in their own cold and damp country, find themselves able to drink large quantities of Italian wines without intoxication, and therefore declare them harmless. Americans gladly believe this, and, moreover, that it is all right, and according to native custom to drink them clear and by the pint; while, in truth, the natives themselves stand aghast at the amount more or less safely imbibed by American and English tourists.

Italian gentlemen almost invariably drink their wine mixed with water, and we have never seen one take more than a small tumblerful at any one meal. Indeed, drunkenness is a vice almost unknown among them. One who is once seen drunk is forever thereafter disgraced, and is shunned by his acquaintances. But we cannot say as much for the Italian peasant, whether he be a resident of the city or of the country. We have heard Americans assert that there is no drunkenness in any country where wine takes the place of stronger liquors. Now, we have sifted this matter thoroughly both in Italy and Switzerland, and are bound to deny the truth of this statement. Why is it then that so little drunkenness is seen by strangers? Because Italian laborers rarely begin their potations until their day's work is done. They carouse from about nightfall until midnight,—when, money spent or credit exhausted, they reel home, and the cries and groans of wives and children soon tell of the fury and brutality which mark the drunkard the world over. Thinking it probable that brandy did most of the mischief, I inquired as to this point. In every case my questions caused surprise, and the answers were always the same: "No! no! It is wine—always wine." But be glad, oh Italy, that this degrading and vulgar vice finds no favor within your borders, save among the poorest and most ignorant of your people.

CHAPTER XXVI.

HABITS AND MANNERS.

THE Roman nobility, whose ancestry have generally derived their titles from their "Uncle, His Holiness," or same lucky and generous "Uncle, the Cardinal," comprises a small part of the population of Rome. They are proverbially indolent, ignorant, corrupt, proud, slaves to rank and show and fortune; and—very naturally, considering the derivation of most of their family importance—obsequious servants of the Pope and his Cardinals. Some few of the Princes are wealthy, possessing immense estates, villas, palaces, collections of art, etc. Others are very far from rich, and are obliged to economize to a degree scarcely credible, in order to keep up the show they worship, and to display upon the Pincio and Corso the absolutely necessary handsome equipage, freighted with charmingly drest wife and children. Of this class, however, I shall say but little. Through diplomatic intercourse we are pretty well acquainted with its peculiarities, and there is but little that can be added to what is already known about them.

From the nobles we turn to the peasanst,—the

"Contadini" of the country, and the lowest class of citizens. We grieve to say that we doubt whether the common people of Central and Southern Italy are a whit more civilized now, in the nineteenth century, than they were in any other age, however remote. We believe that the Coliseum of Rome could be filled to-morrow to its utmost capacity with an audience as eager to witness the death sports of gladiators, or the massacre of criminals by wild beasts, as in the worst days of Nero. We shrink from saying this, and yet we believe it true. The proof is abundant.

The atrocities—mere wanton cruelties—of the brigands which infest the country are well known. They are indeed too loathsome for recital. The frequent assassinations which occur everywhere, and upon the smallest provocations—the fear of each other's vengeance which renders it difficult to secure evidence in case of crime—the cruelty to their animals—from their poor, patient, overladen donkeys to the little blind kittens thrown out in the streets to perish, by being eaten by dogs, or crushed by wheels—their revolting sepulture of their own dead, and still more revolting treatment of dead heretic strangers,—all these are patent facts, and condemning proofs of the semi-barbarism of the classes of which we write.

They are a beautiful race to look upon; but do not trust them. They are pleasing enough when it suits them to be so, but they are as vindictive, revengeful, cruel, selfish, as were ever their heathen ancestors. Why should they not be? Their religion teaches them but little. The Virgin Mary, who is universally the object of their adoration, left them no precepts to guide them, no laws to bind them. God and the Saviour are to them only angry Gods, to be propitiated through Mary, and as she is all-powerful and ever kind, all sin is safe to her votaries. There may be less impurity among them now than when Venus was worshiped, but we doubt if there is less crime of other sorts than when the temples of Jupiter and Apollo crowned the Capitoline and Palatine heights.

Under the head of "Brigandage," much has already been said of these descendants of the slaves and plebeians of ancient times, and we gladly turn therefore to a consideration of the large middle class of the Roman people,—its lawyers, physicians, men of science, men of letters; its bankers, artists, and merchants. Upon this most important and most numerous class depends all progress in the "Rome of to-day."

The Italians of this order, though possessing many other beautiful traits of character and manners, are neither a social nor a hospitable people according to *our* definition of the terms. "Dropping in," unannounced or uninvited, to dinner or tea is a habit very rare among them even in the case of blood relations. We have known a lover and cousin to visit his fiancée daily, for more than a year, and yet never take a meal under her roof. Inquiry only proved this habit of strict privacy while eating, universal, but failed to discover its cause.

We were very unwilling to believe it an evidence of an extreme economy, yet we sometimes admitted the suspicion. And apropos comes a circumstance to my mind, which looks alarmingly toward this conclusion. During a summer spent in the beautiful hills that surround the Campagna, a fete champetre was given by the many Roman gentlemen who found themselves associated there for health and pleasure. To this fete our young people were formally invited, and went. One of them was a young Roman lady, very dear to us all, the other a young American. Upon reaching the park, in whose recesses they found a beautiful dinner spread, it proved that our young American friend was the only foreigner present. She was received with great cordiality, and the place of honor at the table assigned to her. She was toasted and complimented, and made to feel very much at home. But imagine our feelings, dear, generous, hospitable American readers, when we found that the gentlemen had ascertained the exact cost of their entertainment, and apportioned it among all the guests equally, and sent the bills out for collection! It was very droll, and a great come-down to us Americans. Certainly, it cannot but be admitted that the Romans are very great economists, and quite too fond of "pauli." The stranger meets this at every turn. Yet the respectable merchants of Rome, though willing to make a good bargain, we rarely found dishonest; and among artists and professional men one may feel quite as safe as elsewhere, whether in Switzerland itself or among our own people. Our Roman friends assured us very earnestly that dishonesty was rare in the dealings of Roman with Roman; but they admitted and lamented the fact that some classes of their people thought foreigners only fair game, and plucked them accordingly.

Lingerings of the habits and manners of the old heathen times may be traced, here and there, by a careful observer, in the religion, the regulations, and the customs of the modern Romans, and are a continual source of interest, grave or otherwise as the case may be. Most amusing was it to me to hear people declaring "per Bacco," or "per Ercole," when wishing to be especially emphatic. The former expression being used oftenest by ladies, the latter by gentlemen. How it seemed to transport us back into old Rome! How near by seemed the times of Virgil and Horace! Then, too, the ancient pantomimic plays seem to have left their traces in the expressive gestures —often used so mysteriously—which one soon learns to understand. By half a dozen different movements of the features and fingers your companion greets you affectionately, asks you to join him, tells you to beware of some one, says that he is penurious, untruthful, deceitful or dishonest!

The ladies, as with us, keep up a round of calls, during which they discuss, with charming vivacity and grace of gesture, fashion, opera, love and marriage. This last is a subject of intense interest to them all. In our whole experience in Italy we never saw or heard of an "old maid." They are anomalies of nature—shut up in convents.

The men visit rarely, meeting each other constantly on the Corso, in the cafés, at the banking houses, or on the Pincio. They spend their evenings with their families at home, or at the opera; for all Rome has an opera-box, and all Rome uses it. There the ladies display their beautiful toilets, magnificent eyes, teeth, and hair, and—with rare exceptions—fine figures, and statuesque hands. There they enjoy the music, the light, the glitter of diamonds and sheen of pearls, as only these children of the sun can enjoy things which appeal to the sensuous in our nature.

There are occasional dancing parties, card parties, soirees, and musical entertainments, at which young girls only appear under the protecting wing of "mamma," whose maternal care is unceasing at home as well as abroad, and who looks into the face of every unmarried gentleman under sixty years of age to read, if possible, "*eligible partie.*"

A young girl in Italy is strangely fettered. She can never put her foot out of doors unless guarded by a waiting woman or some blood relation, male or female. She cannot even cross the street with her brother-in-law. If she is engaged to be married, she is never left alone with her betrothed, nor can she ever appear in public with him. She generally embroiders exquisitely, and makes for her future lord a great variety of little tokens of love. If she is a musician, she practices six hours a day; if an artist, then under some protecting Cerberus she spends her mornings in picture galleries; if she is literary, she writes harmless verses or improvises; but if, as is rarely the case, she chooses to dabble in the abstract and abstruse sciences, she must be restrained; for under no circumstances must she reason or think—these troublesome privileges being reserved for her father confessor. To be happy, with her means to be married, to go to the opera, to dress well, to have a fine carriage, and to be the mother of many children.

The married women have more freedom, but that social and intellectual intercourse with "the nobler sex" which is permitted to women of mind in other countries, and especially in France, is unknown among them. As may be inferred from these facts, Italian husbands are jealous and vigilant, but, to their credit be it said, they are usually very faithful and scrupulously attentive. Their Italian proverb "Chi ama, tema," who loves, fears, is ever present with them! Indeed, we doubt whether in any other nation can be found more married lovers, or more tender parents than in Italy.

The Italian nature is intense rather than profound, passionate, sensitive, tenacious, quick to resent injury, but true and sincere. When they are faithless, they are careless of concealment. Sorrow is shown in storms of passion and floods of tears, and like tropical clouds, soon exhausts itself by the process.

We have ourselves witnessed scenes almost too exaggerated even for melodrama. For instance, a young married woman in violent hysterics because (we could scarcely help laughing all the while) her husband had praised another's beauty, and had talked with her a few moments about a game then being played by others in the room! The hysterics were real, and the repentant husband was on his knees before his suffering wife, kissing her hands, and recalling her to consciousness with many of those beautiful words of endearment, so musical in the Italian tongue. It was all foolish, but not bad, and an excess of tenderness is greatly better than a lack of it. The love, too, of the Italian father for his children is a beautiful trait. He shares their sports, and enters into all their pursuits, with an ingenuousness and spirit that charms one; and if they are wakeful or sick, he shares with mother and nurse the anxiety they feel and the care they bestow.

Certainly, whatever else they may be, the Italians are model fathers and mothers.

At present the Roman people are little better than slaves to their religion and to their institutions. They have no free press, no free speech. Under the iron hand of Popery they cannot stir, they cannot even lift a cry of oppression. Their wings all clipped—when they attempt to fly, what is the result? Long languishment in some vile prison-house or exile from the bright land they love. The middle class of Rome are, to a man, in favor of the abdication of the temporal power of the Pope—but what can they do? The spies of the cruel Government are everywhere within the walls, and the soldiers of powerful France are at every gate. The Roman nurses within his breast a hope that will not die. He is reserved, taciturn, dignified in his silence. But the old Roman blood courses in his veins, and insurrectionary fires smoulder in every house. To our own mind this oppressed people are greater in their present submission than in their past efforts to be free. In silence they bide until their time come; and come it will, and that soon. Then, their capability of self-government, now shown by their patience in waiting, will be manifested in enlightened legislation, and they will once again be ready to take the lead in the learning and civilization of the world.

CHAPTER XXVII.

SKETCHES FROM ITALIAN LIFE.

We close these chapters on Italian manners and habits by the narration of some incidents that occurred while we were in Rome.

Signore and Signora Matteuci have a lovely family of six daughters and two sons. They are wealthy, and occupy a fine old palace. The Signore is a kindly, intelligent gentleman, and in the grain trade. The Signora, handsome and genial, has spared no pains to bring up her family well. Her daughters are beautiful, but they are also prudent, pious, and industrious. No wonder they were all sought young, and that within about eight years all the six have married and left the stately old home. The last marriage, that of the youngest daughter, made some trouble. The little damsel—then only twelve years of age—was seen by a boy of seventeen, daily coming from and going to school—always properly escorted you may be sure. The young gentleman fell terribly in love with her pretty little ladyship, but nursed his affection in secret for many a pleasant month. Love aiding his sagacity enabled him to become acquainted with the brothers, who invited him to visit them at home. He was thus introduced into the charming family circle, but as the little lady—in pantalets still—whom he went to see was regularly sent out of the room when young men were in the parlors, he had no resource, at last, but to prevail upon his mother to broach the subject with Signora Matteuci, and to plead that he might be allowed to converse with the Signorina. His suit was positively declined on the score of youth and immaturity on both sides, and poor little Laura was sent to a convent to finish her education and forget Raffaello's beautiful and pleading eyes. Month after month passed by, but though good and studious and dutiful, she learned little, grew pale and thin, grew worse and worse, and was at length alarmingly ill. It was clear nothing could save her but home and Raffaello! And so the lover-children met at last and were formally betrothed. Laura's pretty hair had all been cut off during her illness, and now grew in short curls over her pretty little head, but she had gained one grand point, she was at once put into long dresses.

A year of engagement followed, and though the little girl had by no means done growing, the marriage took place in great state at the end of that time.

"Were you at the wedding?"

"No, I could not go."

"Do tell me all about it."

"How can I, when each thing was more beautiful than the other? A pair of beautiful children were married, and all the attendants were young and beautiful too, and the dresses were in exquisite taste. Then the Signora mother looked so handsome, smiling through tears. The ceremony was in the family chapel, and it was lined with flowers, as was every staircase and hall of the palace itself. There were crowds of guests, and tables were spread upon two floors, and covered with good things, all elaborately ornamented. The bridal gifts were magnificent too; and so—and so—the Signora has now married all her daughters."

"What is the bridal trip?"

"They only went to the mountains. The family of the bridegroom own a village up there, and the preparations to receive them were on a great scale, considering it was all done by the villagers themselves. The carriages were met by a procession of all the people, including the convent sisters and their schools and all the priests, and headed by the town authorities. There were banners and chantings and bouquets of flowers, and the gate was festooned with bright drapery, so that it looked like a triumphal arch, and so, too, did the gate of the villa."

"There, now, let me shut my eyes and see it all; and, good reader, will you not try to see it with me?"

Bathed in golden sunshine lies the wide,

prairie-like Campagna. The mountains slope up gently from it as if reluctant to leave its rich, green, swelling undulations. Their bases are all covered with luxuriant orchards of olive and chestnut trees, and with the groves and gardens of many villas. Above these, gray crags and tall cliffs uprear themselves, all glorified by the mist of powdered sunbeams through which we see them.

From the great mountain side juts out a tower-shaped mass of rugged rock, whose summit is crowned with the turreted walls and domes of an ancient stronghold, now the peaceful little town to which we go. Upward, along the winding gravelly road, the strong, sleek, black horses that draw the bridal party pull steadily. The carriage tops are thrown back, and the merry occupants lift their hats and wave their handkerchiefs to the crowd they are meeting just outside the massive old gates. See the people in picturesque and irregular but decorous procession. How beautiful are the soft, dark eyes and shining white teeth that smile their welcomes! Here are the dignified town authorities, and the dark-robed priests, and "sisters" with their various schools. How perfect to the eye is the contrast between the simple, somber garb of all these, and the brilliant-hued costumes of the peasantry, the gleaming jewelry and snow-white head-dresses of the women, and the gay sashes and feather-tipped or flower-bound hats of the men!

The carriages, half full of bouquets, and accompanied by merry words and hearty blessings, pass under the ancient gateway—so ancient that it and the massive walls in which it is set, look as if only a natural outgrowth of the mountain crags they dominate. Through the narrow streets the beautiful train takes its way. On either side, everywhere, fresh flowers and gay draperies. The great gate of the villa has been made to resemble a triumphal arch, so festooned is it with green. They enter the court-yard. The people pause. The carriages pass into the lofty doorway, and the little party alight and receive the formal welcome of the domestics of the household. The bride and groom ascend the stairs, and from a balcony thank the people, who bless them and disperse. Then takes place the entrance into the suite of rooms fitted up for the party.

We see it all! the pure white window curtains swaying in the light mountain breeze; the glorious outlook, across the Campagna to the sea (which lies like a silver border along the horizon), and on either side upon the grand old mountains with their wealth of trees and crags and waterfalls and dark ravines; the tables ready spread with exquisite dishes of cold meats, confectionery, pastries, and especially of beautiful fruits; the ample table linen, the quaint old china, and family silver and cut glass, the old family servants, the old, old hall with its old, old statues, and in touching contrast, the happy and beautiful child-couple and their gay young friends. What a pity these "foreign folk" are so used to such things, that they cannot half know how exquisite they all are!

We have said that among Italians, family ties are very strong, yet the contrary is constantly asserted by careless and prejudiced travelers. Our attention has recently been called to an English work, in which the authoress affirms that nearly every married woman has her "cavalier servente" or lover. This is a shameful slander, and ought not only to condemn the book in which it is found, but to disgrace the writer whose pen wrote and whose head indited it. As we have, however, spoken of married life in a former chapter, we shall say nothing more about it now, but shall turn to the love of children, which is so marked and beautiful a trait among all Italians.

"Think how happy we all are this morning," said a dear young friend to us on one occasion, "our brother Egidio's wife has another little boy."

"Impossible! why it seems to me only the other day that the last little one came."

"Yes. It is true. She has had twelve in fifteen years. Oh, she is so happy, and my brother is enchanted!"

"But are all the twelve living?"

"Ma che! yes. Why not?"

Ma che, be it understood, means something like "How you talk!"

"But she must have three babies now?"

"Yes, but you know two of them are always in the mountains with their nurse. They go as soon as they are a year old, and stay two years. It is more healthy, and the mother sees them constantly."

"Is this frequently done?"

"Yes, when it can be afforded and when there are so many."

"Ludovico mourns always for his eldest boy who died, you know, last summer," said another friend to us one day. "Nothing can distract his mind from his grief. The child had a remarkable talent for drawing, and the walls of his play-room have many of his little sketches upon them, done in chalk or pencil. All these his poor father has had covered with glass, in order to preserve them. He says they are more valuable to him than all the works of Raphael are to the whole world." We had known all the sad circumstances attendant upon the death of the lovely boy of whom his aunt was speaking, and we remember how his young uncle, a noble youth of nineteen or twenty years, had watched night after night by his bedside, administering the remedies, soothing his agitation, himself growing paler and thinner each day, until his darling little playfellow went home to heaven. Ah! people are very human in Italy! and are not ashamed of it—not in the least.

What are the dark characteristics of Rome?

Ah! we know them well. They belong chiefly to its Church and Government. Baseless suspicions, private calumnies, quick vengeance, secret arrests, loathsome prisons, slow justice, fanaticism, persecution, secret and arbitrary powers,—we know of them all, and consequent upon these an universal distrust and fear.

But Romans prefer suffering in Rome to enjoyment away from it. It is to them the one only place in all the wide world. No wonder! For even strangers return again and again to its ancient streets and wide Campagna—all haunted by a mighty Past—feeling that nowhere else, if we except the Holy Land, is the mind so interested, and the sensibilities so touched. "Rome is the abode of tragic peace," say the Germans, and we know of no shorter way of expressing what one feels when under the influence of its magic atmosphere.

THE END.

www.ingramcontent.com/pod-product-compliance
Lightning Source LLC
LaVergne TN
LVHW010147110826
845151LV00002B/446

* 9 7 8 1 4 2 5 5 3 7 6 3 0 *